WOMEN'S STUDIES PROGRAM-UN
1208 OLDFATHER HALL
BOX 880341
LINCOLN NE 68588-0341

D0062478

UN WOMEN'S STUDIES PROGRAM
327 SEATON HALL
BOX 880632
LINCOLN NE 68588-0632

THE FEMINIST CLASSROOM

THE FEMINIST CLASSROOM

Frances A. Maher

Mary Kay Thompson Tetreault

BasicBooks
A Division of HarperCollins*Publishers*

Designed by Joan Greenfield

Library of Congress Cataloging-in-Publication Data
Maher, Frances A.
 The feminist classroom / by Frances A. Maher & Mary Kay Thompson Tetreault
   p. cm.
 Includes bibliographical references and index.
 ISBN 0-465-03302-4 (cloth)
 ISBN 0-465-02354-1 (paper)
 1. Feminism and education—United States. 2. Women—Education—United States. 3. Sex dis-
crimination in higher education—United States. I. Tetreault, Mary Kay Thompson. II. Title.
LC197.T48 1994
376'.65—dc20   94-2158
                                                                                   CIP

95 96 97 98 ❖/RRD 9 8 7 6 5 4 3 2 1

CONTENTS

To our daughters: Chantal M. Tetreault and Sarah Elizabeth Maher,

both born on February 15th, 1969,

and to Matthew Jonathan Maher,

born October 5th, 1971.

PREFACE

THE PROCESS OF WRITING this book has been a testimony to the value and necessity of collective feminist work, and we want to acknowledge the individuals and communities that nurtured this project. It represents to us an ever-expanding network, or web, of relationships and support, encouragements and criticisms, extending through the space embraced by two coasts and a time span of nine full years. This network was initiated in our own collaboration, which had its beginnings in the early 1980s when we launched ourselves into academia. Although we did no writing together until this book, early on we became important critics of one another's scholarship. As we shared drafts of Frinde Maher's articles on feminist pedagogy and Mary Kay Tetreault's on feminist phase theory, we came to value the quality of one another's minds and to trust the other's feminist sensibilities.

Beginning with a pilot study in the fall of 1985 during which we observed in the classrooms of Nancy Porter at Portland State University, Nancy Hoffman and Pancho Savery at the University of Massachusetts, Boston, and on the campus of Lewis and Clark College, we have been engaged together in a rich and rewarding conversation that fanned out from an initial interest in feminist pedagogy to thinking about how knowledge is constructed in classrooms. In spite of our firm commitments we are each certain that if it had not been for the other, the project would never have reached fruition. When one of us flagged, the other felt able to go on; at times it felt like a relay race, with the baton shifting back and forth as each stage was met and each turning point reached. The high points of our work together were perhaps the stolen hours in conference hotel rooms, where, squirreled away from sessions we should have attended, we talked through the data to new realizations and insights.

Throughout the course of most of this study, we were in the habit of calling the professors we worked with our "informants," following the practice of anthropologists. One professor in a workshop pointed out that these teachers were indeed "informing" on the classroom as a heretofore secret world. But as we developed deep connections with the professors, the term, which implies some distance between the researcher and those being researched, did not capture the unusual degree to which they were contributing to the conceptualization of the book. It is for this reason that we use both professors' and students' given names, where permission was granted.[†] We want first to thank the seventeen professor participants. Their willingness to be observed in their classrooms is a rare and generous act, testifying to their own commitments as feminist teachers. But the three weeks we spent with each one was only the initial reason for our debt to them, as we shared with them much of what we wrote at various stages of the project. Throughout the chapters that follow, we illustrate the myriad ways in which their concerns are interwoven with our own. While all of these professors were extremely helpful, we want to thank in particular Laurie Finke, Chinosole, Beverly Clark, and Nancy Grey Osterud, whose comments over the years transformed our perspectives on the whole book.

We also owe a great debt to the students we observed and spoke with. Like their professors, the students not only shaped our analysis but at times helped us rework and transform it. In particular, we gained insights from Nancy Ichimura*, Ron Underwood*, Ned Sharp*, and Cheryl Ibabao at Lewis and Clark College, Elisabeth Stitt and Michelle Barnett* at Wheaton College, Angela Waters* and Wendy Johnson* at Spelman College, Stephanie Jackter at the University of Arizona, and Beatrice Gordon* and Jayna Brown at San Francisco State University.

There were "gatekeepers" at each institution we visited who helped us get there and smoothed our way when we arrived: Myra Dinnerstein at the University of Arizona; Nancy McDermid at San Francisco State University; Sara Coulter and Elaine Hedges at Towson State University; and Beverly Guy-Sheftall at Spelman College, who also arranged for us to stay at Spelman's Alumnae Guest House. Johnnetta Cole, the president of Spelman, welcomed Frinde into her home and to a dinner for her Women's Studies class on the first night she was there. Chinosole turned over her apartment

---

[†] In cases where we used a pseudonym because we were unable to obtain permission or decided to do so for reasons of privacy, we have placed an asterisk by the pseudonym the first time it appears.

to us for a week when we were in San Francisco. In all our visits to unfamiliar campuses, the people we met were friendly, curious, and welcoming without being either intrusive or distant. We learned to feel at home in each place.

The feminist communities at both Lewis and Clark College and Wheaton were crucial to our imagining that we could undertake this book. At both institutions, faculty development seminars in Women's Studies and curriculum integration created a climate in which feminist ideas could be explored and where there were rewards for engaging in feminist scholarship that was interdisciplinary and attentive to pedagogical issues. Our decision to do our research in institutions that had similar grants bespeaks the power of those seminars for us.

Among the colleagues who participated in the seminar with Tetreault at Lewis and Clark College and contributed to her growth as a feminist scholar were David Savage, Susan Kirschner, Jane Atkinson, Jean Ward, and Dick Adams. Her 1986–87 sabbatical laid an invaluable foundation for the research project. The supportive environment for research in the School of Human Development and Community Service at California State University, Fullerton, where she was Dean from 1987–93, made it possible for her to continue the book after becoming a university administrator. Because her Associate Dean, Michael Parker, and the school's department chairs saw research as a legitimate part of a Dean's responsibilities, she was able to carve out time to see this project to completion. Support staff who facilitated the transcription of classroom and interview data included Sandy Archuleta, Nora Velarde, and Kim Yee.

The generous environment of Wheaton College and the support of members of the Balanced Curriculum Project, particularly Bonnie Spanier and Darlene Boroviak, convinced Frinde to pursue her early interests in feminist pedagogy. This backing ensured the space, time, and support that enabled her to work on the project in all her spare time, including a full sabbatical year in 1989–90. The encouragement of the Wheaton project participants, Beverly Lyon Clark, Kersti Yllo, and Bianca Cody Murphy, was crucial at many stages in the research. Nancy Shepardson patiently oversaw the transcription of much classroom and interview material.

We are also extremely grateful to all the people outside the project itself, not directly part of the book but within the web, who encouraged us at every turn. Ellen Schrecker has been a frequent and unfailing source of encouragement and professional advice. Over the years we have been in conversation with many colleagues in the field of education, Patti Lather, Ann Berlak, Jean Anyon, Kathleen Dunn, Kathleen Weiler, and Jean Erdman, among others. Their continuing interest in illuminating what feminist teachers are doing to forge an education appropriate for women has been an inspiration to us. The authors of *Women's Ways of Knowing,* the work that in some ways gave impetus to *The Feminist Classroom,* were enthusiastic and supportive from the beginning. Our prospectus was drafted with the help of participants at their annual Education for Women's Development conference, which brought thirty-five women together once a year for ten years to talk about women's development. Jill Mattuck Tarule, one of the authors of *Women's Ways,* has been a unique combination of friend, sister, and mentor; she has supported and challenged us throughout the years with her comments on drafts of chapters and teacher portraits, her insights about the complex epistemologies of the classroom, her faith that we could pull it all off, and her humor. Jill and Frinde were part of a reading group that at times read drafts of the work, and whose comments were insightful and very useful; we would like to thank Nona Lyons, Phyllis Silverman, Jeanne Paradise, Jane Roland Martin, Blythe Clinchy, and Nodie Oja.

We owe our most recent gratitude to Jo Ann Miller, our editor at Basic Books, and Barrie Thorne, the Director of Women's Studies at the University of Southern California. Jo Ann Miller had confidence in the project from our earliest contacts with her and has been a clear and thoughtful critic throughout. Barrie Thorne, who read the manuscript in its entirety, was particularly helpful in urging us to keep a sense of tension and contradiction, to avoid essentialism and categoricalism, to pay attention to variations within gender, and to attend to complex and shifting social relations.

Finally, we would like to thank our families. Marc Tetreault's feminist orientation to the world has been a central grounding over the past thirty years for Mary Kay's various projects. His work as a painter and his associations with the art world have been instrumental in teaching her about the power of finding and fashioning a particular vision, as she has observed him and a number of artists create their own worlds. Frinde's life partner, John McDermott, has been unfailingly patient, perceptive, and supportive in both material and nonmaterial ways throughout every step of the long march to the finish. His own long experience as a writer helped her persist in the labor of putting parts together piece by piece without losing sight of the whole. (Also, he has done all the cooking for two years.)

Our children, Chantal Tetreault and Sarah and Matthew Maher, all finished both high school and college during the course of this work. They were unfailingly supportive of their mothers, patient and understanding during absences, excited with us at our breakthroughs. Their comments and insights have wound their way through the book itself. Chantal, in particular, helped us see an important aspect of the feminist classroom through her own work in feminist pedagogy. The students we have observed are in their generation; this study, in important ways, is about their struggles, their education, and their future. It is to our children that this book is dedicated.

CHAPTER ONE

Breaking Through Illusion

When those who have the power to name and to socially construct reality choose not to see you or hear you, whether you are dark-skinned, old, disabled, female, or speak with a different accent or dialect than theirs, when someone with the authority of a teacher, say, describes the world and you are not in it, there is a moment of psychic disequilibrium, as if you looked into a mirror and saw nothing. —Adrienne Rich

Infinite vision seems to come from suffering through enforced pain. "Before I got my eyes put out I liked as well to see—As other Creatures, that have Eyes and know no other way." You can run around in ignorant bliss until something breaks through this level of illusion, takes out the "eye" that makes it possible for you to view the world this way, and once you see through it, you can't go back. Trying to face yourself backwards would "strike you dead." —Nancy Ichimura, Lewis and Clark College

THESE TWO QUOTATIONS, one from a poet and one from a Japanese-American college student, are about learning and knowing.[1] They are also about the educational system and the fact that, until recently, the content and pedagogy of American education, although projecting the "illusion" that it spoke to everyone, ignored the needs, experiences, and perspectives of the majority of people in this country—women of all backgrounds, people of color, and all women and men who perceive their education as not made for them.

There is reason to believe that this neglect is being addressed. The second quotation was read by a student in a feminist classroom, in which a thoroughgoing revolution in curriculum content and pedagogy has opened up new educational practices and angles of vision. The aim of this book, an exploration of teaching and learning in the classrooms of seventeen feminist college professors, is to portray the ways in which their commitments to the education of *all* of their students have led to educational approaches that break the illusions and silences, and transform the visions of students like

1

Nancy. These feminist teachers have begun to articulate educational aims and criteria with these newer students in mind, to integrate women's and multicultural content into their curriculum, and to experiment with new, sometimes risky, pedagogical approaches.

Inside the classrooms of these teachers we have discovered a range of varying situations and unique, although representative, stories that illuminate and give concrete form to their struggles over knowledge, access, and power. Each professor portrayed here is responding in her own way to the twin upheavals that have shaken American universities during the past two decades. The first is the demographics of a rapidly changing student body; the second is the struggle for more egalitarian and inclusive knowledge that reflects far-reaching epistemological revolutions in the scholarly disciplines. Although the media has paid much attention recently to both students and curriculum, the pedagogical practices of the teachers who must bring them together have been curiously absent from public debates. We think that classroom settings like the ones depicted in this book enact in vivid form the encounter between these students and the new forms of teaching and learning that seek to include them.

THE CONTEMPORARY CONTEXT

Although the Western educational tradition has claimed "truths" that apply to everyone, it has been considered nonetheless a rather exclusive domain to be mastered by an educated few. Yet, today, as members of formerly excluded groups have entered the university in significant numbers, we could say that some professors, to evoke Adrienne Rich's image, experience moments of psychic disequilibrium when the students they see in their classrooms are very different from those they expected to see. The number of students who complete undergraduate degrees within four years has shrunk dramatically, to about 15 percent of undergraduates.[2] Yolanda Moses, president of the City College of New York and formerly a vice-president in the California State University system, has described the emerging new group as follows: "They are older students (over 28), students of color, (both male and female), part-time students, poor students, differently abled students, gay and lesbian students, international students, and first-generation college goers, to name a few."[3] More than 52 percent of this diverse college population is female.

The structure of institutions of higher education, the curriculum, and the composition of faculties and administrations, have all led to feelings of alienation among these new groups of students. As Moses observed, United States universities "are products of Western society, in which masculine values like orientation toward achievement and objectivity are valued over cooperation [and] connectedness. Universities have been historically upper-class and all white in the make-up of administrators, faculty, and trustees." Research on college attrition has found that the key reasons cited by students for dropping out are not financial instability or academic problems, but dissatisfaction with the institution. Moses remarked that "students leave because they perceive the university as cold, indifferent, uncanny, and not a place they want to be."[4]

One answer to the sources of this dissatisfaction lies in research on women in the academy. Since almost two decades ago, feminist scholars were beginning to notice, and to try to account for, the relatively low achievement, high attrition rate, and classroom invisibility of women students. A widely circulated 1982 pamphlet, "The Classroom Climate: A Chilly One for Women?" took note of "the surprising *decline* in academic and career aspirations experienced by many women during their college years," even though "women students are the new majority of undergraduates." The authors perceived patterns of teacher discrimination against women students in the form of lack of adequate career and graduate school advisement, a paucity of appropriate (female) role models, and the failure to engage females in class discussions.[5] Many studies have since documented the pervasive male domination of classroom discourse.[6]

Although some studies cited women's passive socialization patterns, others observed that many women students (and some men) have educational values and approaches that are at odds with the assertive, competitive, and hierarchical ideology of the academy. Carol Gilligan and Jean Baker Miller, for example, charted models of women's psychological and moral development that placed relationships and caring for others at the center of an evolving self.[7] They challenged the notions of independence, autonomy, and individual rights valued by traditional theoreticians of the healthy, or perhaps male, adult.

In 1986 a model of epistemological development, based on the assumption that "relationships matter" for how we know, was presented by Mary Belenky, Blythe Clinchy, Nancy Goldberger, and Jill Tarule in their book *Women's Ways of Knowing.*[8] Building on and challenging the earlier work of William Perry on the cognitive development of undergraduate males, and using interviews with 135 women from a wide range of educational institutions, they articulated a concept of "connected knowing" based largely on experiential and relational modes of thought. They explained female students' silence and low self-confidence in the context not only of a male-centered curriculum but also classroom discourse that is competitive, abstract, and based on the belief that authentic knowledge is gained only through distance and objectivity. Deborah Tannen, noted for her book on the different interaction styles of women and men, puts it this way: "Male students are more comfortable attacking the readings and might find the inclusion of personal anecdotes irrelevant and 'soft.' Women are more likely to resist discussion they perceive as hostile, and, indeed, it is women in my classes who are most likely to offer personal anecdotes."[9]

Critics have pointed out that these are false dichotomies, which Jill Tarule, among others, has called "gender-related rather than gender-specific." Yet, as Jane Roland Martin has observed, traditional models educate *all* students for the productive processes of society at the expense of the reproductive ones. Both males and females experience an education that divorces "reason from feeling and self from other." This forced split in consciousness, she points out, also underlies the experiences of many ethnic groups in the educational system, who have had to choose not only between English and their native language, between worldly success and being at home, but also sometimes between achievement according to the terms of the dominant society and the communitarian and relational values of a culture left behind.[10]

The work of these writers has focused on students whose life experiences, ways of learning, and cultural values differ from those of the dominant culture for many reasons. Constructed as "different" because of their gender, class, race, and/or culture, the presence of such students has required and supported another major upheaval in the universities today, namely, the challenges to the fundamental "canons" of scholarly disciplines. For years now, feminist and ethnic-studies scholars have proclaimed that the traditional curriculum in American higher education has represented the world in terms of the perspectives and achievements of a dominant minority of privileged white males.[11] They assert that academic knowledge—the knowledge that has defined an educated person—must now embrace the experiences, voices, and concerns of all those who have been excluded from that tradition. They have created new accounts, new theoretical frameworks, and new bodies of knowledge in every discipline, based on the lives of the marginalized.

However, these small gains in curricular change have come under increasing attack by defenders of traditional worldviews. Many academics, led by conservative thinkers such as Allan Bloom, E. D. Hirsch, and Dinesh D'Souza, have recently attacked feminist and multicultural education, invoked "free speech" to protect sexist and racist attacks on women and students of color, and defended the Western tradition on the grounds of its inherent superiority and coherence in the face of what looks to them like a loss of "all standards."[12] From one conservative perspective, "The student should have enough knowledge of his or her cultural tradition to know how it got to be the way it is. . . . For the United States, the dominant tradition is, and for the foreseeable future, will remain the European tradition. . . . However, . . . works from other cultural traditions need to be studied as well . . . [and] the claims of the various minorities should have their place."[13]

Contrast this perspective with that offered by Renato Rosaldo in a recent piece on ethnicity and knowledge. He underscores the difficulty of trying "to discuss ethnicity and otherness without granting comparable attention to forms of domination, including, above all, white supremacy." Exploring the ramifications of this contrasting meaning of the concept of "dominant," he says that many American high school teachers have already discovered the limitations of "American history as usual—Puritans, thirteen colonies, a nation of immigrants, westward expansion, new frontiers."

> Their students ask why, when they look for themselves in the mirror of traditional American history, they see nothing. Asian-American students say that their ancestors came eastward, not westward. African-American students explain that being shackled in a slave galley cannot fruitfully be called an immigrant experience. Native American and Chicano students affirm that, rather than immigrating, they stood still and the border moved.[14]

Feminist and other revisionist scholars such as Rosaldo are trying to come to terms with the political, historical, and cultural contexts of the production of knowledge in the university. Their goal is not to destroy Western culture but to historicize it. As Gary Wills wrote, "multiculturalism is not a deviation from the study of one's own world but a precondition of it. Who knows only one thing knows not even that."[15] This expansion of knowledge to include a variety of perspectives challenges the authority of traditional paradigms, showing them to be embedded in history rather than enshrined truths. Perhaps what disturbs some traditionalists most is that what they have to bequeath to future scholars has recently been revealed to be their own particular viewpoints, not the objective truths they have claimed.

It is in college and university classrooms that these debates over what is worth knowing, and by whom, attain their greatest immediacy and relevance. Furthermore, although the public debates in the media are often conducted by male public figures, the people who are bringing about the expansion of knowledge in the classroom on a day-to-day basis include many female faculty, some of whom are women of color. They themselves face as many obstacles as their nontraditional students, including disproportionate teaching loads, marginalization within departmental power structures, ignorance about and trivialization of their research topics, and extra difficulties in gaining tenure. As one African-American woman faculty member put it in a study of Black women in academe: "Black women are expected to work very hard, be very quiet, and be very grateful that they have a job. White women are expected to be just as quiet, but they do not have to work as hard or be as grateful. White males can do whatever they want." As a result of this kind of discrimination, she goes on to say, "minority men and all women spend a higher proportion of their time teaching and advising rather than engaging in original research."[16]

The relative absence of such voices from the public debates about the curriculum may be partially explained by these kinds of discriminatory practices. But it is still surprising that very little attention has been given to the classroom context.[17] If there is anywhere that one ought to look to find out about the transformation of the curriculum, the ways that students relate to one another, and the impact and significance of the gender, race, and social class of students and teachers in creating knowledge, it ought to be the classroom.

However, the practice of teaching and the concept of pedagogy have always occupied an anomalous position in the academy. Education as a discipline is often demeaned as a "woman's field." The higher the status of the institution, the less teaching and contact with students is required of faculty. The younger and less privileged the students, the more likely it is that their teacher will be a woman. Within higher education, women are overrepresented in low-status institutions with high teaching loads, underrepresented in universities with graduate and research programs. Drawing on a dichotomy with a long and gendered history, we may speculate that research and publications might constitute the "public sphere" of academic life, with relatively clear and visible criteria and standards for competitive success, while classroom teaching may be considered its "private sphere," where success is unsung, relational, open-ended, and difficult to quantify. Research is a high-status "male" activity even when women do it; teaching is a low-status "female" activity even when men do it.[18]

Another reason there is so little attention to the classroom context is that male (and, less frequently, female) scholars are often framing their disputes in a very traditional way. Their discourse is fixed on questions arising from the "mainstream" disciplines and how they are incorporated into the curriculum. What goes on in the more private sphere of the classroom is ignored because most faculty perceive students as apprentices in the faculty's disciplines rather than as learners in charge of their own knowledge. In addition, these scholars see knowledge itself as derived from and dependent upon the scholarly disciplines, the arena where they make their own contributions. They do not tend to see students, especially students different from themselves, as creators of important or relevant insights.

Making a distinction between "mainstream" and "marginal" knowledge, the authors of *Women's Ways of Knowing* write:

> In considering how to design an education appropriate for women, suppose we were to begin by asking, simply: What does a woman know? Traditional courses do not begin there. They begin not with the students' knowledge but with the teacher's knowledge. The courses are about the culture's questions, questions fished out of the "mainstream" disciplines. If the student is female, her questions may differ from the culture's questions, since women, paddling in the bywaters of the culture, have had little to do with positing the questions or designing the agendas of the disciplines.[19]

This study is about the pedagogical approaches and dynamics in classrooms attentive to this question of "what does a woman know?" Our study, because it focuses on the classroom, is not only about revolutions in the way the disciplines frame the culture's questions, but about how a specific group of teachers and students construct and experience themselves as knowers and learners in the classroom. How do gender and diversity shape teaching, learning, and the production of new forms of knowledge? What forms of interaction emerge when such diversities are encouraged, rather than managed or controlled as they are in the traditional academy?

ORIGINS AND DEVELOPMENT OF OUR STUDY

We began this work intending to document the pedagogical approaches and dynamics of classrooms devoted to feminist approaches to learning. Many factors drove us to undertake it. We were each influenced in our early professional lives by the new scholarship on women. As high school Social Studies teachers during the late 1960s and 1970s, we both became concerned about our students, our women students in particular, and the ways in which we thought they were not being served by their education. We began to read the work of historians, literary critics, and social scientists who were undertaking the arduous and exciting work of recovering, naming, and explaining "half of history," half of human experience, and using that knowledge to question the androcentric, or male-centered, basis of traditional knowledge.

We experienced the exhilaration of learning, for the first time, about ourselves. Tetreault edited a high school text of primary sources in women's history.[20]

Having met and shared common interests in graduate school, we began careers in higher education in 1980 and 1981, respectively. Our first academic jobs were at two liberal arts colleges, Tetreault at Lewis and Clark College in the West and Maher at Wheaton in New England.[21] At that time, women's studies programs were exerting a growing influence on the academy.[22] In addition, an increasing number of institutions had begun the process, often with the help of foundation and government grants, of integrating women's history, literature, and other aspects of women's lives into the undergraduate curriculum. Both Wheaton and Lewis and Clark had received such grants, and each of us plunged into curriculum integration work at her own institution with the enthusiasm born of our previous experiences and commitments.

Along with the new models of women's intellectual development, feminist theorists were articulating epistemologies, or ways of knowing, that called attention to women's position of oppression in society as a source of legitimate claims to knowledge and heretofore obscured truths.[23] They used the vast differences in the worlds experienced by men and by women to expose and explore the political and social construction of all knowledge. Some feminist theorists, along with postmodern scholars from other disciplines, have argued that only *consciously* partial perspectives, such as those deriving from women's various positions within society, can guarantee objectivity, an objectivity based *not* on detached impartiality but on an acknowledgment of particular contexts and histories as the ground from which to construct truthful views.[24]

Our encounters with this research, combined with reflections on our own teaching, led us to reexamine what we knew about teaching methods in the college classroom. In traditional approaches, the scholarly expert, having distilled "the truth" from the best minds in the field, transmits it to students. Students learn either through lectures, or by engaging with the professor in a form of so-called "Socratic" dialogue, in which the professor elicits, through a series of probing questions, the right or appropriate answers to the problem posed. Learning is equated to understanding the material in the terms put forward by scholarly authorities. One of the participants in our study, Dorothy Berkson of Lewis and Clark College, in describing her own evolution as a feminist teacher, captured what many others experienced as well:

I used to come into the classroom with a list of questions, and I knew where they were leading. Very Socratic! I don't teach Socratically anymore. I think it's very manipulative. You get the students to come up with the answer you want. Other than getting up and lecturing, which is certainly the most patriarchal form of teaching, I suppose, or authoritarian way, the only way I knew was the Socratic method, and I have just struggled and struggled to get out of it and to find some new way of doing it.[*]

Teachers like Dorothy Berkson and ourselves began to explore new teaching approaches that we called "feminist pedagogies." This new field evolved from many different sources: the consciousness-raising practices derived from the women's movement and other movements of the 1960s, the progressive tradition in American education created by John Dewey, and the more general forms of "liberatory teaching" espoused by Paulo Friere and others.[25] What has made feminist pedagogy unique, however, has been its attention to the particular needs of women students and its grounding in feminist theory as the basis for its multidimensional and positional view of the construction of classroom knowledge. As Maher put it in one article, "we need an interactive pedagogy, a pedagogy which integrates student contributions into the subject matter, just as the subject matter integrates the new material on women."[26]

One mark of this pedagogy is that learning proceeds at least partly from the questions of the students themselves and/or from the everyday experiences of ordinary people, those in the "bywaters of the culture." Dorothy Berkson described a specific transition in her own teaching, as she began to center class discussions around entries from student journals:

I would get frustrated if they didn't take the thing in the direction I thought they were supposed to take it; and so I missed all these wonderful insights that they have to offer . . . they can sometimes come up with the absolute crucial starting point for a really interesting piece of interpretation, and the more they do it, the farther they can take it, the more sophisticated and the better they get at it.

Feminist and liberatory pedagogies aim to encourage the students, particularly women, working-class students, and members of underrepresented ethnic groups, to gain an education that would be relevant to their concerns, to create their own meanings, and to find their own voices in relation to the

---

[*]All material not explicitly footnoted is from our class transcript or interview data.

material. Just as the disciplines are evolving toward multifocal and constructivist forms of knowledge, based on the experiences and viewpoints of all groups in society and not just the most powerful, so does the enactment of these new epistemologies in the classroom draw upon the viewpoints and experiences of students and teachers in new ways.

THINKING THROUGH A METHODOLOGY

This project began as an effort to find and document such "feminist pedagogies" in action, to seek out practitioners who would best exemplify these new teaching methods in their classrooms. Beginning with a pilot study in the fall of 1985, we thought initially to observe professors whose publications had given them national visibility, a kind of stature that we soon realized had little if anything to do with pedagogy. After observing teachers in four different institutions, we decided to limit our study to colleges and universities that had received sizable grants to integrate the study of women and gender into undergraduate courses. We reasoned that curricular revision, and therefore various forms of feminist pedagogy, would be further along in these institutions. We also believed that observing several professors in the same institution would give us a better sense of how institutional contexts shape feminist teaching. Wanting to study a variety of institutions, we chose three liberal arts colleges, one of which is a historically African-American women's college; a research university; and a state university.

Using these criteria, we then selected Lewis and Clark College and Wheaton, the schools in which we taught, as liberal arts colleges. The other three institutions, the University of Arizona, Towson State in Maryland, and Spelman College, all had nationally visible projects and directors of Women's Studies (Myra Dinnerstein, Sara Coulter and Elaine Hedges, and Beverly Guy-Sheftall, respectively). However, as we became further involved in our study and were collecting data at Spelman, we became increasingly aware of the racial homogeneity in many undergraduate colleges, including the ones we had chosen. We decided therefore to add a sixth site, an ethnically diverse state university. We had met Chinosole, the director of Women Studies at San Francisco State University, while doing research at Spelman. After investigating other campuses in the California State University system, we decided on San Francisco State, its diversity outweighing its lack of a gender-integration grant.

At each institution we observed three faculty identified as well-known for their commitment to women's studies and to fine teaching. Our teacher participants, all women, come from a variety of backgrounds: they are middle and working class, white women and women of color, heterosexual and lesbian, married and single, older and younger. They also teach in a variety of disciplines—literature, history, the humanities, education, biology, philosophy, psychology, sociology, and women's studies.[27] We selected our participants based on the following criteria: five years' experience teaching undergraduate courses; an expressed commitment to improving the education of women and ethnic minorities; familiarity with the scholarship on women's issues in their own discipline that was reflected in course syllabi; and a commitment to the analysis and improvement of their own teaching practices. They also had to be willing to be observed in their classrooms.

In our visit to each setting, for a period of three weeks on the campuses other than Lewis and Clark and Wheaton, we gathered extensive campus and classroom observations, audiotaped classes, and conducted in-depth interviews with selected students and each of the professors.[28] We then constructed an in-depth portrait of each professor's teaching based on the different types of data, seeking to describe the various concerns of the teacher and her students and the dynamics of learning in her classroom. Because we wanted to know how each teacher conceptualized "feminist pedagogy" in her own context, we have shown our case study to each participant, and incorporated many of her suggestions into our ongoing analyses.

When we began our study, we had a somewhat simplistic and dichotomized view of the authoritarian, male-dominated, "traditional classroom" versus the idealized "feminist teacher," a notion taken from many early descriptions of feminist teaching practices, including Maher's own. Like the construct of "woman's nature" in some feminist theories, such as Carol Gilligan's, of the early 1980s, this feminist teacher was democratic rather than authoritarian, cooperative rather than competitive, and concerned with "connected" and relational rather than "separate" and rational approaches to learning.[29] We thus framed our analysis of our first classroom in terms of several questions based on categories we had constructed in advance: the teacher's "conceptualizations of gender," the "structure of interactions" in her classroom, and a narrowly conceived dichotomy of the contrast between "rational" and "affective" learning.

When we showed our initial analysis to Laurie Finke, a professor at Lewis and Clark College, and a few of the student informants from her class in Literary Theory, they objected to certain aspects of our portrait, particularly our notion that one student had been silenced because of Finke's overemphasis on abstract and theoretical knowledge. To us their reactions represented ways in which their views "diverged" and "converged" with ours. While not initially questioning the convergences, we began to question the divergences by wondering how we could have been "wrong" about these aspects of our original analysis. We came to see that we had brought our standards of the ideal feminist teacher with us unconsciously through our original questions. Meanwhile we had been hiding ourselves—as knowers, as researchers, as engaged feminists—behind these abstract and categorical questions, still thinking we could describe "what was really going on."

As a result of this first major challenge to our work by the participants themselves, we began the struggle to make our personal positions and research commitments more clear. Believing that the starting point of any research project must be the question "Why are you interested in this?" we wrote our educational autobiographies, looking at ourselves as former female students, feminist high school and college teachers, and feminist researchers. We discovered some of the roots of our own passion, for instance, our longings for the women-centered education we did not have. Of course, we were influenced by the contemporary context in these necessarily brief personal accounts. For example, the themes of silence, voice, and connection that helped define our memories as students, or the theme of authority that came up in our memories as teachers, pervaded our data and readings, particularly of the work of Carol Gilligan; Belenky, Clinchy, Goldberger, and Tarule; and Jane Martin.[30]

As our research commitments became clearer to us, our categorical questions fell away and we began to define ourselves less as distanced and objective observers. We became more conscious of ourselves as personally involved researchers whose social and political positions shaped the research questions that we ourselves constructed. In this process our relationships with our informants became more complex as well. It was no longer that everyone's views either converged with ours (and thus had to be "right"), or diverged (in which case we or they had to be "wrong"), or that there was, in fact, a single "right" or "wrong" about what was happening, but rather that the relationships through which our data and analyses were generated had to be continually examined and revised; those relationships were, in fact, a fundamental aspect of the study itself. Once we wrote our autobiographies, we were in a position to examine these relationships more deeply because we had finally identified our explicit role in them.

Furthermore, we began to see that just as knowledge is constructed in the classroom out of the intersection of different perspectives, rather than found "as truth," so our study would be constructed and reconstructed over time. It would be made of narratives and vignettes of professors teaching, fashioned by us through the process of working with them, rather than a comparative analysis of teaching techniques judged "truly feminist" or not. In this reformulation of our own roles and positions as researchers, we were helped by the work in feminist and postmodern theory, particularly in anthropology, that claimed that a consciousness of relationships like those we have with our participants dislodges "the ground from which some persons and groups may securely represent others." As we came to understand how connected this work is to them and how it evolves because of our relationships, we sought new ways of organizing and representing our data, and of depicting our participants' particular situations and concerns.[31]

In interweaving our questions and concerns with theirs, we have been bothered by nagging issues. Whispering voices in our minds would sometimes ask, What makes this or that teaching practice "feminist"?: Is it the content alone, the pedagogy, or both? Some disciplines, such as literature, have been transformed more than others by feminist scholarship, and seem more amenable to transformations in pedagogical practices. Does this make their practitioners more "feminist"? We saw that we shared with all participants a commitment to taking women students seriously, a consciousness of the extent to which gender is embedded in our social structures, and an understanding of the differing educational needs of different groups of students. We all valued the contribution of feminist scholarship in transforming our teaching. As Dorothy Berkson explained:

> The reason we call this feminist pedagogy is because those of us here who are doing it came at it through thinking about feminist theory. We have chosen to call it feminist because we arrived at it through that route. I call myself a feminist teacher because that is the particular mode of analysis that I use to arrive at what I am trying to do.[32]

Although our ongoing relationships with our informants have made us continue to believe that we can portray a wide variety of genuinely feminist teaching practices, imposing a comprehensive analytical framework, no matter how broad, has sometimes endangered our ability to portray unique individuals and methods on their own terms. These tensions between commonalities and particularities, between shared goals and divergent practices, have remained an issue for us.

The variety of institutional contexts has also shown us that each setting places its own demands on teachers, demands that forced us as researchers to be sensitive to the different constraints and possibilities in each situation. We were made increasingly aware of this issue as we moved from professors at liberal arts colleges who are strongly committed to their teaching, to tenured teacher-scholars at a large research university, to part-time and low-income English instructors at a state university, to women of color seeking to forge a pedagogy of resistance in a culturally diverse urban campus. Feminist professors have been socialized by and have taken on, yet at the same time have often tried to undermine and transform, academic norms. Some tenured academic feminists may be accorded traditional forms of power and respect for their scholarly authority if they "behave" and teach in traditional ways, even as the content of their courses changes. Sara Coulter, co-director of the Integrating the Scholarship on Women, Transforming the Curriculum Project at Towson State University, implied these tensions in a recent letter. "[Feminist] curriculum transformation and feminist pedagogy are not necessarily related," she wrote, "just as not all Women's Studies teachers use feminist pedagogy. Feminist pedagogy is new, radical, and in the early stages of development."[33] Experimenting with new teaching methods and bringing excluded groups into the disciplines exposes the contradictions of traditional scholarly and pedagogical authority, and may impel teachers and their students toward oppositional standpoints that may further marginalize their status. There is no safe place. To come to an understanding of how the classroom is a contested ground in different places, we have sought continually to convey what is on people's minds in each setting, the dynamics of classroom interactions, and how people view the challenges and the prohibitions of their own particular context. Essays on their own teaching by Elizabeth Ellsworth, bell hooks, and others have emphasized that the classroom is a largely unexplored arena for playing out such struggles over knowledge and power.[34]

The most surprising and exciting challenge to our work has concerned the concept of "difference," whether of race, class, culture, or other aspects of peoples' position in our society. Our visit to Spelman first showed us the centrality of this issue in our relationships with these professors, not only in their "difference" from us but, more important, in the ways in which we are "different" from them. How do women of color experience the "feminist classroom"? bell hooks, a noted feminist theorist, articulates a central issue:

> Black students sometimes get the feeling that feminism is a private white cult. The Black students' relentless efforts to link all discussions of gender with race may be contested by white students, who see this as deflecting attention away from feminist concerns. And so suddenly the feminist class-

room is no longer the safe haven many women students imagined. Instead it presents conflict, tension, hostility.[35]

By working with women of color we came to understand that our early conception of the ideal of a democratic and cooperative feminist teacher had been an example of our mistaking the experiences and values of white middle-class women like ourselves for gendered universals. We have been forced to see the relevance of previously unexamined aspects of our own positions, particularly our positions as relatively privileged white women, in shaping the stories we tell. The tasks of attending to the complexity of issues of race, class, age, sexual preference, as well as geographical and institutional context, in each classroom has forced us away from pedagogical generalizations toward the telling of particular stories. In telling these stories, our own roles and positions as narrators must also be visibly marked.

Throughout the writing of this book we have tried to be sensitive to complex relations of race, ethnicity, and culture, sorting out the instances when ethnicity and culture are most salient and marking "race" always as a construct of racism rather than as a biological given. Our participants, as well as other European Americans and women of color, have helped us to see that "race" is the best choice of terms to refer to those economic, political, and social factors that are embedded in the structure of American society and that shape relations of inequality for people of color. African-Americans, in particular, use the term "race" to refer to the tensions between whites and Blacks as a means of responding directly to the dominant discourse by using the term whites use. Because the majority of students we observed were white, we have not identified their race or ethnicity unless the topic under discussion warranted it. We have in all cases identified students of color. We have also used the term "culture" to convey the evolving symbols, behaviors, values, and attitudes that all of us inherit or create for ourselves. The concept of culture broadens our constructs of race and ethnicity because it is not fixed, but rather always evolving within historical and geographical contexts.[36]

FOUR CRITICAL THEMES

In seeking to depict what participating professors and students have shown us, we developed four analytic themes, those of "mastery," "voice," "authority" and "positionality." Because they arose partially from the data themselves, because they captured categories of concerns raised in the literature and shared with our participants, and because they were broad themes that evolved over time, we believed they could organize the relationships we wanted to look at in these institutions and these classrooms—relationships between teachers, their students, and the course materials.

In the light of the struggles over the meaning and purpose of higher education, each of these themes also illuminates a different challenge of diversity. As we define these four themes in relation to our study, we will show how each one has emerged from the classroom transcripts and interviews and in turn illuminated our relationships with our participants. We will also demonstrate how it reflects an important aspect of the participating classrooms, and how it relates to the larger social contexts in which these professors' teaching has taken place.

Mastery

We found "mastery" spelled out in the words of the first woman we observed, Laurie Finke at Lewis and Clark, who has been central in the evolution of our methodology. Her use of mastery in the introductory remarks to her course in Literary Theory led us to see its relationship to the construction of knowledge in classrooms. She said to her class:

> I'm asking you to think in a very different way from the way you have been thinking in most of the English courses you have been taking. . . . But I don't expect you to master everything all at once, and one of the things you sort of have to do is to put aside those neurotic compulsions that we have to always be the master of whatever materials we are reading and sort of immerse yourself in it. I want you to just take off on your craziest ideas and feel free. When you do the reading, I want you to jot down every question that occurs to you, however silly it may sound at the time. Then, when you finish the reading, choose two of the questions that most interest you and try to answer them. Obviously you are not going to come up with definitive answers . . . and as we come together to pool that information we may come up with more definitive answers.

As Finke implies, "mastery" in the educational context has traditionally meant the rational comprehension of ideas on the teacher's and expert's terms. The professor's questions predominate and guide the discourse— according to "questions fished out of the 'mainstream' disciplines." Everyone is measured by the same external standard and is graded in a competitive hierarchy according to their approximation to that standard. In classrooms committed to a feminist reconstruction of knowledge, what new forms does learning take? In some of the classrooms we have observed, such as Finke's, students seek knowledge on their own terms as well as in concert with others—"as we come together to pool that information"—so that individual mastery becomes part of the social construction of knowledge. It becomes collaborative rather than hierarchical. Finke wants her students to make increasingly complex *interpretations* rather than definitive conclusions.

We have also watched each professor wrestle with the relationship between the identities of their students—both as individuals and as a group, what they need to "master," or know, and who they can become as a result. Attention to what different students want or need may mean a variety of approaches and effects. For example, a white student's reading of *The Color Purple* is different from that of a Black student, and poses the challenge of naming and beginning to unlearn racism in order to broaden and deepen her responses. In some of these classrooms the very term "mastery" has become suspect, and its use illuminates the paradox that the traditional curriculum, in teaching students to "master" material and to meet "standards," actually often uses that material to silence and "master" many students instead.

"Mastery" is also an aspect of the study itself. We began with an urge to "master" professors' stories by fitting each one into an overall scheme of feminist pedagogical practices. But as the study proceeded, we came to understand mastery as an interactive construction of meaning with our informants, as described initially by Laurie Finke. Just as her students were encouraged to make successively more complex connections to the material, rather than find *the* "right answer," these professors have helped us to draw increasingly complex understandings of our data, rather than try to fix the "most truthful" portraits. No longer simply looking for ways in which their views diverge from or converge with ours as a test of the accuracy of our accounts, we have sought their perspectives as a means of illuminating aspects of our own viewpoints that may have been hidden from us. That is, they have taught us about ourselves as well as themselves. We have also tried to follow their leads in constructing the purposes of their teaching, rather than imagining and judging them as practitioners of our own ideals. We have hoped to become more their "apprentices," in Elizabeth Spelman's terms, than their masters.[37]

Furthermore, our project has become a collaborative enterprise, in which we, in conversation with each participant, reveal the rich variety of these classrooms. In contrast to the generalized theories or individual classroom accounts that still dominate even the recent literature on feminist pedagogy, we bring these classrooms and their institutional contexts into relationship to each other.[38] From these various standpoints we can begin to construct a range of feminist pedagogies in all their richness and complexity. Our participants' differences and their similarities interact through us, helping us to attend to increasing layers of meaning in each institutional and classroom setting. For example, Laurie Finke's emphasis on student questions was shared by Dorothy Berkson and Grey Osterud from Lewis and Clark but by very few others that we studied, leading us to speculate about the significance of their presence at a liberal arts college whose Gender Studies program had focused on pedagogical innovations. Our collaborative project came to yield an increasingly rich and mutually illuminating set of stories that have emerged from conversation and reflection. We have sought to preserve the texture and distinctiveness that grows from these stories, rather than to construct a unified "master narrative" of feminist pedagogy.

Voice

In terms of the classrooms we observed, "voice" originally meant for us the awakening of the students' own responses. It meant their ability to speak for themselves, to bring their own questions and perspectives to the material. It seemed to connote the connection of one's education to one's personal experience, a connection that members of marginalized groups must often give up when they seek "mastery" through the dominant discourse. As a theme for our work, the concept emerged from our autobiographies, where we had both felt silenced by our educations, and from our keen awareness of "voice" as an important feminist metaphor for women's awakenings.

We have since come to think about these classrooms as arenas in which teachers and students fashion their voices rather than "find" them. As students bring their own questions and perspectives to the material, they use relevant personal experiences to shape a narrative of an emerging self. We have seen how the voices of women and men, of white students and students of color, of those of different ages and sexual preferences, may intersect in the construction of new and multidimensional forms of knowledge.

The ethnic, gender, and class composition of each classroom also creates both possibilities and limitations in terms of which topics are developed and which repressed, suggesting that the etiquette of relations of difference among people is a delicate and evolving matter. Classroom discourses raised difficult questions about the degree to which individuals are embedded in the "identities" marked out for them by the dominant culture. Also at issue are the boundaries of acceptable language about the "Other," and about the ways in which students construct different "selves" and "others" in different environments. The concept of "voice" has helped us to evaluate how different individuals and groups relate to each other in the classroom within the context of these challenging cultural convergences.

Methodologically, in terms of how we have constructed this study, we can now see that we have shaped as well as found our participants' voices. By choosing to highlight certain stories rather than others—for example, Nancy Ichimura's—we have shown muted voices coming into speech. Such choices have included how to present the interaction of classroom data, interviews, and analysis, as well as the juxtaposition of professors and institutions. In each chapter, we have selected not only data but also each excerpt, and example, with the aim of illuminating our major theme and the narratives that represent it.

This process of constructing multiple voices emerged through conversations with participants about both methodology and pedagogy. Laurie Finke told us, "I think your work is a combination of both your voices and mine. I see it as dialogistic. What you have done has been very interesting to me from a theoretical perspective. It is like a conversation, some of me and some of you."[39] Our voices as researchers, then, are also "fashioned"— not "found"—from ongoing conversations with our informants, our data, and each other.

Authority

The authority theme arose for us initially in the context of the autobiographies of our own development as students, feminist teachers, and researchers over the last decade. In writing about ourselves as teachers, we both found ourselves discussing our commitments to social change on behalf of women, people of color, and working-class students as sources not only of our motivation but also of our authority to work with these students, and perhaps influence their thinking and actions. We then began to see the enactment of the teacher's authority as an important theme for examining these classrooms. One of Laurie Finke's students, Ned Sharp, was acutely aware of the ways in which Finke's focus on student questions dismantled the authority with regard to transmitting knowledge that he expected from teachers:

I think that there's plenty of people around here who would like to have an out-and-out debate. And would like to argue with an authoritative voice. . . . There are professors at this school who create the impression that they have authority over a designated body of knowledge. And you go in to get that from them. You have to ask them, "What does this mean?" instead of saying, "I've been thinking this about this." I think Laurie took a big risk . . . she put her personality on the line and absorbed anti-theoretical attacks through her own personality, just like everyone else . . . and rather than getting into this big thing about "boom boom boom you are challenging my authority as the teacher because I'm teaching this class," Laurie just waited and people talked to each other.

As we look at the ways in which some of the teachers gave up certain aspects of their authority as professors in order to make the students responsible for their own learning, we see how much the creation of knowledge depends on the uses of authority, both inside the classroom and within the institution. The nature of each teacher's authority in the classroom can only be understood in relation to both the concept of "good teaching," which is thought to consist of engaging lectures and effective discussion practices, and her own status within the institution. Thus, in asking how she has transformed her courses and opened them up to students, we have also asked how each teacher's authority is constructed by herself, her students, and the university community.

The students we talked to offered no single attitude toward professorial authority. As much as Ned, a young white male, might "go in and get" a designated body of knowledge from authorities who for the most part are delighted to pass it on to him, other students, in the terminology of Belenky et al., would prefer to learn for themselves in the "bywaters." Professors' strategies concerning the use of their authority also vary. However, many of them share a sense of their authority as grounded in their own experience, in their own intellectual encounters with feminist theory or other topics that have personally engaged them, rather than exclusively in their representation of scholarly expertise. For example, Chinosole, Ruth Doell, and Angela Davis at San Francisco State and Margaret Blanchard at Towson State, among others, have had long histories as community activists that they see as profoundly informing their teaching.

We have also begun to think about our authority as researchers in relation to the people we study. Where do we find the sources of our authority to speak for them, and what happens to our authority as we struggle to give them voices in our narrative? What motives, experiences, or histories enable us to do this work? We are motivated to do this study because of the inadequacies of our own educations, because of our knowledge of how poorly served many students are, and because of feeling personally empowered as feminist teachers. Our education in teaching methodologies as high school teachers and professors of education is in sharp contrast to most academics' lack of familiarity with pedagogical theory, and gives us a particular perspective on the central importance of pedagogy in the women's studies movement and in undergraduate education. We share with our informants, furthermore, the experiences of being or having been ourselves feminist college teachers, struggling with the issues of mastery, voice, authority, and positionality in our own classrooms.

More recently we have also understood our authority as intricately bound up in our developing relationships with the study participants and the ways in which these relationships have varied from institution to institution and classroom to classroom. We have struggled to make our aims and qualifications clear to each of them. At Spelman, for example, we were continually asked, "Why are you here?" We have learned that the more we discuss with participants what we are seeing and what concerns *we* have, the more we learn about what is on their minds and what concerns *they* have. The less research authority we assume, the less we are in danger of reproducing the script of what we expected to see and find. In demystifying the researchers' authority in this way, we have become less "objective" and distanced from the participants. The increasing connection we have made with our informants has also given us more responsibility to understand and convey to them our own thoughts and feelings as we go along.

One way of keeping track of this interactive kind of authority has been to try to interrogate our own reactions in different settings. We discovered that it is not only "rational curiosity" that motivates our insights.[40] We have found ourselves feeling, at different times, states of mind such as empathy, compassion and identification, disorientation, and defensiveness, among others. For example, we initially criticized one professor for not directly confronting social-class issues, only to have another participant defend the first from her experiences with a similar problem. As we have named and acknowledged our reactions, we have asked what they tell us about ourselves as well as the situation. We tend to feel empathic when an informant encounters difficulties in a classroom we happen ourselves to be familiar with, judgmental when we know "we would do better," and initially disoriented when professors have teaching problems (or types of students) we have not encountered before.

The authority forged from examining these interactions is one based on connection, even sometimes identification, rather than separation and distance. We have felt ourselves experiencing, painfully at times, Jill Tarule's notion of learning as constructed not only in individual minds, but through the interactions of communities of knowers.[41] At the same time, we must constantly (and partially unconsciously) reiterate the authority we seek to minimize, as we try to disentangle description and analysis from evaluation in our treatment of our informants. The acts of choosing data, juxtaposing and analyzing them, are matters of authorial control. We hope that our portraits give a sense of unfinished business, of vignettes and snapshots of classroom lives that continue and evolve beyond our construction of them at one point in space and time. In this way, we hope to show our authority as limited, contextual, and narrative, part of an ongoing conversation with participants and readers as well.

Positionality

Our final theme is that of "positionality." Postmodern feminist thinkers have seen knowledge as valid when it takes into account the knower's specific position in any context, a position that is always defined by gender, race, class, and other socially significant dimensions.[42] As Laurie Finke put it in the class discussion that fixed the theme for us:

> What is perceived as marginal at any given time depends on the position one occupies. . . . In other words, you have to see centrality and marginality, oppression, oppressor, and oppressed as relational concepts. And so what you have to do is keep the whole thing moving . . . keep seeing it as relational, keep seeing it as position.

The diversity of the classroom environments we have studied has shown us that position, perhaps more than any other single factor, influences the construction of knowledge, and that positional factors reflect relationships of power both within and outside the classroom itself. It has made an important difference in our study, for example, whether teachers and students were male or female, white or African-American, heterosexual or lesbian. And those differences have varied according to the history, region, experiences, and "cultural practices" that brought participants to each classroom and positioned them there.

The concept of positionality has also illuminated our methodology by pointing to the variety of relationships between our informants and ourselves.

Judith Stacey says that ethnographers need to watch out for either the illusion of alliance or the illusion of separateness in relation to their informants, but we find that our different relationships with different informants has posed both of these challenges.[43] For example, the first two teachers we studied shared with us not only a commitment to feminist pedagogy and our common teaching experiences in liberal arts colleges, but a common position as white middle-class academic feminists. Our perspectives changed when Tetreault moved to a large state university, when we observed white middle-class teachers in other state universities like hers, and when we visited African-American teachers in an historically African-American women's college and Chicana/Latina teachers and students in a large and diverse urban campus.

In these settings, our differences from them and from their students forced us to respond to the situation in new ways, and to interrogate our earlier reactions to more familiar environments. In some classroom discussions the emergence of previously marginalized voices offered us sharp challenges. For instance, in a sociology class at Spelman, one African-American undergraduate woman said:

> And also I think it is interesting that we read books by white social scientists, there is a distinct difference and that the passion is just not there. And then I wondered, is it possible, is it possible for a white social scientist to write passionately about my experience, or my peoples' experience? Question number one! And question two, if the passion is not there, is their work relevant? [*There is appreciative laughter*]

Maher was acutely conscious of her own situation as she listened. She wrote in her field notes on this class:

> During this discussion I was extremely uncomfortable, fascinated and impressed by their sophistication. I was also deeply discouraged by the obvious ways in which the racism of the dominant culture made the construction of an oppositional, rather than a complementary, discourse seem so necessary.

The initially defensive reaction of the white researcher, sitting in on a discussion about "white researchers," illustrates our need to criticize our own situations and emotional states as we go along. The student may or may not have intended to convey a message to us; but her statement is a powerful indictment in its own right.

As researchers we must be aware of how the specific teaching contexts—the institutional settings, the classrooms, the interviews—shape the knowledge conveyed by our informants and received by us. Our insights and analyses are shaped by complex relationships with participants, relations based on power as well as on trust and commonalities of vision. As researchers, we come to know what we know because we can articulate our positions vis-à-vis our own commitments and experiences, as well as vis-à-vis our participants, our data, and, ultimately, our readers as well.

The next chapter sets the institutional contexts for our explorations into our participants' classrooms. In the chapters that follow we examine aspects of their teaching in the light of our four themes, using as the bases for our analysis vignettes from discussions, excerpts from interviews, and our own evolving understandings, derived partly from informant responses to early drafts of this book. The juxtaposition of discussions and interviews of contrasting classrooms to illustrate each theme is intended to provide a kaleidoscopic view of the pedagogical approaches and problems we have encountered. The last two chapters suggest some conclusions we have drawn. We hope to create an ongoing conversation with our participants and readers about the complexities and ramifications of the issues raised in these classrooms. They should resonate with our experiences as students, as teachers, and even as parents and children because they are relevant not only to feminism and to pedagogy, but to the construction of knowledge in a more inclusive and democratic academy.

CHAPTER TWO

Creating a Kaleidoscope:
Portraits of Six Institutions

For we have to ask ourselves, here and now, do we wish to join that procession, or don't we? On what terms shall we join that procession? Above all, where is it leading us, the procession of educated men?

—Virginia Woolf

Leslie Flemming's . . . autobiographical reflection on the ways feminist research has transformed not only her work . . . but her life . . . is a narrative whose trajectory will seem intensely familiar to other academic women who came into a knowledge of feminist scholarship after years of unexamined, if uneasy, participation in the disciplines of the patriarchal academy. —Feminist professors at the University of Arizona

FIFTY YEARS AFTER Virginia Woolf gave us her memorable image of the procession of educated men, Leslie Flemming and her colleagues at the University of Arizona wrote of their participation in that procession.[1] On the campuses we studied, it was transformed as the numbers of women in academe increased and institutional attention began to focus on issues of gender, ethnicity, and culture. This transformation set in motion new dynamics among feminist teachers, women's studies courses and departments, and the larger arena of the entire university, dynamics in which our informants participated, holding various positions and speaking in a range of voices.[2]

It became clear to us, as this ethnography progressed, that we had to understand how each professor thought about her feminism in relation to the culture of her academic institution. In each setting, the meaning that professors and students made of their academic culture was an important factor in shaping teachers' pedagogies, students' educational experiences, and the various ways knowledge was constructed in each classroom.

In the following six portraits, we depict the settings in which this interplay between feminist culture and the broader institutional culture took place. All of the professors we observed and interviewed see feminist scholarship and theory as an important source of their teaching and research. However, their feminism interacts with the norms of "good teaching" inherent in each community, commonly held views about how to teach a particular subject, and their own perceptions about the nature and quality of the student body. All of these factors affect professors' beliefs about where and how knowledge is constructed and what they see as the pedagogical possibilities of the classroom. Some believe, for example, that knowledge is produced by scholars like themselves, while others believe it is produced in a community that includes the students as well as colleagues and experts.

We also examine the specific status of Gender Studies and Women's Studies within the culture of each campus, and the place of each feminist professor vis-à-vis her faculty colleagues in terms of relative power, numbers, and influence. Of the women whom we studied, those who worked in institutions where women made up half of the tenure-track faculty had a different and more secure position than those who were a minority of their faculties or were found predominately among the part-time ranks. The female professors and students in the historically female colleges enjoyed a very different sense of their place in the world than did the women elsewhere.

We look at how the professors we studied have been socialized to think about their status and authority in the university, even as they have tried to undermine and transform the conventional sources of this authority. The predominant belief in higher education is that people advance in the academic professions primarily through merit, and that the preponderance of males in higher academic positions is due solely to superior performance.[3] This belief is thrown into question when female and feminist academics relate their own stories. The relative weight placed on teaching and scholarship for promotion and tenure is critical in each context, as are changing standards regarding what constitutes scholarship with the emergence of scholarly work on women. For example, we found that the roles of scholar, teacher, and activist are not so in conflict for women of color as they are for most white women.[4]

This chapter also examines the demographics of the student body in each institution, as well as students' impressions of their school and their experience of gender studies and women's studies within it. We introduce here and develop in later chapters the beliefs we discerned about students' "academic ability" and how they bear on the professors' "constructions" of their students; that is, how they viewed their abilities to learn and create new knowledge. The major criterion for success in higher education is markedly individualistic, with high Scholastic Aptitude Test (SAT) scores and class rank in high school as the measure of a "good" student. We found that although there were a range of opinions in each community, professors in each place shared a predominant viewpoint about the kinds of students enrolled and the academic abilities they brought to the classroom. In our observations of specific classrooms, we elaborate on how professors further "construct" students through their teaching.

THE UNIVERSITY OF ARIZONA:
WINNING A PLACE FOR WOMEN IN THE
ACADEMY AND CURRICULUM

The interaction of the procession of educated men and feminist professors at the University of Arizona has been played out against the beautiful, if stark, backdrop of a semiarid climate, with an expanse of sunny skies and often visible mountains behind the campus. The massive scale of the structures on campus are consistent with the institution's aspirations for national stature. A huge, modern, red-and-blue sculpture by Athena Tacha dominates the east entrance, and two of the most prominent of the 131 buildings are the football stadium and observatory. Among the 3 million books and 2 million other items in the library are specialized publications such as the *Hindustan Times.* The western boundary of the university, where the main gate is located, is abutted by businesses that often cluster near universities—a bookstore, "Kippy's," a favorite lunchtime spot, a Kinko's and a Wendy's. The contrast between the bustle outside the gates and the serenity within is striking. One of the first buildings that meets the eye is Old Main, where the first classes convened in 1891 with thirty-two students and six teachers.[5] At midday, the mall in front of the Student Union is awash with students sunning themselves and eating lunch. Students on skateboards and bicycles, dogs, and Frisbees whiz through this activity.

Here the dominant paradigm of "good teaching" is a scholarly model of "intellectual, consciously 'rational' discourse."[6] The professors believe that knowledge is constructed by discipline-based scholars like themselves and that it is their responsibility to initiate students into that body of knowledge. Consequently, course content rather than students' development is uppermost in their minds. The way classes are organized mirrors this idea of students as passive learners and top-down control. Bells ring to announce the beginning and end of classes. In many classrooms, seats are bolted to the floor. A considerable number of classes take place in large lecture halls where lecturing and "Socratic" methods hold sway. It is not unusual to see a throng of students emerging from the movie theater in mid-afternoon, leaving not a feature film but a biology lecture for more than five hundred students.

However, concern about the quality of undergraduate teaching was in the air when we visited in the spring of 1987, as it has been in the general literature on undergraduate education in recent years. An article in the student newspaper announced the creation by the Arizona Board of Regents of a task force to examine the quality of education at the state's three universities. Various teaching awards were inaugurated in an effort to reward good teaching. In fact, during the semester preceding our fieldwork on campus, one of the feminist scholars we observed in the classroom, Patricia MacCorquodale, received the University Creative Teaching Award. She emphasized its limitations to us:

> Last semester I got the University Creative Teaching Award. . . . The University of Arizona wants to be a research institution, they don't really care about teaching. . . . There's some lip service given to the fact that being a good teacher makes some difference but it really doesn't. There is some movement in the direction of improving teaching. The award that I got now actually goes to people who are teachers. It used to go to people to whom the administration owed a political favor.[7]

An article, "UA said to rank tops in U.S.," in the newspaper, *Lo Que Pasa,* whose primary audience is the Tucson community, captured the University's aspiration to be a renowned research university. In the piece, Henry Koffler, the university president, asserted that Arizona is in the top group of the 3,500 institutions of higher education in the country, noting that in terms of expenditure on research and development, it placed twenty-second among all universities and fourteenth among public institutions. In addition, he noted that the incoming freshmen had record-high average SAT scores.[8]

The feminist culture within this broader institutional culture mirrors the president's ambitions in its heavy emphasis on research. The Southwest Institute for Research on Women (SIROW), an interdisciplinary regional research and resource center, founded and directed until 1989 by Myra Dinnerstein, is among the best in the nation in research and development activities.[9] Despite this focus on research, Pat MacCorquodale emphasized that the Women's Studies faculty were also concerned about their curriculum, if not their classroom pedagogy. In retreats over the years they discussed how courses fit together "so that students aren't hearing the same thing in the sociology and the anthropology and the psychology of women."[10]

Because over 90 percent of the tenured faculty were men, male professors in their "positions as self-defined custodians and beneficiaries of a traditional 'meritocracy'" held great sway over the development of the curriculum and consensus about what constituted knowledge.[11] In this context, the Women's Studies faculty saw their main project as winning a place for women in the academy, both in the curriculum and in the faculty ranks.

Pat MacCorquodale was one of the younger, mostly nontenured, less privileged, feminist women who designed and taught the curriculum transformation project at the university to older, generally powerful, male colleagues.[12] This experience became the spur for her and several colleagues to write about the themes of women's marginality in institutions of higher education, the disciplines, and the curriculum, as well as in the gender politics of the university.[13] They described how they had experienced moments of psychic disequilibrium during the seminars and beyond as they placed their "unexamined, if uneasy participation in the . . . patriarchal academy" in relation to "the truth of the fundamental feminist insight that the intellectual tradition is and has been used to rationalize male dominance."[14]

Leslie Flemming, an associate professor in the Oriental Studies Department, was one of three women who participated in the university's faculty development project; and the seminar's dramatic impact on her intellectual and personal life enabled her to rethink her position in the academy.[15] It was her perception that academic life is not very hospitable to women, that women have a sense that "their very presence in the academy is against all social expectations." Relishing her newly found community of women scholars after years of working primarily with men, she now felt that, after years of relegating women to offhand remarks and brief paragraphs, she could devote her teaching and research to her half of the human race. She wrote about the mainstreaming experience in retrospect:

> Feminist scholarship has made me realize that, despite the usual social expectations and the experiences of most of my age-mates, I have a right to be in the academy, that the struggle to bring and keep me here is not only worth it, but right and just, and that I am indeed helping to effect necessary changes in the roles of women in our society. . . . Mine are the experiences that have been left out of the dominant view of culture.[16]

Among our participants, Flemming expressed the greatest tension about these issues, a tension that had its roots in both her personal and professional life. She recalled her feelings of "terrible isolation" in 1974 as she balanced a career and the birth of the first of her three children. She also endured a discouraging although ultimately successful tenure process. Even though the women's studies seminars helped her to understand the value and importance of women's knowledge and views of the world, she gained no clear conception of feminist pedagogy. Flemming, MacCorquodale, and the other feminists at Arizona felt that they needed to win a place for women at the university on the primarily male terms of scholarly expertise.

Being a student at the university means that you are one of nearly 35,000 students in its undergraduate and graduate programs.[17] The majority of undergraduates are traditional-age college students from Arizona; to be admitted, they must be in the upper third of their high school graduating class. The students we interviewed reflected the population's shift to the sunbelt; all but one had migrated to Arizona from other parts of the country when their parents divorced, for example, or business opportunities attracted them to the Southwest. Despite their large population in Arizona, we saw few Latino students in the classrooms where we observed. MacCorquodale attributed this to the university's failure to recruit and retain Mexican-American students, their poorer preparation for college, and their higher dropout rate. Many who aspire to a college degree enroll in junior colleges with the hope of eventually transferring to the university—an aspiration few achieve.

We found both male and female students to be less conversant with gender issues than their peers on some of the other campuses. MacCorquodale affirmed our perception when she told us that few women on campus had feminist or nontraditional attitudes. Most common were women who "belong to a sorority and come in wearing exactly the right clothes and exactly the right jewelry."

The size of the university and the frequency of large classes create a kind of anonymity for the students. Several spoke of their silence in large lecture classes and their reluctance to speak up in large groups when the professors "have so much material to cover." Although some students found a community for themselves among their sorority sisters, or those who frequented the Women's Center or belonged to a particular ethnic or international community, most did not describe their experiences at the university in terms of belonging to any group, including that of the feminist community. Our interviews with students gave us the impression that they did not in fact see themselves as part of a broader intellectual community, but rather as individual consumers of their education. In this sense they may have conceived of mastery—the accumulation of useful knowledge—in some of the same ways as did most of their professors.

TOWSON STATE UNIVERSITY: TRANSFORMING THE CURRICULUM AND CONSTRUCTING FEMINIST PEDAGOGY ON THE MARGINS

Towson State University, in the words of one of its publications, is the "kind of institution most representative of American higher education—the medium, selective, public, nondoctoral, coeducational university."[18] Originally a teacher-training institution, it became a liberal arts college in 1963. Although the curriculum is a mixture of liberal arts and more professionally oriented studies, the programs with the highest numbers of majors are business administration, mass communication, elementary education, counseling, and psychology. Recruitment brochures emphasized Towson as the best of both worlds, "the best of a large university with a diverse curriculum . . . yet small enough to give you the opportunity for personal growth and a feeling of community."

Like other universities with similar histories, Towson State is known primarily as a teaching rather than a research institution.[19] In the words of Sara Coulter, the co-director of the Transforming the Curriculum Project, "What that gets us in the state is a lower budget and very little respect." This low valuation of teaching within a system of higher education in which prestige and funds accrue to the research settings has reinforced faculty members' experience of Towson State as a lower-status institution. We came away with a general impression of insecurity, a sense of an institutional mission that was somewhat diffuse and underfunded.

When we visited the campus in the fall of 1989, we noted pressure to improve the university's status through more emphasis on research, a process that, in Coulter's words, fed into "the self-fulfilling prophecy of rewarding research and publishing more than teaching [and making us] victims of the system we implement." This shift in emphasis and the fact that promotions had become more scarce worked to limit the time spent with students, even though faculty in general prided themselves on their accessibility to students.

The majority of students are white and of traditional age, many of them transfers from community colleges. Sixty percent are women. The small number of African-American students reflects the racial separation on both the historically Black and the predominantly white campuses in the Maryland system of higher education.[20] Many students are commuters who work their way through college, although in recent years the number of residential students has increased with the building of new dormitories. The students we talked to seemed to see Towson State not so much as a learning community but as a way station on the path to careers, whether in law enforcement, theater, teaching, or social work.

The uneasy "in between" status of the institution within the realm of higher education was mirrored in the composition of the student body by social class; about half the students in the 1986 freshman class were the first in their families to attend college. One professor described the student body as fairly homogeneous; "given the lack of funding for scholarships, you don't have much of a poor class, given our admissions standards are pretty decent . . . we get much more of a broad middle class."[21]

Students themselves were conscious of issues of social class at Towson. In a class discussion, Chuck Sawyer* asserted that the problem with social-class distinctions was that they did not reflect what he determined himself to be, "but what someone else makes of me." Such self-conscious comments led us to see Towson State as a place for upwardly mobile white students, uneasily situated in the class structure of American higher education within a broader society that does not acknowledge class divisions. The recruitment brochure's claim of "opportunity for personal growth" seemed to us to mean an emphasis on individualism apart from a sense of common purpose; the "feeling of community" that the brochure claimed was difficult to discern. This emphasis on the individual was further complicated by status divisions among the students, such as those between residents and commuters, fraternity members and nonmembers.

The campus, although only seven miles north of Baltimore, has a suburban flavor. Large red-brick buildings predominate, laid out around beautifully landscaped, open green spaces and wide walkways. The Student Union, combined with a nearby cluster of high-rise dormitories, gives the campus both a residential air and the impression of providing traditional college social activities. Large posters inside and outside the Student Union announced a variety of activities: Homecoming 1989, a movie series, a sock hop, sports events, and a student trip described as "A Day in the Nation's Capital." The Black Student Union advertised a Homecoming raffle, the proceeds of which would be donated to the Children's Center, a gospel choir concert, and Spike Lee's movie *Do the Right Thing*.

In 1982, *Everywoman's Guide to Colleges and Universities,* a survey and analysis of various educational institutions' offerings for women, ranked Towson with two other schools as highest among institutions of its kind, emphasizing that the majority of campus leadership positions were typically held by women. In addition, it cited the school's strong Women's Studies program, Women's Center, and Affirmative Action program. The Women's Studies program, one of the oldest in the country, was officially begun in 1973, under the leadership of Elaine Hedges, the Director, and Sara Coulter, both full professors in the English Department. Both women had prominence on campus, Hedges as a scholar with more than twelve books to her credit by 1989 and Coulter as a campus leader.[22]

By 1983, ten years after they established the Women's Studies program, the two realized that it was still marginal, and looked for a way of spreading its influence throughout the university. As Coulter observed, "Many faculty regard participation in women's studies as a personal quirk or a leisure-time enthusiasm, like raising dahlias, rather than as a serious area of scholarship." Their solution to the problem was to seek a major grant to integrate the new scholarship on women into the traditional curriculum.[23] More than seventy junior and senior faculty, primarily people who were prominent in the university and many who had reputations as excellent teachers, worked for more than five semesters to revise lower-level survey courses in their disciplines.[24]

In our search for faculty participants, we came to understand that the ongoing tensions about teaching versus research as well as about the status of women's studies were reflected in Coulter's recommendations. When we asked her to identify several faculty who were known for their fine teaching and practice of "feminist pedagogy," she led us to three professors who were marginal both in their departments and in the institution itself, and whose ideas and teaching practices were different from those in the mainstream. This circumstance was partly due to the unavailability of several other potential participants.[25] However, a deeper explanation may have been that, as at Arizona, the project directors felt that changing the curriculum and winning a place for women in the academy were the main tasks of the project. Changing classroom dynamics was a separate issue for them; in Coulter's words, feminist pedagogy was "new, radical, in the early stages of development."

Virginia Gazzam Anderson, a tenured member of the Biology Department in charge of Science Education, initially attended the curriculum-integration seminars at the behest of her department, although she later became an enthusiastic member of the project.[26] By her own admission, Anderson holds a marginal position in her department, due not only to her course assignments in science education but to her innovative, student-centered teaching:

There are people who feel that I am laid back and that I'm not a very good teacher, but they do feel as though the students learn more.

Now, they have been more comfortable since I do it in something that's completely separate from theirs. In other words, when I did it in General Biology, it made people uncomfortable, but when I do it in Biological Literature or Science Education, it doesn't mean that they should have to think about it as an option.

As long as she taught courses that no one else taught, she could teach them in innovative ways.

K Edgington, our second participant, was a full-time writing instructor who had occupied a lecturer's position in the English Department since 1976. As Edgington put it to us, she has probably taught every single writing course offered. The cost of such a varied teaching schedule was highlighted when she told us that her commitment to teaching and activities like editing *On Our Minds,* the newsletter of the Women's Studies program, had prevented her from engaging in the scholarship she would need in order to compete successfully for a tenure-track position.[27] As with Anderson, Edgington's view of knowledge, and of good teaching at Towson, seemed at odds with more conventional views. She thought that "at Towson the ideal is a collaborative effort, where to a degree the professor is a facilitator."

For Anderson, Edgington, and our third informant, Margaret Blanchard, the curriculum-integration seminars helped them to feel more a part of the community, put them in touch with sympathetic colleagues, and created a more supportive environment for innovative teaching than they could find in their home departments. Margaret Blanchard was a long-term part-time writing instructor, whose participation in the curriculum project allowed her to blossom but did not (and could not) solve the problem of her marginality. She described a common situation for many women academics:

I have a temporary position although I have been doing it for fifteen years. I get paid by the course, I have no contract from semester to semester. I have time for my students and my classes and I have time for my own work, so I feel like I'm choosing that, although the price is too high. Being marginal enables you to take risks and to do things. I guess it makes some people more conservative, but for me it is like they can't tell me I can't do this. They aren't paying me enough.[28]

A long history as a feminist political activist in the Baltimore area as well as a successful struggle to increase the pay of part-time teachers at Towson had sustained Blanchard's sturdy self-confidence and her ability to live with her academic situation. However, we were puzzled by a major anomaly between her marginal status and her reputation as an extraordinary teacher. She was recommended to us not only by Sara Coulter but by several other professors in the English Department. Always, when we said we were studying feminist pedagogy, her name came up first. It seemed ironic that in an institution that valued "good teaching," however it was defined, the people whom Coulter saw as good teachers were marginal, relatively powerless, and came from "process" fields, such as writing and education, that are commonly thought of as only transmitting skills and less prestigious than conventional academic disciplines.

The institutional context provided by Towson for the innovative practices we sought was a complex and contradictory one. On the one hand, teaching was valued as it was not at Arizona. In a recent letter to us, Coulter said about her colleagues, for example, that "the faculty as a whole agonize over their syllabi, keep long office hours. . . ." But, she went on, "They may also mostly lecture, agree with your U. of A. professors that their job is to command a body of knowledge, perceive all the new areas of knowledge, like Women's Studies, as a threat to the integrity of academia, and reject instructors like Margaret as lacking standards." In this context, the faculty development grant, although very influential in the evolution of the curriculum at Towson, did not emphasize pedagogical issues. And yet, on the other hand, it was the influence of the grant that created an atmosphere of tolerance and acceptance, if not total inclusion, for teachers like Margaret Blanchard, K Edgington, and Virginia Anderson.

LEWIS AND CLARK COLLEGE: RETHINKING COEDUCATION AND RACIAL DIVERSITY

Since 1982, Lewis and Clark College has hosted an annual Gender Studies Symposium in which students are actively engaged as planners and panelists, giving 80 percent of the papers. Appearing on panels with feminist scholars from around the country are student presentations on topics such as "Women Writers after 1800," "Men and Women in Relationships: Two Responses to Gilligan," and "Social Relations and Ideologies of Reproduction," as well as media presentations on "Women in the Nicaraguan Revolution" and "Women in India." This public display of students as authorities in regard to a body of knowledge is a by-product of an institutional pedagogy that views students as well as professors as creators of knowledge.

The three feminist professors we observed at Lewis and Clark have a persistent concern with the social construction of knowledge from new and different perspectives, particularly those of women but also including those of students. A hallmark of their pedagogy is the practice of beginning with the students' questions rather than the common approach of asking the professors' questions.[29] The English professor Dorothy Berkson's embrace of students' interpretive capacities, described in chapter 1, is representative of the other two professors we worked with as well.

This pedagogy reflects not only their beliefs about the students' role in the construction of knowledge, but how they fashion their own roles, making careful distinctions between their engagement with the subject matter and their performance as teachers. Nancy Grey Osterud, an assistant professor in the History Department at the time we observed her class, told us how she had come to realize this distinction during a discussion of a basic concept in the field of gender studies. She had assumed that the students (about half the class) who were silent just needed time and opportunity to become equal participants, and did not realize that they felt unprepared to join a discussion that presumed so much knowledge and experience with regard to gender issues. She said:

> This became a self-reinforcing pattern, so I did not become aware that some students were confused until later in the term, when many had worked their way out of the initial difficulty by themselves. . . . *In this instance, my engagement with the subject matter interfered with my performance as a teacher.*[30]

This kind of pedagogy illustrates a major shift from perceiving students as knowers only in terms of the teacher's notions of knowledge to viewing them as learners in charge of their own questions. These professors expected students to fashion their voices, discover their own authority, and engage in creating knowledge with the teacher and with each other.

Laurie Finke, of the English Department, recalled feeling like an outsider until she came to understand the "unwritten notion about what constitutes good teaching here . . . which emphasizes discussion, self-development of the students, and working them toward some kind of independence." The vehicle for her development as a teacher and her education into the culture of teaching was the weekly seminar in which faculty members who taught in the Gender Studies Program came together to talk about their pedagogy. (She had been teaching at the college for three years when we observed her classes during the 1986–87 academic year.) As she put it, "Being on the first Basic Inquiry team was virtually a lesson in pedagogy. We got to try out a lot of stuff and we got to talk to each other about what we did."

Because they viewed the classroom as an important setting for the construction of knowledge, both Laurie Finke and Dorothy Berkson saw their teaching and research as part of a symbiotic relationship. Finke taught a course *and* wrote a book on literary theory.[31] Berkson's curriculum-integration work took the form of pairing female and male texts around themes and issues in nineteenth- and twentieth-century America. As she experimented with the pairing of texts in her courses and saw how they fed both the students' and her own thinking, she conceived of the idea of a book comparing nineteenth-century male and female writers.[32]

Lewis and Clark began its history as Albany College in 1867, residing initially in the Oregon town of that name, and moving to its present location in Portland in 1942. When you leave Interstate 5 and take the road leading up to Lewis and Clark, you begin to climb through an area of huge pines, and for a moment you think you've entered a deep forest that will go on forever. But suddenly you come to the top of Palatine Hill, and in the clearing you catch your first glimpse of the college. The playing fields and the bleachers seem diminutive in comparison to the tall trees. Both the main gate, a former carriage house of a major estate, and the Manor House, where the administrative offices are housed, are of English Tudor architecture. Despite the New World, "new money" opulence of the Manor House, and its beautiful natural environment, with a perfect view of Mount Hood on clear days, the majority of buildings on campus are modest. With the exception of the science and humanities buildings, many of the faculty offices and classes are housed in little more than temporary constructions and prefabricated bungalows.[33]

From its earliest history, the college characterized itself as providing an equal education for women and men:

> The student body numbered eighty-six, forty-three women and forty-three men. Albany always received women on equal terms with men, never keeping them separate in academic work or making special rules for them, as in some neighboring colleges. . . . The only concession made to the women was that English might be substituted for higher mathematics.[34]

More than a century later, the college still prided itself in being an institution that was not only working to balance the curriculum with regard to gender but also providing an "equal education for both women and men within a single curriculum." However, a 1982 report, "The Issue of Gender in the Lewis and Clark Curriculum," which was later published as "Reassessing Coeducation," expressed caution at being too euphoric about the institution's progress toward gender equity. It detailed how women and men were receiving different educations although they had access to what was considered a single curriculum. The sexes diverged in course selection as men gravitated to the sciences, business administration, political science, and economics, and women were concentrated in the humanities, the "softer" social sciences of psychology and sociology, and in one science, biology. The authors of the report concluded that a truly liberal contemporary education would "offer women and men equal access to the same curriculum, and at the same time ensure that the curriculum is not limited to male-defined values and concerns."[35]

The impetus for this report, as well as a renewed interest in women's issues, was a four-week faculty development seminar in women's studies held in the summer of 1981.[36] Over the next several years, feminist faculty members, including Mary Kay Tetreault, explored the implications of feminist scholarship for their disciplines, the nature of knowledge, and the content of their courses through a coalition called the Women's Interest Group (WIGS). They also harnessed the energy ignited during the seminar toward further institutionalization of gender issues through a reconceptualization of the college's mission statement.[37] By 1984, a Gender Studies Concentration had been formed, with the explicit purpose of addressing "the intersection of gender, race, class, and culture." In these efforts all three of our participants were active, Dorothy Berkson having joined the faculty and the Women's Interest Group in 1981, Laurie Finke in 1983, and Grey Osterud in 1984.

Because of this widespread exploration of gender issues, it was common for students to expect course material to reflect feminist questions. Many students we interviewed narrated a story similar to Carole Reagan's*, who as a senior recalled how she was "blown away by a women's studies class I took my freshman year." She also found herself in sociology and anthropology and English classes where every professor was a feminist. She said:

> There is an assumption that everybody in the class is either feminist or sympathetic toward women's issues and very conscious of gender roles. . . . I guess tipping things over and looking at them from an entirely different point of view has opened up other channels of my mind.

However, echoing the authors of the report on coeducation, Ted Michelini, a chemistry major, said that this focus on gender occurred more in the humanities than the sciences: "I had a Women's Writers course that was very interesting. I kind of feel like in the sciences I do miss out on a lot of things that women would have anything to do with."

One of the challenges at an institution where 85 percent of the students are white is in integrating issues of race, culture, and gender. By 1987 there was a persistent concern on the part of some faculty to racially balance the curriculum and to "aid in the movement toward racial justice by advocating respect for cultural diversity and self-determination of all peoples."[38] Grey Osterud was in the forefront of this effort. However, she left Lewis and Clark in 1988, in part because she could not accept the limitations she discovered, "limits rooted in the fundamental nature, social location, and ideology of this institution." To Osterud's mind, the very focus on student perspectives that characterized the Gender Studies Program was a part of the problem. While this emphasis "passed as feminist because it seemed to be supportive and sisterly, in practice it reinforced the exclusion and subordination of people of color."

> The culture of our gender studies program validates personal experiences and suppresses the expression of differences that challenge other peoples' perspectives. People feel empowered to speak of their own experiences, and construct theory on that basis, and that is good. But they do not feel impelled to include other peoples' experience in their explanatory frameworks, . . . and when the other people insist that their experiences too must be taken into account, they respond with barely-concealed hostility.[39]

This meant, as she put it, that whatever interracial communication took place occurred "as a result of the determined yet patient efforts of students of color themselves." Like most Americans, white students at Lewis and Clark regarded race as a problem of nonwhite people and held them responsible for solving it. Ron Underwood, an African-American senior history major, believed that whites think that "the Black experience is too far away from our lives, so far away from our lives that we can't, as whites, talk about it." He wondered what it would be like if there were no Black people in the room because "I'm usually the only Black student in classes and I always wonder what they're going to say about Black people when I'm not in the room. To what extent are they going to come in and objectify Black people because I think that's what a lot of the root of racism is."

Cheryl Ibabao felt invalidated as a Filipino-American as well. She said: "I wish we would try to imagine ourselves to be something other than white upper-class people. . . . *We've been focusing on Black and white America and the thing is that Black and white America doesn't exist."*

WHEATON COLLEGE:
BUILDING A "GENDER-BALANCED"
ENVIRONMENT FOR WOMEN AND MEN

Wheaton was established in 1834 by Mary Lyon, the founder of Mount Holyoke, and prides itself on having been one of the oldest women's colleges in New England until it admitted men in 1988. These origins are visible today in its pastoral, almost unworldly, aura. Arranged around a long green central quadrangle, the buildings include a prominent and classic Greek Revival chapel, a large library, also with Greek columns, and groups of nineteenth-century red-brick buildings housing dormitories, classrooms, and the administration. Down a small hill lies a lake, complete with geese, around which are several newer dormitories built when the college expanded in the 1960s.

Driven by declining enrollments, Wheaton College changed in the fall of 1988 from being an historically all-women's college to becoming a coeducational institution that would still preserve the values of the original community.[40] In 1983, President Alice Emerson captured those values when she wrote:

> Women's colleges were founded on the belief that what women do matters.
> . . . it is our reason for being. Faculty members at colleges for women believe
> it is important for women to be educated to undertake significant work in
> the future. This combination of factors made women's colleges the logical
> institutions to pioneer on behalf of integrating the study of women into the
> curriculum.[41]

The pioneering to which Emerson alluded took the form of the Balanced Curriculum Project, launched to integrate the new scholarship on women into introductory courses. It was conceived and driven by the administration, a factor that spoke for the uniquely woman-centered nature of the institution.[42] Not only the president but the provost and just over half the one hundred faculty are women.

Over the more than ten years since the project began, there has developed a broad culture of support for gender equality and a gender-equal education. It was work on the project and a subsequent Feminist Theory Study Group that brought the newer, overtly feminist faculty together as an intellectual and social community, including two of our participants, Beverly Clark and Kersti Yllo, as well as Frinde Maher.[43] These feminists soon became central to the institution, in a place where faculty wield a comparatively large amount of institutional and curricular power and responsibility. As Clark noted, members of the theory group are "past and present chairs of the Tenure Committee and the chair of the Educational Policy Committee," which deals with curriculum decisions for the college.

This generation of feminist faculty have gone through several stages in evolving what it means to offer a gender-balanced education—first to women and then to both women and men. The first phase of initial curriculum integration, during which over half the courses in the colleges were revised to include women in some way, gave way to a concern several years later with the racism and exclusionary frameworks of the early scholarship on women. The next phase was to add non-Western and cultural-diversity requirements to the Wheaton curriculum. In the third phase, the gradual move toward a curriculum balanced by "gender, race, class, and culture" was interrupted by the decision to become coeducational.

We began our work at Wheaton in 1987 knowing that this last year of single-sex education would mean a heightened awareness of imminent changes in the culture of feminism.[44] One of the students, Elisabeth Stitt, described her sense of this unique, and disappearing, female environment: "I didn't have to look at the other [masculine] side of the question because the other side of the question is not present in your daily life to be forced to look at. . . . I'm absolutely immersed in this women's community. . . . A typical male figure here is just a shock to the system."

Because of this "shock to the system" about to take place the next year, because of the national reputation of the Balanced Curriculum Project, and because of the, by now, longstanding commitment of the faculty and administration to the education of women, the college embarked on an official mission, still under way, to develop a new model of coeducation that keeps women and issues of gender at the center of their enterprise. According to the Task Force on the Learning Environment, its rationale is "rooted in our awareness that women and men are, from birth, socialized differently, treated differently, and generally expected to behave differently." The goal is to establish "a learning environment in which the pursuit of a strong liberal arts education is facilitated for women and men by a sensitivity to gender issues on the part of faculty, staff, and students."[45]

The other central aspect of Wheaton as an institution is its focus on teaching, and on the classroom as an important arena where knowledge can come from the students as well as the professors. With administrative encourage-ment, a series of monthly teaching workshops was initiated in 1982 to explore general issues in teaching.[46] One of the areas of discussion, sparked by landmark studies of women as knowers and learners such as *Women's Ways of Knowing*, was the notion that different approaches to learning could be part of classroom epistemology. In the words of the task force report, classrooms would "offer a range of learning experiences and approaches to accommodate and value student diversity . . . cooperative interchanges as well as arguments . . . topics addressed experientially as well as theoretically."

We saw these distinguishing qualities of the institution—an emphasis on teaching and the centrality of gender—reflected in our informants as they helped to shape and were shaped by the college culture. In terms of her own background and place at Wheaton, Beverly Clark, who described her-self as having "a pretty strong feminist inclination" when she started teach-ing at the college, saw the Balanced Curriculum Project as supporting and extending her development as a feminist.[47] Clark described the culture of feminism at Wheaton as focused on exploring what in many places is a "bywater," namely, the production of knowledge from a self-consciously *gen-dered,* student-centered point of view.

> We are engaged in the social construction of knowledge in a teaching and learning community. We want to know what the discipline is doing, what the department is doing, what I am doing about the con-struction of our students' identity. We have a history and a commit-ment to develop new knowledge, but we aren't mainly a research institution. Our knowledge is a collaborative knowledge built into the deep structure of our courses.

A second participant, Bianca Cody Murphy, who joined the Psychology Department in 1986, was drawn to Wheaton because of the institution's clarity about its values. She felt that the college was "an atmosphere that was conducive to the kind of teaching I like to do . . . and and I loved having col-leagues I could talk to about how I teach. I think most people would agree that gender is central at Wheaton, and that we pay attention to teaching."[48]

The culture of feminism at Wheaton also helped make it possible for her to be an "out" lesbian, both as the faculty advisor to the Gay and Lesbian Student Alliance, and in her classes. She pointed out to us recently that the student handbook not only "affirmed diversity," but explicitly supported the *visibility* of lesbian and gay students, staff, and faculty members. She said, "It's pretty impressive. It's one hundred steps beyond where every other place is."[49]

The supportive environment for feminism at Wheaton also enabled Kersti Yllo, in the Sociology Department, to take a self-consciously radical and consciousness-raising stance in regard to her teaching. Her feminism dates back to her undergraduate days at Denison University, where she took her first women's studies course and decided to study family sociology.[50] She told us in an interview that she enjoyed the role of interpreter of radical feminist views to others. Indeed, she is able at Wheaton to not only infuse all her courses with feminist content, but to teach a course, based on her research expertise, entitled Violence Against Women. This advanced seminar, taught every other year, culminates in a series of campus-wide presentations on topics such as battered women and date rape; and many students who take her course work in local battered-women's shelters and on hot lines.

The students at Wheaton seem very homogeneous to the visitor's eye; they are largely white, middle class, and of traditional college age.[51] As an overwhelmingly residential campus, the college provides much of the students' social as well as academic and extracurricular life. With coeducation, they even tend to stay around on weekends; the campus used to be deserted as the young women sought a social life in nearby Boston and Providence, Rhode Island. While their academic credentials place the students as average academically, our teacher informants found them often diverse and challenging, and some very bright.

Stanley DeSilva was among the 80 men, out of 1,100 students, who enrolled in the fall of 1988. Asked about his sense of the importance of gender at Wheaton and the kind of male the college wanted to admit, he described "a male student that was aware of the traditions of the school, a male that didn't want to come in here and suddenly assume the traditional male role, a male that was willing to gradually . . . become integrated with the community."

In general, students' viewed Wheaton as an environment in which there was tremendous support for their development as women (and men) and a strong sense of their teachers respecting them as knowers and even experts in their own education; like their professors, they felt that they were constructors of knowledge. However, those views have changed with coeducation, reflecting the strengths and weaknesses of the shifting experiences of homogeneity and diversity.

The uniquely female environment that Elisabeth Stitt described so positively in 1987 was balanced by a quite common sense among students at that time of being isolated from the "real world." The women's communities forged in the classrooms of the single-sex Wheaton were those of middle-class white women, even though all the syllabi we looked at included material on women of color, gays and lesbians, and other less "mainstream" populations. Yet, in the absence of a significant number of diverse perspectives, marginal voices tended to be silenced, or subsumed. Echoing Ron Underwood at Lewis and Clark, Michelle Barnett, the only African-American student in Clark's Feminist Criticism class, observed: "White women often say that they might not be able to understand a Black woman's experience. In conversations with other Black women at Wheaton, we get the sense that white women cop out. . . . They say that your experience is 'too complex' for us to understand."

Thus the sense of Wheaton as an oasis was built not only on its strengths—a unified commitment to women's lives and potentials—but also on its whiteness, which was not changed by coeducation. Many faculty members realize that the challenge before the college now is to apply the issues of difference posed by the presence of mainly white men to the wider domains of race, culture, class, and other forms of diversity. Perhaps students like Stanley DeSilva, who were attracted by the admissions office's attention to diversity and openness about "their multicultural orientation and minority recruitment" will be instrumental in moving Wheaton beyond, in his words, its "preppy, Waspy" reputation. But given that both students and faculty still include very few people of color, the concepts of "woman" and "man" that are constructed at Wheaton are primarily still middle class and white.

SPELMAN COLLEGE: CREATING OPPOSITIONAL KNOWLEDGE FROM BLACK WOMEN'S STANDPOINTS

In the fall of 1989, Johnnetta Cole, the president of Spelman College, taught a women's studies class with Beverly Guy-Sheftall, the director of Women's Studies; it was held in the downstairs den of the president's house. During our visit to the last class of the semester, the group of twelve students (out of seventeen enrolled) and their professors sat informally around a big table. The students gave reports on fieldwork they had undertaken with a number of community agencies in the Atlanta area such as the National Black Women's Health Project, a women's shelter at the local YWCA, the Witness/Victim Assistance Program, Narcotics Anonymous, and a family-planning clinic.[52] Many of the students noted that these agencies served predominantly African-American populations.

Mentioning the need for more African-American volunteers, the student whose project involved the YWCA remarked, "How long will it take for white people to stop taking care of us?" The two teachers peppered the presentations with brief, supportive comments, often stressing the commonality between people in the room and the people outside: "You can see yourself in these clinics," said Guy-Sheftall, or as Cole put it, "I think, that's *me* down there." At the end of the last session there was an outpouring of appreciation for the course. Guy-Sheftall remarked, "This is really a feminist class, seeing you all speak, get empowered, get analytical about your lives"; Cole added, to appreciative groans, "I might trade the presidency for this!"

Five years later, this scene of an activist teacher-president and her Women's Studies class still stands out. Spelman College was founded in 1881 as the Atlanta Baptist Female Seminary by white New England missionaries, whose purpose was the education of "young Black women just out of slavery and eager to acquire educational skills." Today, Spelman's purpose is still to empower Black women and enable them to succeed on their own terms in the larger society. The institutional transformation produced by Cole's presence as the first African-American "sister" president in the history of the college was built upon feminist work that began with the founding of a women's studies program in 1981.[53] Within this framework, professors and students alike worked to construct a comprehensive vision of the world from the standpoint of a group that always was placed at the bottom. Gloria Wade-Gayles, one of the professors whom we observed, said that teaching at Spelman brought to mind a West Indian proverb: the herb most used and most thrown away is the Black woman.[54]

The vision of these feminist professors was of teachers connected to their students within a safe, yet embattled, haven away from the restrictions imposed by white society. Mona Phillips, whose Sociology of Women course we observed for one week, spoke to her students about their position in terms of a metaphor—the "dark enclosure" of gender within the "narrow space" of race:

> We have, as Gloria Gayles says, always been conscious of the narrow space—the narrow space. The only interesting question is the ways in which we have negotiated the dark enclosure within that narrow space. You can take that theoretical construct and [use it to] make sense of Black women's history.[55]

The Spelman campus, a series of tall, wide, red-brick buildings, is arranged around a spacious central quadrangle that gives it the air of a New

England college, although the trees and flowers everywhere bespeak the South. One has indeed the impression of being in an enclosure, a green and quiet oasis, which is reinforced by a high chain fence that surrounds the campus and divides it from the housing project that lies just beyond its gates.[56] A large and elegant Greek Revival building, the Sisters Chapel, marks one end of the Spelman quadrangle. Alongside it are the president's house, where the Women's Studies class was held, and classroom and office buildings. Several dormitories lie across the quadrangle, among them Abby Aldrich Rockefeller Hall.[57]

Before Johnnetta Cole's arrival, the college had been primarily known as a prestigious setting for Black women to become educated young ladies. The majority of the faculty used to be white, as were most former presidents, although in recent years the balance had reversed. A former student and director of the Honors Program, Ethel Githii, drew these contrasts in an interview on National Public Radio:

> We were white-gloved and hatted whenever we left the campus. . . . We were perfect models of what, and some will not be happy with this description, of what the finest and best in white schools should be. [But] the standards of quality for students now are not limited to those set by whites. We now have a president who looks like us. And we can follow her example . . . and it's wonderful.[58]

Cole herself, in the NPR interview, voiced her commitment to challenging Spelman's elite image, saying, "One of the things that we (emphasize) at Spelman is the sense in which these women are very connected to African-American communities. So within that group of women that we select, we insist that there be some women who are [according to Mary Bethune's phrase] 'diamonds in the rough.'"[59] In the same interview, Guy-Sheftall elaborated on the importance of having a college president who is concerned about Africa and says it's all right to identify yourself as an African-American. Not only were more students wearing "afros" and braids, but there was much more emphasis on Black Women's Studies from an international perspective, and on a curriculum engaged with cutting-edge issues of race and gender.

This new vision of putting African-American women at the center was paired with Cole's explicit and much quoted concern that Spelman women use their education to "build sturdy Black bridges into the very communities from which we have come and into those that surround us," always keeping in mind their ties with other Black women, and with Black men and children. In an interview in 1988, she asked: "How can we call ourselves either educated or leaders if we turn away from the very reality that a third of Black America lives in poverty?"[60]

The Spelman of 1990, then, seemed to be an institution in the process of remaking itself. Drawing on an older tradition of community service by Black women, the new leadership placed Black women's identities, and their commonality with the larger Black community, at the center of their model of learning and leadership. Mona Phillips described a unique concept of Black womanhood emerging from the overlapping dimensions of African-American women's lives: "home overlaps with community, overlaps with the workplace . . . and by community again I mean residence, neighborhood, and the larger African-American community."[61]

In searching for the impact of the institution on teaching practices and students' educational experiences, we found that for our faculty informants, if not for all teachers at Spelman, the most important feature of this new community ethos was its political epistemology: our participants found knowledge and truth in those stories and concepts that explicitly served the needs of the Black community. Knowledge was understood as serving a unified and cohesive African-American community, *against* the expertise of white scholars, which was seen as deeply racist and historically destructive of Black lives.

There were two powerful aspects of this epistemological stance. One was the clear understanding that truth was political, positional, and linked to the struggle for social change. The other was its communal and supportive nature. Learning was not understood to be an individual attribute or achievement; rather, the emphasis in classes and in interviews was on the collective mastery they would need in order to succeed as Black women and, in so doing, help the men and children in their wider community. Teaching and learning were tasks that were not simply intellectual, but also emotional and political—matters of community survival.

Both Phillips and Wade-Gayles saw the need to create for their students an "enclosure" of intellectual encouragement and emotional support. Phillips offered her students a constant listening ear, often turning up in the cafeteria at breakfast time for informal "office hours." One student called Phillips's class a "family." An article in the *New York Times Magazine* cited Wade-Gayles in its depiction of Spelman's nurturing atmosphere:

> At Spelman, for example, if a student's work in Dr. Gloria Wade-Gayles'
> class is falling off, the student is far less likely to get a failing grade than an

invitation to come talk with her professor about what is wrong. [Said Wade-Gayles], "If a family member has lost a job or something, I give the student space. Teaching at Spelman is not a bottom-line kind of thing."[62]

Within this nurturing atmosphere, we also noticed the inevitable tensions that arose in the course of developing a cohesive oppositional knowledge. In their lives, as in their construction of knowledge, professors and students had to confront the positions of white people, Black men, and the rest of the Black community. In addition, there were divisions within the Spelman community, such as those based on social class and wealth. One radical student mocked others who walked around in fancy clothes, or carried shopping bags from stores such as Ann Taylor. "We have Black people who are so scared of giving up their credit cards," she said, arguing for the Black community to engage in self-help economic projects. Yet, another activist student was engaged in community organizing in the housing project just beyond Spelman's fence, believing that in this way she was mitigating the hostility toward Spelman students.

The students whom we got to know all had an extremely strong sense of Spelman as the supportive and engaging place that faculty participants sought for them. Moreover, as part of their sense of Spelman, they were very conscious of the role of these faculty members, and others in Women's Studies, in putting Black women's concerns at the core of their education. Angela Waters, a senior English major and poet in Phillips's class, put it this way: "I went to an all-Black high school, but I think that the differences between my high school and Spelman is that here I am introduced to a lot of stuff about Black women."

Finally, the students we interviewed perceived themselves as different from other Spelman women in their feminism, even in their social activism, and regarded their feminist teachers as playing a critical role within the institution. Wendy Johnson described many Spelman women as passive, or unwilling to speak up for fear of being labeled as radicals. In contrast, she felt Phillips's students were different "because we are not going to sit by and just accept anything":

My awareness has been so heightened since I set foot on this campus, especially about Black male domination over women. . . . We are Morehouse's cheerleading team, their support, and they are called the house and we are called the yard! You leave your house and come to the yard to play.

Marta Thomas*, who grew up in an upper-middle-class suburb in New Jersey, struggled at Spelman with issues of social commitment, relations with white people, and other difficult personal issues. But she was eloquent about the college and its effect on her as a student and a person. After ongoing debates with other African-American friends who attended college with whites, she believed none of them understood what they were missing. But she concluded, "I don't think they'll see it now, they'll see it in ten years. . . . It's so much more challenging here for me than at a white school."

SAN FRANCISCO STATE UNIVERSITY: WOMEN STUDIES FROM THE PERSPECTIVE OF WOMEN OF COLOR

While we were on campus in March 1991, we noticed a striking display outside the Women Studies office: a montage of photographs of professors in the department, who are predominately women of color. Accompanying the display was a Xeroxed packet, "Women of Color Classes," consisting of course descriptions written by students. As shown in the following excerpts, it promised an education focusing on an expanded, internationalist view of women's lives that does not separate the color from the woman:

TRANSLATING WOMEN'S EXPERIENCE THROUGH WRITING: Let the double vision of Chinosole, as an Afro-American, and Osa Hidalgo, as a Chicana, be a catalyst for a rainbow Women of Color womanist expression that gives you all the space and paper you need to write according to your own personal intuitive and practical needs. The course is tailor-made for the individual, with ample and plentiful commentary on your writing. . . . from the tiniest problems of mechanics, such as comma splices, to the grandest evocations of poetry!

LITERATURE BY WOMEN OF COLOR: Finally a course that studies our sisters: twentieth-century contributions from African-American, Latina/Chicana, Native-American and Asian-American/Pacific women! . . . Guided by Merle Woo, an accomplished author, these meetings will be filled with insight and analyses.[63]

INCARCERATED WOMEN: This course will take you through the history and politics of incarcerated women. You, as the student, will investigate the reasons behind women's overwhelming presence in the prisons, jails, juvenile detention centers, and mental institutions of the United States. . . . When you finish this course with Ericka Huggins and Angela Davis, you will have developed a greater understanding of the spiritual and emotional effects of all women imprisoned physically and mentally in this society.

Our conversations with Chinosole, the Chair of Women Studies, led us to see these photographs and descriptions as a barometer of the goals set by herself and her colleagues. Struggling against their "uneasy participation in the disciplines of the patriarchal academy," they also experienced an uneasy participation in feminist scholarship until they were able to fuse this knowledge with cultural studies, specifically African-American and Third World scholarship.

When we initially described their work as building "oppositional knowledge," Chinosole objected, for she believes that such a conceptualization makes male-dominated Eurocentric knowledge too important and does not capture how relevant this new critical and political knowledge is to the social conditions in which we live. More important than opposing the dominant discourse, she wrote, is "opening up the simplest facts about ourselves, understanding distinct social and cultural continuities, adding to the threads of knowledge, finding new modes of understanding, different goals of education." Chinosole and her colleagues are building feminist/womanist theory that redefines some of the basic issues in women's studies by uncovering the ways in which race, ethnicity, class, gender, and sexuality interact and illuminate each other. Of utmost importance to the department faculty is developing an inclusive knowledge that goes across cultures and beyond the boundaries of the United States.

Carla Trujillo, one of the teachers we observed, was a lecturer at "State" and one of the people whose photo was part of the montage of Women Studies faculty. Very conscious of herself as a Latina within a diverse student community, she recalled her first impressions of "State":

> I spent the first three weeks getting used to the "State" system, which is intensely different from the University of California system. There are very different class dynamics. I spent my time walking around with my eyes open all the time because the students looked like me, everybody was predominately from a working-class background or worked full-time or they were putting themselves through school just like I did.[64]

Her sense of her own position is tied to growing up as a Latina in California, which she experienced as a situation of unequal power relations that "tries to take away what we have within us by telling us that we are inferior, or no good, or that we won't succeed." As a result of her own personal and social background, Trujillo works to empower students to be true to their potential.

The Women Studies Department at San Francisco State, which first offered courses in 1970–71 and gained approval to offer the B.A. by 1976, did not always take this stance toward women of color. Angela Davis, the feminist scholar and political activist, began teaching in the department in the late 1970s. She recalled how at first, as the only woman of color, she felt she was criticized because of her efforts to integrate an analysis of racism into the analysis of sexism that she and the program founders presented. As Davis put it, "I can remember when I first tried to put them together . . . the assumption was that there was something called gender, or somebody called woman, and bringing those concepts together was seen as a challenge to the prevailing conceptions of feminism. . . . Quite a few students criticized me for speaking about racism too much." Davis saw these patterns change when Chinosole became Chair and began to develop the program to reflect the diversity of the student body and thus attract larger numbers of women of color.[65] To Davis's mind, it's the only women's studies department in the country on a historically white campus where it is possible to focus in a serious way on the contributions of women of color.[66]

Like many other women's studies departments, the one at State had its genesis in community activism. However, over the years the department conformed more and more to the disciplinary values of the academy. Feeling a sense of urgency about the problems in their communities as well as their personal histories of political activism, Chinosole and her colleagues saw the need to return to those earlier community ties because of their importance to theory building, the rendering of services to the community, and their potential for transforming the university. Chinosole summarized her position when she said: "We need this reality check, we need this accountability, we need this comprehension. This has got to affect the theory that we do. Community work cannot be done by phone."[67]

We were conscious of State as an urban university the first time we rode the trolley to campus. As the trolley made its way to the university, cars began to fill with students of all ages from a complex mixture of cultures that reflected the diversity of the student body.[68] No ivory tower, San Francisco State is the most ethnically diverse and class-conscious of the institutions we visited, and it has a large and visible lesbian/gay presence. Once the trolley—which runs parallel to the main entrance to the university—stopped, the throng of students spread out across the tracks to their destinations on campus. The trolley is an apt symbol of the physical and social connection of this educational environment and students' other, equally full lives at work and at home.[69] Although a broad green commons is situated at the center of campus surrounded by the library, the business school, and the student union, the school has a bustling, city pace at all hours.

What is most important about the institution's status as an urban university is the extent to which many of the economic and social issues of our cities are played out on the campus.[70] Faculty, administrators, and students are struggling to build an inclusive university in which the historically unequal power relations among diverse groups are made explicit. Beatrice Gordon, an art major who is African-American, focused on the challenges and tensions posed by so much diversity when she imagined what it would be like to be a student at Spelman:

> I'd like to experience a Black college because it would be like home in many ways. Whereas here, you're constantly trying to build a home and it's constantly being attacked, if not torn down. I would imagine at a place like Spelman your needs are met at a deeper level. I could look around and identify on a level where there's no words.
>
> Here, everyone is trying to develop words and find the right words and that's what exhausts you. . . . There comes a point where unity cannot exist on this campus because it can go so far, [then it] dissolves and branches off. So everything becomes disunified again, until we find that common thread, but then that is going to dissolve and break.
>
> In the classrooms . . . there's just so much diversity that you have to decide which point of view you are going to stick to. Are you going to spread yourself thin with each point of view? At Spelman, I think that the amount will narrow itself down, not only because you're women but you're African-American women.

Beatrice's perception that boundaries always had to be defended and that knowledge construction was embattled is accurate not only personally but institutionally. The context in which some faculty and students were attempting to build a "home" for students like Beatrice was one in which the politics of knowledge were politicized in a much more overt way than in the other institutions we visited. The courses we observed frequently began with announcements of political or antiwar speakers, rallies, and teach-ins.

This highly charged political culture had its origins in the student strike of 1967, called to institute Third World Studies and open enrollment at the university. Ruth Doell, a full professor in the Biology Department and one of our participants, recalled how the strike politicized departments:

I went out on strike (as a part-time lecturer) and that influenced my career enormously. It was a definitive event and it made for political repercussions for many years. I was on strike in a division that did not believe in the strike. I worked with colleagues afterwards who thought I was pretty radical, and more than radical, undesirable. There were a lot of people who were fired over that and who didn't survive. I've always thought I was lucky, very lucky, not to have lost my job.

Following the strike, however, Doell was "punished" with what was considered an undesirable course schedule. Instead of teaching upper-division major courses in microbiology, she was assigned Biology 100, which, according to Doell, "was not considered very prestigious. But I found it absolutely fascinating to teach non-majors."[71]

The academic year when we visited, we witnessed sharp contests for knowledge and power on a number of fronts, as groups sharing conceptualizations of race, ethnicity, and gender sought to build consensus and political clout by asserting common interests, knowledge, and demands. Numerous times we heard students introduce their remarks in classes by saying, "As a white, Jewish, lesbian feminist," or "Because I am an Asian-American, working-class woman." In no other institution did we find such a consciousness of positionality both *outside* and *inside* the classroom, as if people somehow understood the particularity, and limits, of any one view of knowledge and truth.

However, these struggles over identity politics can become divisive and painful, and in 1990 open conflict was apparent in a number of arenas. The student newspaper carried articles about the dispute between the Black Studies Department and the Political Science Department over the latter's addition of a course in Black politics to be taught by an expert in the field who is African-American. Students shut down President Robert A. Corrigan's fall convocation, in which the first honorary doctorate was presented to an Asian, to protest state budget cuts and what they believed was the president's attempt to dismantle the School of Ethnic Studies. As a protest against U.S. involvement in the Gulf War, students built a shanty town, "Little Baghdad," which remained standing after the cease-fire as a way of provoking discussion about the war. The most tense moments occurred when campus police in riot gear surrounded the unit. The Vice-President for Academic Affairs, Marilyn Boxer, who did pioneering work in women's studies, was subjected to a vote of "no confidence" after she and President Corrigan denied promotions to eight faculty members in various departments and she rejected a recommendation for an additional tenure-track appointment in Women Studies.

Although Women Studies has been less protective of its "turf" than some departments, it, too, has a long history of contentious relationships among groups with different standpoints, who have tried to articulate and solidify demands around the claims of different categories of gender identity. More recently with the budget cuts, divisions have arisen because women of color, to an extent, control both tenure lines and lecturer positions. Part-time lecturers have become increasingly insecure as their needs are weighed against those of tenure-line faculty and curricular requirements. Beatrice Gordon is right when she suggests that forging a diverse women's studies community is a constant and exhausting challenge.

Despite these internal conflicts over power and ideology, the general campus atmosphere, the pathbreaking approach of the Women Studies Department, and Chinosole's work toward community building allow for radical departures that nourish a diverse, nontraditional faculty, curriculum, and students.[72] For students, Women Studies is a unique and treasured place in the university. Jilchristina Vest, a Women Studies major of mixed African- and European-American ancestry, said she "got her politics" at State. She described Women Studies in this way:

> For the first time you're not the minority, you're the majority. It's just nice being in a classroom with people who are literally your peers, literally from similar cultures and similar backgrounds, . . . just to be around people that you don't have to explain yourself to all the time, and you're not like this specimen.

To return to Virginia Woolf's metaphor that introduced this chapter, we have attempted here to outline the institutional assumptions and cultures that have shaped our informants' participation in "the procession of educated men." Before we move the procession into specific classrooms, we want to highlight some aspects of institutional culture that are critically important for feminist pedagogy to flourish. First is the extent to which innovative, student-centered teaching is valued in the institution. Except for Women Studies at San Francisco State, teaching was most innovative at the three liberal arts colleges, in which feminist professors were at the heart of the institution. At other campuses such as Towson State University, where the norms of good teaching remained more traditional, where two of our participants had yet to complete their doctorates, and where all three informants came from less prestigious disciplines such as education or writing, feminist teachers were marginalized. Another important factor in fostering feminist pedagogy is the extent to which the campus climate is a comfortable one for women, as measured, for instance, by the degree to which it is safe to be overtly feminist, or the extent to which top administrators signal the importance of matters of gender, ethnicity, class, and culture. Finally, the period during which women's studies first blossomed on a campus makes a difference in terms of the curricular emphasis on gender and the appeal of gender studies programs to the widest variety of students. We attribute the presence of men in feminist classes at Lewis and Clark more than at any other institution partially to its Gender Studies Program, which is based in feminist theory. Enrollment in its introductory course, The Social and Cultural Construction of Gender, is typically divided equally between women and men.

CHAPTER THREE

Mastery

━━

"What could you possibly learn by studying us?"
"What would happen if what was inside us were to enter the world?"
—Carol Gilligan

If you want to take a class with women, with people of color, . . . come to the Women Studies Department and start learning about things that they told you you didn't need to know. . . . learning about me, instead of learning about them, starting to learn about her instead of learning about him, it's a connection that makes education education.
—Jilchristina Vest, a student at San Francisco State University

THIS PROJECT EVOLVED in the context of two decades of feminist criticism of mainstream academic disciplines, for their exclusion and denial of women's traditions, history, and experiences. (For a representative list of these works, chapter 1, note 11.) In Gilligan's question "What would happen if what was inside us were to enter the world?" and Jilchristina's talk of "learning about things they told you you didn't need to know," are intimations of the costs and challenges, both to themselves and to their culture, of repressing women's knowledge.[1] Here also lie the beginnings of a reconceptualization of education from women's points of view.

The dominating themes of the traditional disciplines also teach students, both overtly and by implication, about themselves. Stories are legion among women, people of color, and the poor, who can recall the "lessons" they learned, not only from textbooks, but from teachers and fellow students, about their inferior and marginalized places in society.[2] Chinosole recalls an early "lesson" and her reactions to it:

Being dark-skinned in America, very dark-skinned, and confronting the fact that everybody was making wrong judgments about me; when I was about seven, I decided, well, if this country is wrong about me, they must be wrong about everything else. So I took a counter posture on everything. When I heard that capitalism was good, I went to read about Lenin when I was [about] twelve. I heard that God exists so I picked up a book by Bertrand Russell when I was fourteen. Anything they said was right about Western civilization, I rejected.

Revelations such as this—that "they" were "wrong about me"—have empowered the teachers and students with whom we worked to challenge the position assigned to them by society and the traditional curriculum. In struggling for knowledge that would help them to place themselves in the world they are learning about, they have reframed the idea of mastery. No longer limited to the acquisition of knowledge on the terms of the experts, the notion of mastery has been expanded by our informants to mean the *interpretation* of knowledge from the new perspectives of students, women, and other marginalized groups whose lives represent "the bywaters and tributaries" to mainstream academic culture.

Through a series of excerpts, this chapter illustrates some of the ways knowledge is reconstructed in feminist classrooms, despite the forces of tradition that continue to hold sway. Much of the discourse we actually observed was, of course, concerned with transmitting content. Conventional views about what happens in the classroom reflect the belief that the material of knowledge can be expressed and understood only through rational discourse. In this context, "pedagogy" signifies "teaching methods" that will transmit the *content* of knowledge. But, for us pedagogy means the entire process of creating knowledge, involving the innumerable ways in which students, teachers, and academic disciplines interact and redefine each other in the classroom, the educational institution, and the larger society. Pedagogy also acknowledges the nonrational aspects of knowing, what Laurie Finke has called "the pedagogical unconscious," and how unconscious dynamics affect conscious discourses.[3]

What, then, happens when women's knowledge enters the world of interpretation? These feminist classrooms have given us many new insights from women's lives. First, we have noted changing definitions of academic knowledge, as professors extended their range of themes and topics, and looked at old material in new ways. Second, we have seen the redistribution of expertise and the widening of sources of authority: knowledge can be produced by all groups in society, including students, rather than solely by the academic disciplines, experts in a field, or teachers.

This redistribution of expertise opens up further issues. In conventional views, knowledge is created mainly with approaches such as rational analysis and scholarly detachment, which are thought to have little connection to personal concerns. But if students' own lives, stories, and questions become sources of knowledge and insight, it is possible to form new relationships between these personal narratives and broader theoretical frameworks such as gendered analyses of society. Some of the professors we observed explicitly used the tools of emotional insight and intuition to help students formulate their own stories. For instance, Margaret Blanchard's course at Towson State was entitled Women and Intuition. Gloria Wade-Gayles, from Spelman, told us that the essence of learning for her is emotional growth, "discovery of the self and discovery of others around you." How are such new "ways of knowing" enacted in the classroom?

Reinterpretations of knowledge, and the processes of knowing, also came explicitly from the viewpoints of groups previously silenced in society, often leading to different views of reality. Ron Underwood holds that "oppressed people . . . are better at ripping apart the disguises," an idea in harmony with other theories of radical pedagogy, such as those of Paulo Freire, and with Renato Rosaldo's notion that "victims of oppression . . . can provide insights into the workings of power that differ from those available to people in high positions."[4] We have seen not only individuals resisting the "lessons" of the dominant culture, but communities of learners in the process of constructing new insights together. All the teachers with whom we worked sought to empower their students, in their immediate settings and beyond, to claim the full participation in society that some groups have been denied. Some of them understood that this full participation could change the way the education system reflects and interprets society. Jayna Brown, a student at San Francisco State, after hearing each student talk about what brought her to a course entitled Wild Women in Music and Literature, wrote: "There's something very revolutionary going on. There's a very powerful thing happening . . . all we're doing is reconstructing the world."

In reconstructing their teaching, each one of our informants wrestled with the forces that shaped both its possibilities and limitations: the structure and content of her academic discipline; her personal and intellectual history and its influence on her choice of academic topics and pedagogical approaches; and, of course, the professor's construction of the students and the perspectives students brought to the classroom. The feminist pedagogies that we encountered in various institutions represented a range of possible constructions of knowledge, from establishing a "toehold" within a traditional discipline, to creating courses based on feminist concepts, to expanding the boundaries of academic knowledge itself.

RECONSTRUCTING ACADEMIC KNOWLEDGE
FROM A FEMINIST PERSPECTIVE

In our first vignettes we juxtapose two professors in the same discipline, sociology, but as taught in sharply contrasting contexts. This pairing illustrates that the process of challenging and then reconstructing knowledge is shaped not only by context but by the extent to which you believe the discipline serves all people equally. Our first illustration is taken from a course taught by Patricia MacCorquodale in spring of 1987 at the University of Arizona, an institution where the contrasts between traditional mastery and its feminist redefinition seemed particularly sharply drawn. Professors at the university viewed the undergraduate student body as "average" and "not intellectually alive," and their teaching as an authoritative body of knowledge that had to be transmitted partly because they were concerned, as one informant put it, with "what every graduate student needs to know."

MacCorquodale's introduction to the academic disciplines began early, but she described hers as an uneasy participation.

I always felt left out in the classroom; the "chilly classroom" personified much of my educational experience. I went to schools that were high-powered, competitive, intellectual places where verbal battles were the name of the game, and I always knew that I didn't want to do that. It wasn't that I couldn't—I had been a debater in high school. But I wanted to create classrooms where that wouldn't happen to my female students.

In graduate school it became even more of a gender issue because the male faculty and the male graduate students were into all this sort of ranking your competitiveness, and it was not a good experience.

Reflecting on the evolution of her teaching, she talked about her increasing awareness of the need to bring the students into the learning process:

When I started teaching I just wanted them to learn the material and get a grade. . . . But it was boring. The students didn't really relate to it at all. I wanted them to be able to think about it in terms of the context of their own lives. So then I started using more examples and trying to find things that would somehow allow them to personalize the material.

To MacCorquodale, sociology is a discipline that, although grounded in people's lives, moves beyond individual concerns by collecting data and developing theory in order to generalize about human experience. The use of personal examples does not invalidate social-structural generalizations, but, as MacCorquodale put it, "if there's enough individual experience that contradicts the categories, then the categories themselves need to be changed." However, rather than using student questions or concerns to challenge assumptions in the discipline, she sought to make sociology more relevant to their own lives. She sought to create a bridge between the accepted pedagogy of her institution, a model of "intellectual, consciously rational discourse," and one that more directly took account of students' personal concerns.

The Sociology of Sexuality course that we observed in the spring of 1987 enrolled ninety-three students and met in a large lecture hall with tiered seats arranged in semicircular, graduated rows.[5] The topic they were discussing on a day we were present concerned changing conceptions of homosexuality. MacCorquodale asked the class to speculate on some Freudian interpretations: "How might a Freudian approach explain these kinds of patterns? That some people end up having partners of the same sex?" The students gave a variety of answers; and, as teachers often do when they are looking for specific answers, she fended them off until one satisfied her. "Freud wouldn't quite make it like that," she responded, or, "that's not quite what he would say." When a student finally suggested an unresolved Oedipal complex, MacCorquodale both accepted it and elaborated on her answer:

Right, that they didn't resolve those complexes that have to do with identification, and Freud thought that people were attracted to the opposite-sex parent, and they are able to resolve that and identify correctly with the parent of the same sex.

But this kind of question-and-answer mode did not satisfy her desire to bring more student concerns into the classroom, to "personalize the material" for them. As a result, she invited the students to prepare questions and comments for the next class, and "I'll do like Johnny Carson and try to answer them, so there will be a chance for you to ask the things you probably really want to say and know, but I know it's difficult for you to ask them in this big group context."

She began the next class with some of the questions that the students had come up with; one of them asked why there is a greater stigma attached to male homosexuality than lesbianism. A freshman named Richard Doyle* suggested:

In our society men have to be macho, and if you're not macho that's bad; women have a more free range of emotions they show, that they may act, but men have to act a certain way.

Although his response was a detached generalization, this young man spoke more personally in his interview with us, reflecting a common feeling among males that their experiences are denied in courses such as this: "She says all the bad things happened to women in our society and makes it sound like everything's great for men, which to some extent I agree with but . . . I really envy women in some ways. They're free to show their emotions in a lot more ways. Men are not allowed to." Although MacCorquodale supported him here, saying that women do have more flexibility in their roles, she turned back to the students and asked them what they thought. A twenty-six-year-old woman named Stephanie Jackter, who thought of herself as a feminist but didn't admit to it because of its "antimale connotation," replied quite fervently:

I totally disagree with that. I would say that there are probably just as many female homosexuals in America as there are male homosexuals, [but] they're closeted because the very strict interpretation of femininity in this society is, in order to be a woman you must be fertile, feminine, and have an interest in men. For a woman to show an interest in another woman is highly taboo in this society. Highly taboo.

MacCorquodale proposed an empirical answer: "I guess we can make arguments for both sides, and it's sort of an empirical question, you can find out what people's attitudes are, but there's certainly some ways that the female role is very restricted."

To us, this question-and-answer session represented MacCorquodale's efforts, against the grain of the discipline, to fashion a more personal approach to knowledge by using student questions to frame the course content for that day. In her regretful narrative of her own education as "the chilly classroom" and her lament that traditional lectures don't relate academic content very well to real life, she was reflecting a discomfort evocative of the contrast between male and female modes of discourse noted by Tannen, Belenky et al., and other feminist scholars who focus on women's conversations as "negotiations for closeness," support, and friendship.[6]

However, the large size of her class and the institutional context also limited the ways that MacCorquodale could bring students into new relationships with the material or construct with them a critique of mainstream sociological views. Stephanie Jackter described to us the institutional constraints on feminist teaching at Arizona. "I feel that Pat has to walk on eggshells in teaching the class. It's very difficult for me to even express what those are but that's one of the reasons I am very talkative in class. I try to bring up issues that stretch the boundaries that she as a teacher can't pass over."

Implicit in MacCorquodale's handling of student questions is the notion that sociological knowledge is constructed by researchers like herself, and that it chiefly concerns objective truths can be verified through the proper research methodologies. Their questions, which she took seriously, were located at the bottom of an informational hierarchy and considered in the context of the authoritative knowledge conveyed by the discipline. Students could use sociology to "think about things in terms of the context of their own lives," but they could not use their positions or concerns to critique sociology in turn. As Stephanie Jackter noted, the boundaries of the discipline, and the authoritative role of the teacher at Arizona, remained intact even in this innovative classroom.

In contrast to the notion of knowledge developing within a disciplinary and research hierarchy, the professors whom we observed at Spelman College demonstrated a persistent concern with the social construction of knowledge from new and different perspectives, particularly those of women of color. In constructing knowledge from the standpoint of Black women, they reflected the work of African-American theorists such as Patricia Hill Collins and bell hooks in transforming feminist theory.[7] Students were perceived as central in this endeavor, because of both their academic ability and their experiences as Black women. President Cole's vision "that when you walk into a classroom the expectation is that you will soar," that you will "take off and . . . surpass even your own expections," is an expression of the institutional commitment to these young women whom the dominant culture persistently devalues.[8]

Mona Phillips of Spelman told us that she had spent the period of her graduate education developing an oppositional stance to the field of sociology. She saw early on that sociology, as practiced by mainstream scholars, was not about her, and thus could not claim the objective truths it sought for itself though empirical investigation. This was the basis for her development as a self-consciously Black and feminist knower. As she said in an interview:

I never felt comfortable with objectifying, making objects out of who I was, and I guess what never happened to me is that I never saw a

Black person as separate from me. . . . This doesn't mean that I'm any less objective and that I don't recognize within-group variation, I'm just saying that when I say we and I'm talking about low-income Black folks, I understand that my experience is the same, yet different. I know that very clearly, but I can still say "we."

This self-consciousness and empathy with all Black people was also reflected in her wish to have students identify with the Black women who, for generations, had created coherent stories about their own lives. Phillips wanted them to see that "we are part of an historical context, and that the questions they are asking are important because they've been asked before." She also wanted to strengthen the students in their own choices and commitments:

I don't want them to be afraid of hearing their own thoughts, not just in the classroom but when they're with their own kids . . . or in some relationship. I want them to be able to make choices, to come to grips with the right and wrong in their lives, and take it and face it and say, "OK, this is not right in this relationship or whatever, I have to do something about it" . . . that's hard, that's really hard . . . and if they are serious about social change, they should take part.

Phillips's notion of mastery was interdisciplinary, in which sociology, biography, and history were all valid and interconnected sources of information. Her students, as Black women, were themselves sources of the knowledge they would use to construct theory together.

The class we observed at Spelman in the spring of 1990 was in a course called Sociology of Women with an enrollment of fifteen undergraduates. Students sat informally in a circle with Phillips at a seat in the front. After introducing two books on African-American women's history, she evoked students' visions of alternative theoretical frameworks in which to discuss that history.[9] Considering "those issues, those concerns that Black women have been concerned about all throughout history," she focused on one issue in particular: "the question, the eternal question, of race and gender, which is more important?"

In the next class, discussion of a reading assignment quickly led to a dialogue dealing with knowledge, the academic disciplines, and the construction of "truth." One student commented that she preferred literature to social science:

A literary picture includes the author's depiction of society and all kinds of roles, whereas the social scientist tends to be more objective ... but no matter how objective his or her vision [is] she is only going to pay attention to certain things. So I'm thinking that a literary character is just more creative—I've found that it's easier for me to identify with *The Women of Brewster Place* 'cause I'm a Black woman than to see a thing saying "Black women do this, that, and the other" because it seems like all clumped together ...

This and similar reactions to a writing assignment turned into an examination of different ways of knowing as well as the many places where knowledge originates. Issues of mastery here were at the outset identified with personal response. The students were grappling with the question of who were the authorities on their own lives because, like Phillips, they could not rely on the expertise of traditional social science. Phillips must have seen a deeper concern here because at this point she changed her emphasis to consider the passionate engagement of Black social scientists in their work. "What I'm hearing you say," she broke in, "is that what you miss from some of the sociological stuff is the passion":

But if you look at some point at our later sociologists and some of the work that they do, the passion's there—if you look at Bonnie Dill's piece, the passion is there, ... but one reason is because she is a Black woman writing about Black women, and so the passion is there. Du Bois, the passion is there on every page.

Interpretation, for this teacher, derives from connection, from the fact that the writer shared common experiences, as a woman of color, with her research subjects, just as Phillips shared common experiences with her students. The discussion took off at this point, deriving energy from students' eagerness to explore this issue. The student who spoke next carried Phillips's implication further, by asking "whether it is possible for a white social scientist to write passionately about my experience, or my peoples' experience?" With Phillips's encouragement, she went on: "The thing is I guess it comes down to truth, I don't know, you know I ... " At this, Phillips jumped up and wrote "TRUTH" on the blackboard, and the following dialogue ensued:

FIRST STUDENT: I think that traditionally and historically [researchers] that have tended to examine Blacks generally, Black women, Black men,

Black families, have always first started out as seeing them as deviant, and pathological, and you're this, you're that, and we knew that that wasn't us, and so it was sort of like blinders, that type of research, 'cause it was traditionally done by white men, and I mean we weren't, it wasn't done subjectively. And I think there is a possibility that social scientific research can be done that *is* relevant, that *we* might learn from, by whites, but I don't think that they can enter the subject in the same way that Toni Morrison or Gloria Naylor can.

SECOND STUDENT: You know, and like it is a search for truth, the ultimate truth, by white social scientists, and my question is, Why didn't the Black social scientists get to define the truth first?

FIRST STUDENT: It's sort of, like, to legitimize the theory, because when we say it, they don't listen.

SECOND STUDENT: . . . it's like we still have colonized minds.

These students were affirming the value of constructing knowledge from their own standpoint, against "truths" of white social scientists that claimed they were "deviant" and "pathological." They were expressing the need, in Chinosole's words, to "open up the simplest facts about ourselves." They were also openly struggling against the power of the dominant culture's claims to truth. Phillips pushed her students to be critical of the scholarly texts they were reading because those texts denied their reality:

We create the knowledge, and just because our creations are not in places where knowledge is held, which is in textbooks, that doesn't mean we didn't do it. . . . When you talk about Black women's lives from a [white] feminist perspective you really don't read about our mothers, our aunts, our sisters, all the women we know.

This group was able to offer a stronger criticism of sociology "from the margins" than was possible in MacCorquodale's class at the University of Arizona. Here students challenged the sources and aims of sociological knowledge, and explicitly used their own life experience, as well as inter-disciplinary knowledge, to do so. Phillips's class demonstrated a concep-tion of mastery not as the acquisition of conventional knowledge but as more culturally positioned interpretation—or reinterpretation—from the perspective of a previously silenced group.

The combination of an intimate classroom setting and an institutional context historically designed for the support of Black women at Spelman were both important, but perhaps the unique motivation in this classroom was the pressing need of students and teacher for an alternative means by which to locate themselves in the world. As Phillips herself put it, "What I would eventually like to do is find a place for ourselves in the world, in a world of Black women, women of color. I would like that very much." This vision of a unique place and role for African-American women not only helps them to fashion a strong voice for themselves as individuals, but can also serve the larger Black community. In this classroom, both teacher and students were creating a communal and egalitarian, rather than individualized and hierarchical, form of knowing.

INTERDISCIPLINARY AND FEMINIST INTERPRETATIONS

By moving to two other institutions—Wheaton College and Lewis and Clark—and by shifting course offerings, we explore further how content and institutional setting interact with the personal and intellectual histories of both professors and students to redefine mastery in yet other ways. Here the issue does not concern explicit cultural resistance to a mainstream discipline like sociology, since the course content itself is feminist; Bev Clark at Wheaton and Laurie Finke at Lewis and Clark both taught feminist literary criticism.

Our focus in Clark's class is on students' struggles over new and feminist readings of texts. Although at the time Wheaton was all female like Spelman, Wheaton students are predominately of European American descent. Our faculty informants saw them as academically average, traditional young women whose minds needed exposure to alternative ways of viewing the world. While these professors shared Phillips's concern for the production of knowledge from self-consciously *gendered,* student-centered, and personal ways of knowing, their conceptualizations of education were more individualistic, less reflective of a particular community than were those of the professors at Spelman, who envisioned knowledge always in the context of the Black community's persistent struggles for self-definition against white oppression. Beverly Clark reflected her subjective orientation when she told us:

> I want to do two things that are rather contradictory; I want to empower the students, and I want to shake them up . . . I want to encourage them to take risks, and to the extent that they feel com-

fortable, they may be willing to take some risks that will shake them up.

At the time we observed, Clark was struggling to articulate her own position regarding theoretical approaches to literature by American and French feminists, and was using her Feminist Criticism course to explore these issues.[10] The language she used to describe her own engagement with the topic corresponded to her description of the goals she set for her students. She said, "It is a tremendously exciting course that shakes me up in a lot of ways. I find the American criticism empowering me, and the French criticism shaking me up." Clark's sense of what constitutes feminist knowledge was constantly at play with her belief that all knowledge, including her own, is partial, contextual, and diverse.[11] This interpretation of her discipline—literature—is in sharp contrast to both MacCorquodale's and Phillips's views of mainstream sociology as a more stable body of information and theory.

This evolving and decentered epistemological stance also guided Clark's pedagogy. She modeled her own feminism for the students as a personal intellectual journey, so that they too would feel free to explore and modify their own positions. Students initiated class discussions by raising issues in oral presentations of journal entries or brief papers. The topic one week, early in the semester, was "Do Women Read Differently?" As was typical in Clark's class, each work by a literary theorist was paired with a piece of fiction or poetry so that "we can reflect on the literature in light of the criticism." That day, the thirteen students in her class had read a piece by Judith Fetterley urging women to be "resisting readers," who should particularly distrust male-written texts for their views of women.[12] The literature selections that week focused on feminist reinterpretations of classic fairy tales, including a provocative short story by Angela Carter, "The Company of Wolves," which suggests that Little Red Riding Hood seduces the wolf in order to save her life.[13]

Elisabeth Stitt, a senior English major from California who was studying to be a teacher, started off the class with a journal entry that reiterated a common theme of Wheaton as a feminist environment. She expressed confusion and dismay at feminist worldviews because they threaten to sever her connections to her former life and, especially, to men.

Elisabeth quoted from her journal:

Feminist criticism . . . is another one of those topics that one is almost required to be interested in at Wheaton. I find feminist theory somewhat scary. At Wheaton I have learned mostly about the differences between men and women. Certainly women should be autonomous and their experience should be recognized. But if women relate mainly to a women's canon, because it more closely reflects our experience, on what ground do we meet the men in our life? Does feminist criticism help build bridges between groups? Between men and women? Or does it tear down bridges? . . . A woman who in the 1980s is scared of what she might discover by looking at her own experience! I make myself sound stupid.

Martha Johnson, a sophomore, echoed and extended Elisabeth's concern:

I could see the elements of sexism [that Fetterley saw] but I also felt that my mother and grandmother couldn't see it or they said you can push this too far, and I was very torn between what I had been brought up to believe by my mother and grandmother and what I was learning in the class.

Praising the students for the honesty of their reactions, Clark turned the discussion to the Carter story, asking what they thought of the sexual encounter between Little Red Riding Hood and the wolf in this version of the story: "Is she simply out to save her life, or is she seducing him?. . . How guilty is she?" Susan Cotter*, another senior English major, said jokingly, "I knew I was in trouble, I'm not sure I knew quite what to make of the end, when she rips his shirt off." This remark initiated an extended discussion, in which Anne Painter, another senior, responded:

OK, let me just see how to put it . . . she was a curious young girl, she was coming of age anyway, and . . . she was really kind of excited, hoping, half hoping, that he'd be there, open the door . . . and so basically [she] doesn't have any say, but just the last part, where she starts laughing, it's like she's getting the better of him almost, playing his little game almost, going along with it.

The following conversation ensued:

CLARK: She saved her life.
ELISABETH: That's what really struck me, all of a sudden it's like she's taken in the whole situation, she has supreme confidence . . . it was a gesture of

removing the clothing, interrupting the connection, the control that you have over me.

ANNE: (*quoting from the story*) And she "laid his head on her lap." And she is really taking control over the situation, where he was really in control over her . . .

To raise the alternative viewpoint, Clark responded:

How about those of you who did tend to see it as a rape? (*long silence*) We've already talked about some things—she saw the tuft of her grandmother's white hair in the fireplace, she's in danger of death. . . . There are some things she can do to exert some control, but the whole situation of being placed in—you know—it's either death or a fate worse than death, OK? She knows how to play it, but she's still in that situation, and that's a part of my gut reaction.

It is interesting that none of the students took this position, or agreed with the "rape" hypothesis. Although Clark linked the issue to unequal power relations between men and women, she ignored the discourse of sexual empowerment that engaged Anne and Elisabeth. Shortly afterward she summarized her own reactions:

I think the question Carter raises for me is whether in the kind of white middle-class feminism that I sort of wanted to get into, I'm ignoring certain aspects of the subconscious . . . possibilities for violence, that are going to erupt in some way. Am I somehow—Is the world not as nice as I would like to make it? [But] I could ask the question, is she feminist or not? Is she rethinking opportunities, reimagining possibilities for women, or is she simply enmeshing us deeper into patriarchal structures? So it's a story that disturbs me on a lot of levels, there's the initial issue of rape, there's also—I don't like this killing off of other women. And a grandmother no less (*laughter*).

This passage exemplifies the way Clark modeled the act of interpretation for her students. She displayed her emotional reactions to the story; it's "disturbing," maybe even on a subconscious level. She also explored *why* it was disturbing in terms of her feminism, and then showed how her reactions could be extended to a more analytic approach to the material: Is Carter feminist, or not? This thinking process illustrates how the construction of feminist knowledge includes the exploration and interrogation of emotional respons-es, just as, in Phillips's class, student and teacher "gut reactions" were part of the process of creating new interpretations.

But this class discussion also displayed the complexities of expressing "what is inside us" for different women. Students were "resisting readers" in several ways. Their ambivalent responses reflect the confusions and yearnings of many young women coming of age in the mid-1980s, who worry that by giving themselves over to feminist views of women's oppression they will be risking a loss of freedom, and of pleasure as well. As Jill Marts, a Lewis and Clark student, said: "I resist the framework that confines women who are feminists. [Like Emma Goldman] if I can't dance I don't want to be part of your revolution." These students saw in the feminist version of Little Red Riding Hood a sexuality that could be read as an exertion of female power, of a new kind of feminism, rather than a submission to helplessness or a "fate worse than death."

While she did not immediately explore these partly generational differ-ences between her students and herself, at the end of the discussion Clark suggested that they return to the issue raised by Elisabeth Stitt's journal entry, "whether you want to read as a feminist, . . . that there's somehow something comfortable in not having to think about these things." Susan Cotter said that she got really mad "when I read about an author who is sex-ist, and you just have to grin and bear it." But a few others echoed the fears of Elisabeth and Martha. Michelle Barnett, a sophomore and the only African-American student in the class, spoke poignantly about her fear of the isolation she would face if she became a resisting, feminist reader:

> I'd be cutting myself off from the two other types of readers, because you have the way men read, and then you have the way women read, until they take this class (*laughter*). And then the way women read after they take this class (*more laughter*)! . . . Just even going to Wheaton College, it's almost as if I've separated myself from all the other people at coeducational institutions, the women—there are the men in those institutions and the women in those institutions, and then there's me.

Michelle felt doubly at odds, perhaps triply, because of her race. She left unmarked here the racial aspects of her isolation, and, in fact, in her inter-view, looking over this transcript, she said, "I didn't say anything about race then, on purpose. I kept silent about race at first in the class." Becky

Hemperly, a senior, finished off the discussion by saying wistfully, "It was almost like, these are things that had occurred to me but nobody ever wrote them down before. But it was like, a feeling of disappointment, like saying well I'll never read that the same way again."

Bev Clark's class dramatized for us the contradictions and ambivalence inherent in reading differently as a woman, which is a new form of subjective knowledge, personal and autobiographical, coming from women's lives rather than from a search for the intellectually most sophisticated reading. Clark wanted her students to combine their subjective reactions with emerging tools of analysis, and to then form a more broad-ranging set of connections with feminism and literary theory. Both Clark and Mona Phillips wanted students to construct a knowledge that was useful to them—in Phillips's case, a knowledge that was socially directed toward serving the African-American community; for Clark, a knowledge more focused on personal development that would enable students to reach a wider appreciation of feminist issues.

It is striking that the strongest resistance we saw to feminist interpretations of texts occurred in classroom discourses, like Clark's, that took this more individualistic approach. Allowing students to see mastery as related to individual empowerment also infers seeing the oppression of women as a source of personal disempowerment and loss. At Lewis and Clark, a female student in Dorothy Berkson's course on Women Writers was overhead to say: "Does this class depress you? I've been in severe depression and my roommate said it's probably the class. Same thing in each book—they are all hanging themselves." Elisabeth put well her individualistic goals for learning and her resistance to the message that she heard:

I'm only taking the class to connect it with myself, but I mean basically that's the only reason I get into any class. That and Bev . . . [Partly] I want this class to provide the solution. The class says absolutely that you have to [look at women's oppression]. I mean face it, I'm not doing it, resist it with every grain of my body—thinking about it makes me feel sick.

Could feminist knowledge about women's oppression, without the security of a community or larger social purpose such as that shared by the students at Spelman, be too frightening and too isolating for some young women, particularly heterosexual white women, who value their relationships with men? Elisabeth exclaimed, half-jokingly: "Bev might think it's better to blow apart the world, not peel it off like the layers on an onion. But here you just put a bomb in the center of the onion and go bang." We were reminded of the idea of African-American feminist theorist Patricia Hill Collins—that, within a common gender oppression, white women's subordination has been created through a history of seduction by white men, in contrast to Black women's subordination partially through rejection by them.[14]

Perhaps this helps to explain why personalized forms of interpretation probably did not have the same effect for the lone student of color in the class. Michelle, who shared her classmates' resistance to the isolation inferred from feminist approaches, still must have found it hard to respond to arguments that did not recognize racism as well as gender oppression.

At Lewis and Clark College, Laurie Finke's senior seminar in Literary Theory raised very different questions about the sources and ends of feminist knowledge, in particular about the relationship between explanatory theoretical frameworks and the role of student perspectives in shaping those frameworks. It was in Finke's class, in the fall of 1986, that we first observed the pedagogical shift toward beginning classroom discussions with the students' questions rather than the professor's, which represented to us the priority that some feminist teachers give to students' questions and concerns.

Like Bev Clark, Laurie Finke saw her course as an arena for working through her own research questions and thus viewed her pedagogy as an opportunity to gain mastery along with her students:

> In this particular course it's not a question of "I'm an expert and now I'm going to fill you in." It's "this is what I work on and you're working on it with me and I don't know where it's going to go. I may get a brilliant idea in the middle of class and go off on it. But it is difficult material and I don't expect you to 'master it.'" I don't expect them to come to class understanding it and they're not going to get the final word from me because I'm not sure what it is.

The professors at Lewis and Clark thought highly of their students, who were "average" according to national norms. Dorothy Berkson saw them as disaffected, bright underachievers who didn't excel in a more competitive learning environment. Defining "good students" as those willing to struggle with ideas, Berkson thought that the culture of feminist pedagogy at Lewis and Clark enabled students to "ask different kinds of questions and to think in new ways." Finke noted that "in this group you can pick out the students who are still at a very relativistic stage in their life . . . and I'm acutely aware how different their sense of literature is from mine." She wanted to wean her students away from the notion, common to many undergraduates, "that they have to master everything they read . . . [or] they can't have any questions about it." Thus she conceived of discussions as guided by her students' ideas and questions:

> The idea is to make them more aware of when they have questions and how they can ask them for themselves. . . . By forcing them to come up with some kind of provisional answer, you encourage them to begin to think of themselves more as independent learners than just something that information gets processed through. I'm trying to reach a point where everyone feels they have equal access to whatever the agenda of the day is.

Nine students were enrolled in Finke's class, four females and five males, three of whom we later learned were in their late twenties or thirties. Reflecting Finke's emphasis on questioning, the course goal, as stated in the syllabus, was "to survey some of the terrain of modern critical thought in hopes of developing a scholarly awareness of the significant questions that have been and are being asked about criticism." Feminism was one form of literary criticism explored in the class, along with structuralism, poststructuralism, and psychoanalysis, among others.

The class from which the following excerpt is drawn focused on discussion of the ideas of a prominent French feminist, Julia Kristeva, as analyzed by Toril Moi in her book *Sexual/Textual Politics*.[15] The initial topic, Kristeva's treatment of language, was "derailed" when Finke used the word "class" to illustrate how the same term can have different meanings. This led to an extended argument about whether women could be seen as a class, in which two males, Ned Sharp and Ralph Goodman*, fought vigorously against that idea, and one female, Jill Marts, defended it. Ralph, a thirty-five-year-old who referred to himself as a "former SDSer," began by saying: "I'm rejecting sexes as defined as classes; I think classes are defined by economics." Jill replied, "Right, and economics is defined by gender."

Jill was twenty-eight years old and had held a variety of different jobs, mostly "women's jobs," up to now. Paying for college by waiting on tables, she had also been a secretary and a seamstress. Ralph's next several remarks, that "gender is defined by economics," that "it has less to do with, you know, sexual oppression in itself as it does [with] what's called power, or acquisition, or ownership," made her bristle. She responded, "That seems so irrelevant to this—you argue it's power and acquisition, but the fact of the matter is a high majority of women are making less money." Ned Sharp, a senior English major, soon came to Ralph's defense, asserting at one point that "if you look at gender you will see all women as being oppressed." What he did *not* say was that "if you look at gender, you will see all men as being privileged." Indeed, while Ned and Ralph were arguing in a way that obscured males' advantages as a group, Jill continually referred to women's material deprivation. However, because of the force of the males' arguments, women, not men, were under attack here.

As the discussion became stuck on the issues of gender and class as competing binary oppositions, Finke tried to resolve it by introducing and defining the concept of positionality:

> What we need is a description that is not based on categories but, as Kristeva says, on positionality, on relations. No group is in and of itself oppressed or marginal. It's only in relation to something else. So that, for instance, women we can say are marginal compared to men. But black women are marginal compared to white, middle-class women. There is no center. . . . What we need to do is keep the whole model in motion.

Margaret Collins*, a student whose concern with language initiated the original discussion, responded:

> One thing I thought about when Kristeva was talking about marginality—how it was positioning relations to man, the center, how the patriarchal center was going in a straight line. I think that if Kristeva sort of went one step further and created not only the wedge she talks about in language but a web that goes beyond language. Because in a web, a binary opposition doesn't really have a chance to survive.

Margaret, like Jill, was searching for ways out of the binary oppositions that oppress women. Finke responded to Margaret's point by quoting Moi on Kristeva, what she called "my favorite line in the book":

> "What is perceived as marginal at any given time depends on the position one occupies." It's that simple. You can take the poorest, most oppressed group in this country, and they are going to be central compared to almost anybody in, say, Ethiopia. You have to see cen-

trality and marginality, oppression, oppressor, and oppressed as relational concepts.

The rest of the discussion was marked by two themes. One was Jill's concern that "this kind of approach or attitude can be dangerous for feminism," by which she meant that women's oppression could be ignored in the relativism of such a positional approach. The other was Finke's warning against seeing the women's struggle as divorced from other social struggles: "I mean, how does feminism keep from creating a white, middle-class feminist movement which is completely ignorant of what is happening in racial or class struggles?" At the end, Finke said, "You can't privilege one over the other," and Jill concluded, "yes, but what I'm saying is there's a real danger to thinking theoretically and ignoring the practicality of what is really going on."

We can trace Finke's role in the process of knowledge construction as she moved back and forth between being a class participant and "expert." Since the discussion was set on its course by student questions and concerns, she did not attempt to reformulate it until she saw that the students were stuck. She then laid out the concept of positionality to enable them to think relationally about gender, class, and power. However, because of classroom dynamics, the gender oppression evoked by Jill was given a back seat to points about the importance of acknowledging the positionality of different forms of oppression. We see this partly as a function of the males' assertion of economic class as the main oppression, by which they were able to ignore the issue of male privilege. Ned Sharp represented many male students who deny their privilege but also fear its loss. He told us he preferred Kristeva's call to deconstruct the hierarchies over "feminism's idea of a feminist self," which he viewed as "a limitation on the human self." Better to erase all differences than risk the reversal of the hierarchies that a feminist self implied. Because of the absence of any ethnic minority students in the class, any chances of discussing racial oppressions were also minimized here.

But Finke also played a role in resisting the direct discussion of gender oppression. Jill tried to focus on the working conditions of women in society and concluded, "I think there is a real danger to think theoretically and ignore the practicality of what is really going on." But whereas Clark and her students drew on their personal reactions in order to fashion a subjective, even emotional interpretation, Finke wanted hers to speak theoretically, to move beyond personal perspectives to a comparison of approaches in the abstract.

This led her to ignore the illustrative significance of her own students' positions in society as sources of knowledge in the classroom—their standpoints as males and females, as members of a particular social class, or as people with workplace experience. Thus male privileges were enacted, not least in their vocal domination of the discussion, but they were not criticized. In an interview, Finke said that she wanted to give her students access to the theoretical questions she herself was wrestling with. She indeed urged them to give up traditional forms of mastery of the subject matter and to ask and answer their own questions. But her emphasis on theory, even though it was a theory of positionality, divested the discussion of the experiential, positional groundings it might have employed to move students beyond the dichotomies of gender and class.

Comparisons between Clark's and Finke's class are very illuminating. On the surface, they have only the topic of feminist literary criticism in common, since Clark seemed to focus on exploring personal reactions to literature as a route to theory, whereas Finke focused on the theory itself. Clark's all-female group comfortably traded personal impressions with each other, allowing disagreements, or different readings, to be aired, whereas the males and females in Finke's class engaged in an argument that sought a "right answer." The second class displayed a more traditionally competitive form of mastery.

But, in the ways in which feminist knowledge was being constructed, similarities between the classes are equally striking. Both discussions represented attempts by female participants to introduce and formulate their personal narratives, in the light of sometimes dismaying insights about the oppression of women. Both groups struggled with the problem of explaining women's experiences in the world, such as seduction and rape, or women's economic oppression, in terms of different theoretical frameworks in order to interpret, and possibly change, gender inequalities. Does seduction of the wolf represent female agency or powerlessness? Do women belong in one class category, or many? Both discussions revealed quite sharp divisions between students and teachers around these issues. In neither class were the *differences* in students' and teachers' positions, such as differences of age or race in Clark's class or workplace experience in Finke's, interrogated as sources of their knowledge. The discussions enacted, but did not explore, the tensions between the meanings of "woman" or "women's oppression," as abstract categories, and the differences in women's lives that elaborate these meanings.

EXPANDING THE BOUNDARIES OF
ACADEMIC KNOWLEDGE

Several of our teacher participants have pushed their interests in women's lives beyond the structures of academic disciplines. To examine the feminist construction of knowledge beyond disciplinary boundaries, we turn to classrooms at Towson State University and at San Francisco State University. Margaret Blanchard's course at Towson, Women and Intuition, which we visited in the fall of 1989, was a creative writing course that emphasized individual growth and collective processes rather than specific academic content or skills. Students were challenged to define intuition together, and Blanchard used her extensive knowledge of the emerging field of women's spirituality to help awaken their creative powers.

Like the majority of her colleagues, Blanchard visualized Towson students as not merely average, but "mixed" in terms of intelligence and preparation. She also felt that women, in particular, had been shortchanged by the educational system and needed to be encouraged to express themselves and expand their thinking. She said in her interview:

> I want them to broaden and see other possibilities, other points of view. I don't focus so much on skills because I think people learn what they need to learn if you give them the opportunity. . . . I like to encourage people to experience something and then reflect on it and then come to deeper understandings. Some people really need guidance beforehand, especially in something new to them like this. They need to know that their intuition is real, that I'm not making it up.

Because the course was aimed toward individual development, Blanchard, like Bev Clark, had different goals for each of the twenty-eight students, women ranging in age from the early twenties to sixty, and including three African-Americans. "For one student to speak in class once in the semester would be a major breakthrough. For another student to listen may be key. . . . I try to structure it so that each person can find her own way and her own breakthrough."

But this individual development was both dependent on and crucial to the development of the whole class as a community. Blanchard's success was captured by one student, an outspoken career women in her mid-thirties named Diane Jones*, who told us:

77

I took the course to evolve to a point where, with other people, we can better understand what [intuition] means. We are all kind of searching for a definition together, so when someone comes up with an experience or an idea or maybe a role they see intuition playing in their lives—Margaret recognizes the value of our learning from each other, not just learning from her.

To foster these aims, Blanchard structured the course to include writing and drawing assignments for spurring students' imaginations, a wide range of readings on the subjects of women's thinking and women's intuition, and finally class discussions for sharing the fruits of their explorations. Blanchard felt that all these aspects of the course were important and worked together. "I think probably the writing and drawing are the most important, their own personal engagement with their own issues and with the material, and the other two are ways of amplifying that . . . expanding it into a more diverse, more complex context."

This class, in its pedagogy and its unusual timing—it met on alternative Saturdays for three hours—underlined its contrast to Towson's other offerings. Its success was partly a function of its marginality at Towson—students found it a refuge from their other, more traditional and male-identified classes. For example, Joan Hammond and Lillian Massey, both in their sixties, had experienced discrimination elsewhere because of their age and gender. In an art class a professor said to them: "If you're a senior citizen and if you are not serious, you don't belong here. You're wasting our time, using our equipment."

In the class discussion we observed in the fall of 1989, Blanchard began by asking students to "note in your journals something that you think needs to be healed. It can be something that you have personally experienced, some wound or some social ill that needs to be healed." She went on:

So what I'd like to do is a little bit of a guided imagery where you get in touch with some part of yourself—a child self, the hurt child, or the angry child, some emotion that you don't like . . . or some positive part of yourself that needs more recognition. We talked about how we incorporate or internalize sexist attitudes, all the negative self-images that we get from that. If instead we discover some positive strength, then we could neutralize that.

Positive images could be used to counteract internalized forms of sexism; and, in fact, a major theme in the course was the tension between internalized and direct, external, forms of oppression experienced by women. Blanchard then began a series of guided-imagery drawing exercises, in one of which the students were to find a conflict in their lives, a kind of "either-or" or "no-win" situation, "some kind of double bind." Then they were asked to find a symbol, "something that represents each side, and draw a picture of each one."

A discussion of the drawings followed the exercise. Joan Hammond had an egg, the symbol of life. Diane Jones had a brick wall in a storm, and a clay pot for growth. Kathy D'Angelo*, a younger student, said that she was graduating in January and was scared of the future. One student told the story of her growth and her husband's stagnation in terms of her springing out: she drew herself like a corkscrew, or the top of a jack-in-the-box, and her husband as stagnant, crouched at the bottom of the box. "He's content with his own little world," she said, "and he's not growing." Throughout the ensuing discussion, students supported each other by commenting favorably on each other's imagery, a pattern that was very common to this class. Often they discussed problems in their personal relationships.

Blanchard next made a point about the processes by which the construction of new knowledge, or new interpretations, can shape and transform rather than just reflect reality. She told the class:

> You can take an image like the images that you've come up with now, you can develop them into stories, in other words, you can spin them out into time, and in time, then, things can change, things can happen, that will transform the images or will transform the actual experience. Sometimes you can transform the image itself and get a new insight.

She then used an example from her own experience of menopause, arguably a fairly taboo subject in most college classrooms:

> I think I'm going through menopause, and trying to work with images of menopause which are extremely negative. Like of drying up. They talk about it as the next stage of life next to death . . . So I'm trying to transform that experience in terms of how I view it; I mean the negative aspect is not so much the experience itself but how I look at it to begin with.
>
> I heard in some places you can't become a shaman—one of the wise women of the tribe,—until you've gone through menopause. So I thought that makes it more like an initiation, not the end of your

life, and the image of the crone is a very positive image. So those images have sustained me, even though it's been difficult; it's made it more positive.

A student immediately responded, "Isn't that what menopause means? You lose a certain part of yourself, you don't have your period, and you have new opportunity." The ensuing comments seemed almost to be comforting Blanchard. These exchanges are mostly between the older women, those past menopause:

JOAN: It's like the freedom to go on, no regrets—it's like being out of jail (*laughter*).

LILLIAN MASSEY: I was never really concerned, I didn't have time to think about it.

BLANCHARD: It's just exactly as you're saying, it's a real transformation, moving on to the next stage. If the dragonfly wanted to stay in her shell, it would be extremely painful and she would eventually die, but if you move on to the next stage, and let that flowering or new emergence come, that could be delightful.

LILLIAN: You're taught that your purpose in life is to have children. Once you accept it doesn't have to be . . .

JOAN: You can move on to other things.

ANOTHER STUDENT: Like that joke about birth control: you take an aspirin and put it between your legs.

ANOTHER: When you get a little older, your knees can relax (*Much laughter at both these comments*).

This discussion is a powerful example of what can happen in a classroom when women's questions are no longer relegated to the "bywaters" of the culture, and silence is broken about formerly taboo topics. Perhaps explorations from such tributaries as this one have made possible some of the transformations in consciousness we have seen in other places. Although the class did much reading in women's spirituality, psychology, and epistemology, the focus remained on the students' own lives. The emphasis was on an epistemology, or way of knowing, that differs sharply from traditional analytical models. As Blanchard said about intuition:

I am interested in (it) because I think that intuition is a way to bring all those different personal perspectives together. It is a way of unifying without making everything or everybody the same. (At least that is how I am defining it.) It provides a way we can have both unity and diversity, at least in vision.

Intuition doesn't, in itself, solve anything. You still have to make choices and take action, personal and political, because some things are better—more loving, more just—than others. But intuition helps you get down to a deeper level. Each thing (or person) has its unique reality, and yet they can all be mingled together without losing their individuality.

Intuition can function not only to facilitate personal growth, but also to bring together different perspectives, different ways of seeing the world, in an evolving web of relationships and meanings. As in the example of spinning out an image in time to create a story that might change a situation, Blanchard's epistemology reflected the insight of Margaret Collins, in Laurie Finke's class, about the relational web, beyond patriarchal language, that can challenge conventional linearities. However, we worried that this emphasis on intuitive learning reinforced the conventional gender dichotomy that this group often discussed, between rational, objective forms of thought, which they asserted were favored by men, and the more "connected" ways of knowing that women used, although Blanchard told us that male students in the past had done very well in the course.

At Towson, a diverse women's community was constructed on the margins of the university curriculum. Even difficult real-life problems could be approached in the context of this community, in which internalized feelings of oppression could be addressed, for example, by transforming mental images of negative thoughts and feelings, and also alleviated through the support of other women. By interweaving multiple perspectives through the telling of particular, personal stories, and by reconciling dichotomies by means of constructive imagery, Blanchard sought to help these women resolve the conflicts in their lives.

The students shared this sense of community participation. For example, younger students particularly appreciated the older ones. Margot Borders*, a Black woman in her thirties, told us that "the older women, when they say something about life, I listen and keep it in the back of my mind. 'Cause they just come out and tell you how things are." Joan and Lillian relished this role. "I'm not sure if our age doesn't encourage the younger ones to talk," said Joan. "We're supportive, if their parents or their professors are not."

Both of the African-American students to whom we talked also told us that Blanchard's low-key approach had made them feel at home. Hattie West*, a twenty-two-year-old, said that "in this class you learn to appreciate yourself. . . . It's like I'm in a class that I'm in with a bunch of friends that I don't know yet." She described disagreements as "being cushioned, like 'I understand what you're saying but I just happen to think. . . .' I hate disagreeing when someone's feelings get hurt." Hattie also felt that, "there's not too many places in regular society where you would be able to hang out with people of so many age groups and different backgrounds." To Hattie, Blanchard's subjective approach to societal issues helped students to think creatively about social change:

> It sometimes seems like feminist teachers just push all this stuff on you, but Margaret just sort of eases it in. In this class there's like this little voice of hope. Things have been wrong but they can be better. . . . Like with the black and white thing—I'd say look at me, I'm Black and I can do this, in a peaceful way and say you're wrong, this is what can happen if you just calm down a bit. . . . Almost, if you're peaceful you can move faster. I feel like water. Water is peaceful but it has lots of power and it can move very fast.

Indeed in many of the classes we observed, particularly those that were all-female, students tended to support each other's contributions and to minimize their disagreements. This pattern of individual support and respect sometimes led to the repression of unresolved conflicts among participants representing widely different social positions. But for Blanchard's class, the focus on personal problems and interior and intuitive processes meant that broader social conflicts became less relevant in terms of their Saturday-morning community.

At San Francisco State University, it was the voices of people new to the academy, people determined to change its definitions of knowledge, of power, and of themselves, that breached the boundaries of traditional disciplines. The Women Studies faculty constructed their students as consciously positioned subjects and actors whose race, class, sexual orientation, and gender gave them the authority to contribute to the evolution of knowledge in the classroom and the responsibility for political activism outside. An acute consciousness of their diversity created a community climate that undermined the provincial tendency among American academicians, including white feminists, to master only knowledge created by white American theoreticians.

Chinosole noted that no one can go into a classroom of Kenyan, Jewish-American, Filipina, Indian, German, and European American students and act as though white North America is the center of the universe: as Chinosole put it, "with such students and a faculty largely consisting of women of color, "multicultural is no ism, it just IS."

Besides student diversity, two other factors informed Angela Davis's and Chinosole's ideas about the kinds of knowledge their students needed. First, their knowledge of and commitment to African-American and Third World scholarship preceded their uneasy participation in academic feminism. It was only when they were able to fuse these two bodies of knowledge, one nontraditional discipline with another, that they were able to move on to building feminist theory. Second, each one of them had a long and dramatic personal history of working in their communities to resist racism and sexism. Chinosole spoke to us of the significance of their activism:

> We often find ourselves at critical moments as catalysts. It's because of the position that we have been in in this country historically, . . . we don't have in-between spaces, you either capitulate or you fight. We cannot walk about in this amnesiac, somnolent state that the majority of the population walks around in.

The course we studied, Wild Women in Music and Literature: Cross-Cultural Women's Literature and Culture, was designed to show how culture and gender interact to combat oppression by looking at such African-American cultural expressions as women's blues and autobiography. Chinosole said:

> What we're trying to do in this class is find out what is feminist in a particular cultural environment. So that's why the blues and autobiography as radical art forms are points of departure for an understanding of African-American culture, which is a prerequisite for defining and evolving this Black feminist theory.

The course emphasized African-American women's political and activist traditions, continuing the work that Davis began in the early 1970s with the publication of "The Black Woman's Role in the Community of Slaves." This tradition has been described by Alice Walker as "womanist," by several of our African-American participants as "what Black women have always done," and by Angela Davis as "the role that the African-American women's community played in forging what we now call feminism."[16]

Students were exposed to a variety of multidisciplinary printed materials—feminist literary theory, autobiography, and books on the blues—as well as new sources of knowledge: the blues themselves were reconstructed as texts in feminist theory.[17] An audiotape of blues music that students compiled and circulated spoke worlds about African-American women's experiences: love, resistance to oppression, sexual preference, violence, anger, racism, homelessness, poverty, lynching, and work. The blues tradition, as Patricia Hill Collins has pointed out, "provides the most consistent and long-standing text of Black women who demand that Black men reject stereotypical sex roles and 'change their ways.'"[18] Ida Cox's song, "Wild Women Don't Have the Blues," is a feminist call to women to move away from being male-defined and male-dependent. As Jilchristina Vest put it: "Once you understand one song by Ma Rainey, you understand an entire realm of things that happened during Ma Rainey's time and that is very useful in everyday life."

Students were asked to use modes of inquiry taken from Black feminist cultural theory as a point of departure for constructing knowledge about, for instance, Jewish-American, Native American or Irish women's culture. A striking example of these connections occurred in a class following a session on African-American blues singers as precursors of feminism. After a discussion of the blues, Lori New Breast, a graduate student who is a Blackfoot from Montana, described how she was struck by the similarities between the blues and "a similar tradition among Indians . . . that has really developed since the 1890s, called the Forty-Nine Songs":[19]

These songs are about what our experiences were like in the late nineteenth to the early twentieth century. There's a bunch of love songs about meeting new men and women from other tribes, because now you're in these institutions where the tribal boundaries are stretched, where children are relocated to schools. And with the car, you now have tribes that normally didn't come to each others' celebrations who can go 1,300 miles to Oklahoma and be part of the Southern Plains. There are also songs about institutionalized violence, about anthropologists, about the predatory academic practice of studying people as subjects, other than recognizing their human qualities. And protest songs.

At this time we suddenly heard sirens in the distance. This was the first class following an incident between the campus police and students who were protesting the Gulf War by building a shack on campus called Little Baghdad. Both Chinosole and Davis spent a significant part of the previous weekend at the site to support the students and insure their safety. Echoing Lori's statement that these songs mark an absence of "constitutional protection" as well as "institutionalized violence," the sirens were an eerie reminder of police visibility in ethnic-minority communities. Lori prevailed over them to speak of the importance of creating knowledge and meaning through community, and vice versa.

> Our discussion last week reminded me so much of my family's experience and the way that you keep your community alive, not by lamenting what is past, but you still keep on creating. It's the whole concept of rebuilding your community, or looking for strategies to heal yourself in these situations based on your tradition.
>
> It is that whole thing of having your voice heard by redefining who you are in context. Yeah, I can't be like my great-grandmothers, I mean, I just am who I am. And you can hear these songs, this art form at different gatherings like academic or mental health conferences, any celebration you go to. . . . But these Forty-Nine Songs, I look at them like a bridging of new traditions and old traditions, and I see it as a way for tribal people to try to reconcile and still create traditions in the community . . . to create expression that is ours, [something that] is not defined in a history class or any department or academic circumstances.

The idea that voice, identity, and knowledge are achieved only by understanding one's own situation—that is, the importance of positional knowing—is a theme noted by many other students, and taken up in more detail in chapter 4. Because this kind of knowing is not typically available "in a history class or any academic circumstances," these students and their teachers worked hard to transform their education. Lori argued for knowledge based on a common history and purpose, and directed to the explicitly social goal of "rebuilding your community."

The questions that followed in response to Lori's account were primarily factual—"What tribe are you? Why are they called the Forty-Nine Songs?"—almost as if the class were groping for insights into Lori's thinking. But Angela Davis focused on the songs' evolving and communal quality: "Are they continually being rewritten, is it possible for someone to write a part of one?" Lori replied, "Yeah, or to just make them up right when you're doing it in a group." "So it's everyone's," Davis went on, "you can improvise." Lori gave an example:

> Last summer in San Francisco they had a Native American health conference . . . this man asked if he could play this Forty-Nine hand-drum song about his daughter's recovery from alcoholism. It was in English and in his native language. . . . It's flexible, it's not like the Star Spangled Banner, you can't play around with that too much (*laughter*).

In concluding the discussion, Chinosole suggested comparisons to blues improvisations, "so this as a class will become increasingly cross-cultural. And as you think of examples outside of the African-American experience . . . we'll slow down and then we'll analyze it from a theoretical point of view, what does that mean theoretically?" This is the kind of cross-cultural approach Chinosole meant when she said Black feminist theory "is a radical departure for many other related theories."

Lori's presentation is an eloquent example of a form of knowledge that is evolving and that evokes multiple meanings. The interpretive frameworks she used are neither universal, on the one hand, nor particularized, on the other, but rather "partial" truths specifically grounded in a community of discourse. Her description of the Forty-Nine Songs also challenged the traditional assumption that texts must be fixed and attributable to one author working in isolation. In a call for such expansive and diverse worldviews, Chinosole explained the multidimensional perspectives of feminist education in terms of the demise of the Copernican view of the earth as center of the universe:

> We must break through our own kind of Copernican fallacy, by building curricula and shaping pedagogy to admit that the royal "WE" of males, of European-trained, or of citizens of the U.S.A. is not at the center of the universe. . . . As one approach, we can move beyond local and national points of reference to an ever-expanding appreciation of various universes.[20]

The questions that guided the discourse in this course on Wild Women expressed what the professors and students knew as women of color, showing how feminist theory could be pushed beyond the limitations of white American thinking.

MASTERY AS INTERPRETATION:
SOME CONCLUSIONS

Stepping back to view this whole array of classes, we see that each professor pushed against the boundaries of academic knowledge to forge new interpretations of the world. The novelty and imaginative range of these feminist "ways of knowing" embraced themes from homosexuality to female sexuality to menopause, modes of discourse from journals to drawings to song, and trenchant criticism of mainstream academic approaches for ignoring African-American lives, or the fact that "a large majority of women are making less money."

Whereas Pat MacCorquodale tried to use sociology at times to help students formulate their own questions, Laurie Finke, by shaping the whole classroom discourse around student questions, allowed them to work on constructing a "theory of their own." Bev Clark and Margaret Blanchard worked with students' psychological and physical experiences of the female body. By using literature in her sociology courses, Mona Phillips acted both within and in resistance to mainstream academic sociology as she constructed knowledge in opposition to that of "white social scientists." Chinosole and Angela Davis seem to have moved beyond feminist quarrels with traditional literature; rather than setting up oppositional readings of literary texts, they expanded the idea of the text to include diverse "texts" of the oral tradition.

However, inextricably bound with celebrating the power of "women's knowledge" to reshape the world are questions about its nature. In a perennial oscillation, feminists struggle to define "women" without imposing permanent attributes on them or ignoring their profound differences from each other, which in some contexts seem more important than gender similarities.[21] In the classrooms we have viewed, this tension lies between the unquestioned value of "women's knowledge," on the one hand, and, on the other, the multiple interpretations of what "women's knowledge" may mean.

What are the costs of celebrating women and feminism outside the particular contexts of race, culture, and class? As we have mentioned, it seemed difficult for women in the predominantly white classrooms we observed at Wheaton and at Towson State to place their hopes and disillusionments about personal relationships within other contexts of social privileges and/or oppressions, especially those of race and social class. For Margaret Blanchard's students, such important differences in societal power positions were treated as personal, individual affairs. By contrast, the students at San Francisco State were continually pushed to see the personal as inevitably political, communal, and international, due to the diversity of the student body and the consciously political stance of their teachers. To them, "woman" as a category did not exist apart from the racial and cultural dimensions of women's lives.

As these classroom groups struggled for feminist interpretations, they also often encountered the persistent tendencies in our culture toward formulating dichotomies and "we/they" thinking. The women of color at San Francisco State and at Spelman faced the contradictions of their "intersectionality," in Kimberle Crenshaw's term, at the crossroads of race and gender oppression. To forge a Black feminist interpretive framework is to resist its constant erasure through both the racism of white feminist theory and the sexism in the Black movement. This opposition of race and gender, created and enforced from the outside, led Phillips to ask "the eternal question, of race and gender, which is more important," while other African-American teachers insisted that it is impossible to separate the two issues.[22]

The construction of a collective identity as Black women at Spelman drew upon individual commonalities that, at the same time, worked to conceal important differences among students and teachers in terms of social class and region, among other dimensions. This group also had to explore, as we shall discuss in more detail, the dynamics of their strong alliances and yet necessary struggles with Black men. At San Francisco State, knowledge was perceived not so much as oppositional—against white knowledge or against men—but as developing from within the group in response to their own diversities, and their need, as Chinosole said, "to open up the simplest facts about ourselves." Difficulties with interpreting the category "woman," traditionally associated with and imposed by privileged white women, appear not only in considerations of "gender and race," but also in looking at gender and class, as Laurie Finke's class reveals. That these issues, so endemic to feminist theory, would crop up in these classrooms is not so surprising. More problematic has been our own difficulties in interpreting them. For example, learning to listen to our informants at Spelman and at San Francisco State, we became aware of our own oscillation as we tried to comprehend the varieties of ways in which women of color deal with the dominant culture's construction of the "black/woman" divide.

Another difficult dichotomy, both for our informants and for us, concerns the widely held notion, expressed by Belenky et al., Tannen, and others, that women and men learn differently, in discourses dichotomized as intuitive, connected, subjective, and supportive, on the one hand, and as rational, separate, objective, and combative, on the other.[23] Again, this opposition both illuminates and obscures the complex process of creating meaning in the classroom. We saw many instances of both men and women demonstrating stereotypic female and male behaviors. Blanchard's class even talked about this dichotomy as a given, and certainly in Finke's class the males' discourse was both abstract and combative. But the stance of male students in these feminist classrooms was in the service of a position no less specific and personal than Jill Marts's for being hidden for view. Their angry tone of voice was certainly "emotional." Arguments based on abstractions and universals perhaps reflect a cognitive style indicative of privilege or academic training, not maleness: for example, some middle-class white women students we observed used an abstract concept of "women" to obscure their racial and class privilege at the same time that they personalized their experiences of gender. New forms of interpretation that explicitly take account of the different positional and cognitive aspects of multiple "ways of knowing" demonstrate that both men and women use narratives, their emotions, and analytical tools in various ways and in many different voices. In the next chapter we will focus on the complex dynamic of "voice" and its role in the construction of feminist knowledge.

CHAPTER FOUR

Voice

So when they met, first in those chocolate halls {of Garfield Primary School} and next through the ropes of the swing, they felt the ease and comfort of old friends. Because each had discovered years before that they were neither white nor male, and that all freedom and triumph was forbidden to them, they had set about creating something else to be.
— Toni Morrison, *Sula*

It's so hard . . . as a woman of color . . . to come up with the language, and say, "I'm going to write this" . . . but voice is in everything, and I think it's about class and race and gender.
— Jayna Brown, a student at San Francisco State University

IN HER NOVEL *Sula,* Toni Morrison put her finger on what her central characters, Nel and Sula, were up against once they discovered that the world of "freedom and triumph" did not include them; they had looked in the academic "mirror" described by Adrienne Rich and saw nothing. In contrast, Jayna Brown, who had purposely gone to San Francisco State to "find a place with people who are on my side, who shared some cultural perspective with me," was searching for a community, like the one Nel and Sula had created for themselves, within which to create herself. She found classrooms where she was free to find her place in the world, to fashion her own voice, and to imagine "something else to be."

We entered Jayna's classroom as well as others with a heightened interest in the theme of "voice," in part because of our own work as professors but also because it has been an interesting concept for feminists for more than a decade.[1] In terms of those questions we raised in the previous chapter in relation to multiple interpretations of feminist knowledge, we now consider the evolution of students' voices specifically as a means of self-expression. The first issue of voice raised in feminist classrooms concerns the development of students' identities as gendered individuals, which for female students means the emerging consciousness of themselves as women. Male students, too, had to come to see themselves as gendered, as they confronted, through their encounter with the experiences of females, their own positions as men.

But gender is not the only category through which people construct a self. We were also struck by the multiplicity of identities around which students fashioned their voices. These students encountered some of the difficult and painful dimensions around which identity is fashioned in this culture, namely, ethnicity and racism; sexuality and sexual preference; and, in a more muted way, social class. Their discussions of gender reflected varying degrees of attention to "difference." Many students struggled with balancing individual selfhood and group membership, with definitions of "self" and "other" and the "we/they" dichotomies that both liberated and constrained them.

Young women are also facing the "pleasures and dangers" of female sexuality, as demonstrated in Bev Clark's class. In more than one of these classes, students spoke of sexual abuse and violence in public for the first time, initiating painful dialogues that brought "unspeakable things unspoken," in Toni Morrison's words, into the public arena of the classroom. A student in Mona Phillips's class recalled that when she told her story of abuse by her father, "I started talking about what had happened and before I could get three words out, everybody was in tears."

A third issue concerns the connection between the evolution of voice and the languages of experience and theory. The shift from private stories, often painful ones, to a more public discourse often demands that the students bridge the large gap between these two languages. Discussing the discrepancies that often exist between the public language of classrooms and the private language of journals, Grey Osterud observed:

> I had collected their journals, and what was going on in their journals
> . . . was a tremendous amount of processing of personal experience.
> Writing with a lot of feeling, very eloquent but very private voices. . .
> and we hadn't made a way in the classroom for them to speak in those
> voices. . . . But when I see this tremendous discrepancy between two
> kinds of language, one in journals and one in large group discussion, I
> know there's a problem.

These private and public voices evolved in a complex interplay between the individual, the group, the teacher, the academic discipline, and the institutional context. As the processes of personal development and the construction of multiple identities of gender, sexuality, ethnicity, and culture came into contact, teachers and students were engaged in shaping each other's voice. To the extent that classrooms became communities of discourse, dialogues (and the identities that fed and grew out of them) were shaped by permissible and/or impermissible topics, concerns, and experiences; they evolved by negation as well as affirmation, by means of silence as well as expression.

VOICE AND PERSONAL DEVELOPMENT: FEMALE STUDENTS

As we take up the complex issues of voice for female students we are struck by the multitude of barriers that females face throughout adolescence and early adulthood. Beginning about age eleven, the psychologist Carol Gilligan observed, girls learn to internalize the gender expectations of the dominant culture, dismissing their own emerging sense of themselves: "As the river of a girl's life flows into the sea of Western culture, she is in danger of drowning or disappearing."[2] At puberty, girls also learn that becoming women includes subordination to male standards. Elisabeth Stitt, at Wheaton, captured how her development was complicated by gender relations:

I think I have a conflict about the old expectations, about how I should be relating to men. In the traditional model you are different or special, treated as a female as opposed to a person. I am still desiring traditional relationships, [but] I'm not able to conceive of them anymore. I could have handled the nineteenth century very well. Somebody could have given me a role and I would have fulfilled it.

All of a sudden I am confronted with, will men value that? Will they recognize the essential me, above me being female? I want to be attractive, and I want people to find me attractive, but I want them to look beyond the packaging.

Numerous stories about females in their college years confirm that many, in the face of such contradictory messages, do indeed disappear and remain silent in the college classroom. Gilligan noted that a woman's later education may hinge on the retrieval of her "twelve-year-old self—a journey linked with the recovery of voice and therefore with psychological survival."[3]

In many of these classes we have seen female students experience a second rite of passage, as over and over again we heard them extol these courses as opportunities to hear and learn about themselves for the first time in their education. Typically they might recall how they were "blown away" in their first Women's Studies course, "thinking that such a word as misogyny exists or how ingrained patriarchal thought is in our society." One of the students at Lewis and Clark, Carole Reagan, put it like this:

> Tipping things over and looking at them from an entirely different point of view has just opened up other channels of my mind. I can't even say what a mind-blowing experience it is to feel like I have the freedom and the confidence to look at things in a different way, to turn things inside out, and to write in a different way.

They spoke of several common sources of their awakenings: the course materials on women, the personalized and interactive discussions, and writing assignments in which they were able to make connections that had eluded them before. Students often selected these courses because they were explicitly interested in exploring feminist issues in their own lives. Angela Waters, a student in Mona Phillips's class, put it very simply when she said that "it makes a difference to me that we are studying *The Women of Brewster Place* and the sociology of women because I can relate to that experience. . . . It just helps to know that the issues they are addressing are pertinent to me."

This learning was also valuable because it took place in communities that encouraged students to develop ideas aloud and together. Susan Cotter, in Bev Clark's class, spoke for many when she said, "If you can say what you mean, it will help you understand." Listening to female students in the classes we explored in the last chapter, we heard several themes of development emerging. The first concerned the struggle to create a consciously female self, and the ways in which classroom discourse provided gender constructs by means of which students could fashion their voices as women. Margot Borders, a thirty-year-old woman in Margaret Blanchard's class, recalled a story she wrote about dancing on eggs as a way of capturing the risks of getting through life: "I had to be careful because I was walking on eggs and if I broke one I would be punished . . . I had people saying do this and don't do that. . . . I would say the eggs are about life itself." She continued:

> Margaret had us focus on these feelings within ourselves, and that's something I never do. I just push it aside. I grew up in the Catholic church and you're not supposed to feel anger, hate, be selfish. But it's OK to focus on these things and experience those things. That's what I'm finally doing now. And it helps.

However, it was often difficult to apply the insights gained in class to life itself. Here the language of personal experience and the language and categories of feminist theory both coincided and collided. Susan, for example, saw herself as using feminist ideas to negotiate a personal journey, worrying as she anticipated her future that feminism might conflict with "the pragmatics of going out into the world and working." She went on: "I feel like I'm trapping myself in patriarchy by doing that, but that's what I want to do someday, and if feminism and working and living can't coexist like that, then you have a problem."

Students also found themselves confused by these new ideas, placed outside of traditional roles, and in conflict with others, even other women. As Martha Johnson remarked during a discussion in Clark's class, "I was very torn between what I had been brought up to believe by my mother and my grandmother and what I was learning in the class"; Michelle Barnett echoed these reflections in her interview:

> I remember my mother saying to me, "Don't bring this feminist mess into my home. You're confusing the issues." And my friends would say, "You're taking this too far. Let's be serious." We'd all go on in class; then we would talk to others and get confused again.

Our interviews with students revealed profoundly contradictory responses to the issues posed by feminists like Gilligan. Some students learned to fashion conscious feminist voices for themselves, especially through formal writing assignments in which they made the transition from traditional mastery to personal interpretation. Michelle described such a breakthrough:

> I remember when I felt really insecure about my paper, and I went to Toni Oliviero [another faculty member who sat in on the course], and she said, "You're not trusting yourself." My paper was on Toni Morrison; she's not a feminist but she's a womanist. Morrison writes about the Black family reaching down and lifting up the Black males—she creates strong female characters. In the end my paper all came together. I was *so proud,* truly excited!. . . [I had] the feeling that I'd overcome something.

A similar breakthrough happened for Jill Marts in Laurie Finke's course in Literary Theory, where some students had trouble with abstract theoretical language. Jill, who sometimes argued with the male students, told us that "more and more, I find I am able to pull away from personal experience through theory." Her frustration was tied to returning to school after eight years and "having the worst fear of writing in the world." Jill saw Finke as responsible for her overcoming this fear by convincing her that she could "write with my own voice"; like Michelle's, her awakening was tied to a particular writing assignment:

> We were writing and writing in our journals, and I was really comfortable writing there but was still struggling with writing papers. [With my paper on feminist theory] my rough draft was just a synthesis of feminist theory in general. . . . I didn't come up with anything [new], it was more like a book review. So then I got to the point where finally . . . the last paragraph contained the idea for my paper.

Stuck there, she went to Finke's house in desperation the night before it was due, as part of a public presentation of student papers for the Gender Studies Symposium.

> Laurie said, "You know things, you only need to learn how to get it out." She said something like, you know you have all this stuff, here is this one sentence and it is great. It could be the beginning sentence. Try writing the paper in your journal. I went home and went to bed. I had to present the paper at 9:30 in the morning. I got up at 4:00 and wrote until 9:00 in my journal. I was organized. I got up there and read it and it went real well.

Oliviero's observation that Michelle was not trusting herself and Finke's insight that Jill's main theme was in the last paragraph of her paper illustrate that for both teachers, the writing process provided a necessary bridge between the personal language of journals and the issues of feminist theory. Their insistence that students find a personal voice to interpret feminist theory enabled their students to make connections that had eluded them before. Instances such as this led us to see that a crucial difference between traditional mastery and feminist interpretation is the acknowledgment of voice, through which students connect their personal uniqueness, their original thoughts, to broader feminist ideas in order to create a gender identity.

Implicit in our readings of the interviews is also the notion, elaborated in *Women's Ways of Knowing,* that students tend to proceed from a "subjective" stage, in which knowledge and meaning is lodged in oneself and one's own experiences, through a detached "procedural" understanding of "critical" or analytic modes of thought taught by the disciplines, to a more fully realized "constructed" epistemology in which they become knowers and agents who integrate the claims of intuition and reason, self and other. While the younger women we spoke to seemed to view the ideas they encountered subjectively—"What does all this mean for me?"—the older students recognized the importance of knowledge constructed by others. Jill Marts, Margot Borders, and Midge Crowe from Beverly Clark's class had experienced mature life events through which they could interpret the ideas about women's lives that they encountered in the classroom. Midge had returned to school after many years raising children. In her interview she remarked that "the younger women in the class would say, Why do I need to know this theory?" But unlike the younger students, she valued the variety of external perspectives precisely because of their difference from her own:

> I really liked finding out that I was limited. . . . I [had] thought all people were alike, but what I really believed was that they were all like me. Even Black people. Black people can be like Black people—their own cultures, their own ethnic views. I always thought in terms of myself.

In teasing apart the different aspects of students' identities that formed their classroom voices, we must also consider the influence of race, class, and culture. As we have seen, women of color and white women spoke in very similar ways about the impact of these classes on their lives. But while white students like Midge were able to embrace a consciousness of others' lives, most continued to see themselves primarily as individuals defined by gender but not race. The perspective of students of color, on the other hand, always embraced race as well as gender, understood "difference" as part of their norm, and tended to project a vision of a collective consciousness that transcended their individual identities. As Jayna Brown of San Francisco State put it, "voice is (always) about class and race and gender."

Thus the students in Mona Phillips's class valued her emphasis on theoretical frameworks for understanding *Black* women's lives. Angela Waters, who was a senior and an acknowledged feminist, told us that the voice she was creating as a writer was made possible by her acknowledging a conscious identity as a Black woman: "I don't think writing can afford to be genderless, colorless, classless. . . . If I don't address those issues in my work then

I'll live in some kind of duplicity that will get me in trouble eventually."
Speaking of Phillips's goals for her students, she explicitly linked an understanding of "Black women's unique viewpoint" with the breaking of silence,
and the collective rather than individualized discourse that would result:

> [Mona wants us] to get a woman's perspective. We're recognizing
> that we do have a unique viewpoint and we bring race into it and we
> understand our suppression and reasons for our conservatism, and . . .
> why sometimes we won't talk in a classroom.

For Marta Thomas, a sophomore at Spelman who was brought up in a
largely white upper-middle-class suburb in New Jersey, the development of
voice was linked not only to race and gender, but also to issues of social class.
Like Angela, she identified with the categories of Black womanhood developed in class: "Black women, feminism, and the issues that face Blacks—it is
a race and gender issue. And how they should be incorporated, it is just
everything in life." Acknowledging that it's hard to be both middle class and
Black, she told us that "It's like on the one hand [other Blacks say] oh you're
so good, on the other hand, you are betraying us, you don't care, you sold
out." In class one day she asserted that it is important that Blacks and whites
learn to understand each other. When some students disagreed, saying that
"we don't want them to understand us and we don't need them to understand us," she resolved not to say anything, becoming quite self-conscious
about her own voice in relation to the collective one.

Although, after this incident, Phillips encouraged her to speak in class
and called on her regularly, she told us that "sometimes I'm really active in
the discussions and sometimes I just sit and listen because I don't necessarily
agree, I mean I haven't come to that understanding yet. Sometimes I feel
that I have so much more to learn, just about being Black. . . . I think I am
able to express my opinions without feeling ashamed, or afraid of it, or afraid
of the person's reaction." But her voice seemed more tentative than those of
the others. It's as if the more militant students, like Angela, who brought to
the course deeper reflections on the racism in their lives, were teaching
Marta that divisions among themselves should be suppressed in order to construct a unified voice for Black women. In this process, some aspects of her
identity, such as her class position, were muted as she struggled to shape a
new and more politically conscious identity.

As shown in Marta's predicament, the capacity to develop a sturdy and
coherent voice can be threatened by a classroom environment that encour-

ages students to talk about some aspects of themselves but not others, reflecting, in Diana Fuss's terms, "the hierarchies of identity within each speaking subject."[4] Michelle Barnett needed to define a feminism that was different from that of her white peers at Wheaton, and that would somehow take account of her experiences as a Black woman. But she felt silenced on issues of race in classes at Wheaton, and made a conscious decision not to comment about race, "holding out as long as I could":

> I was so conscious of making comments about other issues, so that my comments about race wouldn't stand out. You think that they think it's because you're Black, but then you think you could just be paranoid.
>
> I remember feeling [about the discussion of Toni Morrison's *Sula*], "Should I say this? Should I take on this subject? Can I make this statement without making it a racial one? No, I guess not." I wanted to discuss it [the issue of race] but I also didn't want the discussion to focus on me. I wanted to bring it up, but I didn't want to carry it along.

The burden of Michelle's isolated position imposed limits on what she could learn about feminism. Yet, she appreciated Bev Clark and what she was trying to do, despite the all-white context that led her to suppress crucial aspects of her identity.

In the course called Wild Women in Music and Literature at San Francisco State, as contrasted with the more homogeneous classrooms of Spelman and Wheaton, the exceptionally diverse range of women enabled students to speak always with an awareness of the roles of gender, race, and class in both their individual and collective identities. Since Women Studies faculty were committed to building a program based primarily on the perspectives of women of color, the white students, who were half the enrollment in this class, were clearly apprentices in the construction of multicultural knowledge. In the discussions we observed, white students tended to be silent, while African-American students and the professors explored the issues. Indeed, Zahra Mfume* perceived that the white students in the class "feel really out of it," because in this place they were not in the position of privilege: "I said, well, now you know what it's like. There's a time for privileging, and it would be nice if everyone could be privileged all the time, but it just doesn't work that way."

Finding and fashioning a voice in that class, as in others, happened not only through classroom discourse. Sherri Tucker, one of the European American students who did not speak while we observed the class, published an article from her term paper for the class. Later she wrote to us:

> That course remains the most profound learning experience of my entire scholarly experience. I was a Creative Writing graduate student when I took the course and now I am a final semester Women Studies graduate student, writing a thesis on all-woman jazz and swing bands in the 1940s.[5]

Ginnie Richards*, the only white student we interviewed, enthusiastically adapted to the role of learning from others. A graduate student getting a master's degree in Women Studies, she contrasted her experience at State with the intellectually elite undergraduate education she received at Brown University. She felt challenged at State, she told us, because here she did not experience "this sense of separation I felt at Brown." The teachers were approachable in a genuine way: "They give us respect, and they demand respect as well, as people and not as Madonnas who bequeath their knowledge, their wisdom, to us."

Ginnie, who had gone through the difficult but exhilarating process of coming out as a lesbian at Brown, acutely felt the distinction between the languages of personal experience and of abstract theory. According to the feminist theory she learned at Brown, if she knew it intellectually, then she knew it spiritually. She came to believe that "if I have the words for it," then she had the right to say, "I'm right, and you're wrong. And that's what I did with people and situations. If you try to live that way, you end up, I think, on a personal level, hurting yourself."

Ginnie believed it was the consciously multiethnic and politicized context of San Francisco State that empowered her to regenerate her sense of herself and her social activism. Although she didn't relate this explicitly to her sexuality, she said that it was at State that she was first able to experience her self "whole": "There's not this sense of separation that I felt at Brown. . . . I didn't realize how much that hurt me until that wasn't true any more, which is here."

This integration of voice in Women Studies classes around issues of both gender and ethnicity was not true, however, of all the classes at San Francisco State. "Wild Women" was often the only class in which the African-American women were not a minority, and several students related struggles in other classes to get the professor to discuss African-American history or women's issues. Zahra spoke of this as a "hassle": "you really have to have a lot of energy to do it." She said, "I need to have at least one Women Studies or Black Studies class a semester; to have to deal with that kind of stuff you need to have something where you feel comfortable." In Beatrice Gordon's experience, the other fields she studied were male-oriented, "and white male at that." Like many others, she saw Women Studies as trying to "reach this balance where women could not only find themselves but find each other." Jilchristina Vest enlarged upon this theme:

> [In this class] there's no limit to my internalizing it, and understanding it, and really being able to become more functional with it. By contrast, the more I learn about it [Eurocentric knowledge] the more dysfunctional I get. . . . I felt it was constricting me and making me more confused and making me more ignorant, if that's possible, because I couldn't relate it to anything.

The traditional discourse silenced her, not only because of the subject matter, but also because of her preference for "connected" relational learning often observed in women students. For these students, the "Wild Women" class offered a chance to create a personal identity in a community of women who were engaged in the same task.

The challenge of constructing, or reclaiming, a consciously positional voice was particularly complicated for students like Jilchristina Vest and Jayna Brown, who are of African-American and European American descent. Jilchristina spoke of the importance of the language of identification at a place like State, where so many students were of mixed race and culture. Recalling that she used to identify herself as "mixed," she concluded, "That doesn't say anything. [Now] I call myself African, yeah. An African in America. Because I'm not necessarily an American under this system, but that's a whole other thing."

As at Spelman, these students were able to fashion their voices as African-American women. But they seemed more aware than at Spelman of the differences among themselves, and the necessity of building connections as "women of color" across these differences. In fact, they tended more to use the phrase "women of color," identifying with a wider group of women than simply African-Americans. A key aspect of this consciousness was not only the wide range of cultures in the student body at State, but the way they interacted in this particular class. For Jilchristina "you were guaranteed to get chills at some point in this class" from being with "a diverse group of women with so many points of view." Although they did not necessarily share the same ideologies, they could "work together as a collective and . . . we're all women and that's so empowering."

It is the diversity among women, reflected in the student body, course materials, and classroom interactions, that enabled each student at State to see her identity "whole," rather than having to sacrifice some aspect of it in order to fit into the class. Because students could see themselves both reflected by and in contrast to each other, each one could imagine developing a voice that reflected her gender, her sexuality, her race, and her culture. In turn, they were prepared to stretch their perspectives to embrace many complex "others."

MALE GENDER IDENTITIES:
STUDENT INTERVIEWS

We turn now to the question of how male gender identity is linked to the theme of voice. How, for example, do male students confront questions of gender inequality? What were their perspectives about the languages of experience and theory? Our interviews with male students at Lewis and Clark enabled us to explore issues of male gender identity. Although men in Gender Studies classes were probably a self-selected group who were not comfortable with conventional definitions of masculinity, they could not avoid confronting gender inequality in the ways that whites can often avoid dealing with racial inequality. Most were able to work through the implications of feminism for men's lives, partly because a large number of male faculty taught and took action around gender issues, and because topics on gender were integrated into the introductory General Studies course. In addition, because these men had to listen to women who were assumed to have authority, they were in a position similar to the European American students in Wild Women in Music and Literature.[6]

Male students were often ambivalent about participating in classroom discourse that drew on personal experiences rather than universal principles and abstract concepts. Ned Sharp summed it up this way:

[I have to decide] from my own knowledge and my own desire to debate issues, to have a critical, combative discourse rather than supportive . . . group therapy. There are people in the class right now that I would definitely like to engage in an academic debate and to try to break down the consistent habits of their thought that don't seem to be leading them anywhere—but I've ended up dealing with discussion in a sort of facilitative, to my mind, smarmy type of way.

Ralph Goodman, too, complained that in Laurie Finke's class there were "only colorless, valueless, dynamics . . . with no evaluative stance whatsoever." These two men pinpointed their discomfort as deriving not from the subject matter but from the anecdotal voices and collaborative learning processes that they associated with Finke's and Osterud's classes. They missed playing the "doubting game"—a technique named by Peter Elbow in which ideas are put on trial to see whether there is a loophole, a factual error, or the omission of contrary evidence—and felt that evolving discussions, inclusive of different voices and interpretation, were often not going anywhere. Although Ned told us in an interview that he was no longer engaging in combative discourse, Osterud saw him continuing to challenge other students' ways of thinking: "What he learned to do was to be very careful not to seem to invalidate women's views; he challenged the way they were thinking while at the same time being very clear that he was not saying they weren't thinking well. He was much less concerned about the men, with whom he reverted to his debating style. The men didn't feel he was invalidating them by arguing with them. They were used to separating themselves from their ideas."[7]

The focus on personal experiences also forced men to confront their own experiences of being male, or being in the position of "the oppressor." Ted Michelini, a chemistry major in Osterud's class, spoke of discomfort at times when he found the topic excluded him from the discussion. His reaction was to "take a nonemotional stance toward things, to play the devil's advocate, be more critical of some of the theories than perhaps was helpful." He felt scared and ill at ease as he heard female students talk about painful experiences with men; he resisted identifying with women as victims and realized that his male identification was "more distinct" than his identification with women. He sometimes thought of himself as caught in the dichotomy of two polarized positions: the rapist or the rape victim.

But Osterud's class, Feminism in Historical Perspective/Feminist Theory, offered Ted different ways to conceive of his role and to behave in class:

There were a lot of times I just had to tell myself, just bite my tongue, just sit there, and that was more helpful than anything. And it's sometimes hard for me to remember that. I usually try to think, "Wow, which point of view will be best for me to take here?" Sometimes it's hard for me to realize that no point of view would be best for me to take. I can be as helpful saying nothing as I can be saying something.

Osterud believes that Ted modeled alternative standpoints for the other men in the class, a dynamic that was difficult to observe because the male students tended not to interact with one another. Although it may have been merely etiquette, the men did not sit together and did not speak directly to one another. "Male bonding" was absent.[8]

Interestingly, the discomfort that these men expressed about the personalized discourse did not lead to their silence in class. Their valuing of critical discourse in the academy, the entitled position of males in the outside culture, and their socialization into dominance in the classroom all combined in helping them to speak more often than their numbers would indicate. For example, Beth Sanchez noted about Grey Osterud's class: "It's been really funny to just kind of see women sit back and let the men dominate it—I mean here we are talking about feminist theory and letting men dominate the conversation."

Acting on what they learned in previous gender studies classes, a few men consciously restrained themselves. Jamil Mustafa, a very articulate and frequent participant in Dorothy Berkson's class, said he tried not to dominate class discussions because "I know how I feel when someone really monopolizes the time, because I sense that there are people in the course who are a little bit shyer and would like to contribute something, and if someone like me constantly talks, then they get intimidated."

Like Jamil, Ted appreciated this new kind of feminist education. Ted used eloquent imagery to convey his journey from the abstract to the personal, grounded, and concrete.

I find that in classes where gender is explored, it's sort of as if you admit that you're walking in quicksand and stop gazing at the sky and begin to realize what your surroundings are, and then that's when you can . . . communicate truly with people in the class. You have to come out and admit that you're a human being and that you are set in this matrix. You have to deal with some of your foundations before you can jet on and deal with the impersonal and oceanic.

For Ted, the personal language of the discussions forced him to turn his gaze from the sky to his classmates and to the unfamiliar knowledge and voices they represented.

BREAKING THROUGH SILENCE

The classroom can also be a place in which previously silent students are encouraged to express the strong identities they often suppress in a culture where they feel alienated. The idea of giving voice to "muted" groups within a dominant culture was enacted in the following class at Lewis and Clark, in which the teacher's pairing of the languages of experience and theory challenges a gifted student to publicly articulate her identity for the first time.

Dorothy Berkson's 1987 class, called Women Writers After 1800, included seventeen women and five men ranging from freshmen to seniors. The course introduced students to some feminist literary theory, followed by nineteenth-century novels and poetry—*Jane Eyre, The Yellow Wallpaper,* and poems by Emily Dickinson, for instance—and concluded with works by Marge Piercy and Alice Walker. The major themes explored in the class were enclosure and entrapment, womens' perception of themselves in a patriarchal culture, and the strategies they used to try to overcome their oppression.[9]

On this Friday afternoon, Berkson began by asking if anyone had written about Emily Dickinson in response to the discussion of her poetry in the previous class. Nancy Ichimura, a Japanese-American woman from a small Finnish community in southern Washington, who often sat quietly at the edge of the room, nodded, and was asked to read. Nancy based the first part of her journal entry on a poem that begins, "I'm Nobody! Who are you?"[10]

> I couldn't help thinking of the idea of a mute culture within a dominant culture. A "nobody" knowing she's different from the dominant culture keeps silent and is surprised to find out there are others who share this feeling. But they speak only to each other and hide otherwise. This is what it must have been like being a woman and thinking against the grain. But don't tell! At least if you are silent and no one knows, you can continue to live your inner life as you wish, your thoughts at least still belong to you. If "they" the somebodies find out, they'll advertise and you'll have to become one of them.
>
> But to be somebody! How dreary! How public! She says "To tell one's name the livelong day to an admiring bog!" What is a name? . . . Names don't really tell you anything about what a person is like. So when you become a somebody and buy into the dominant culture, you have to live in their roles. You could call yourself a wife and the admiring bog says lovely, yes. You could call yourself a spinster even, and the bog would still admire you because you fit. But

what if you don't want to be any of these things? Well, then you stay a nobody. Nobodies, though silent and secretive at least have their peace, their solitude and are free from the judgment of the bog. (This could also be read about genius.)

Nancy then turned to some comments on Dickinson's poem that begins "Before I got my eye put out," which is poem 327 in the Johnson edition:

> But looking at [poem 327] it's problematic, there is a price to pay, and it isn't always voluntary.[11] Infinite vision seems to come from suffering through enforced pain. "Before I got my eyes put out I liked as well to see—As other Creatures, that have Eyes and know no other way." You can run around in ignorant bliss until something breaks through this level of illusion, takes out the "eye" that makes it possible for you to view the world this way and once you see through it, you can't go back, trying to face yourself backwards would "strike you dead." I'm not articulating this well but it's like growing awareness.
>
> A silly example: It's like watching a Walt Disney movie as a child where Hayley Mills and these other girls dance and primp before a party singing "Femininity," how being a woman is all about looking pretty and smiling pretty and acting stupid to attract men. As a child I ate it up, at least it seemed benign, at the most I eagerly studied it. But once your eye gets put out and you realize how this vision has warped you, it would split your heart to try and believe that again, it would strike you dead.

When Nancy stopped reading there was silence; it was as if the class itself were "struck dead." Berkson attempted to help the students engage Nancy's ideas by asking her to summarize, but Nancy's journal entry proved too complex or too painful for the class, because of her powerful images and her experience of the intersection of gender and race. After a few unrelated comments, Berkson reviewed the concept of a mute culture within the dominant culture, and related this issue to the idea of positionality:

> When you have cultures where one group dominates over another group—and this could be men over women, masters over slaves, one class over another class, it doesn't have to be men and women, it can take any number of configurations—any time you have that kind of a cultural situation, the suppressed or what he [Ardener] calls "muted"

culture will often be silent in some very significant and profound way.[12]

By pointing to oppressed groups in general, Berkson broadened the theme's focus, also intending to help students defuse the impact of Nancy's emotionally charged statement.

Just when it appeared as though no other students were going to speak, two women—Jennifer Bowen*, a senior and a class leader, whom we later learned had an abusive childhood, and Darcie Tokioka, another Japanese-American student in the class—took up Nancy's themes. Supported throughout by Berkson's interjections, which gave this exchange the back-and-forth feel of jazz improvisation, Jennifer reminded her peers that if you are privileged by the dominant culture, you have to play its roles to keep its benefits: "You can't have it both ways. That's the price you pay." Darcie's remarks centered on the tensions of being in a minority and yet retaining your autonomy precisely because of not being thrust into the majority:

> When I read it, [I thought Dickinson is] proud of being a nobody, she's a person, she's someone other than the majority. She is kind of shocked when she finds that there is actually another person who doesn't want to be part of the majority also. When she says, "Oh how dreary to be somebody," it's like "oh how dreary to be part of the majority." You don't stand out, you just kind of go in and mix with the majority. Whereas when you are a nobody you are someone. . . . You don't have to answer to anyone and you can just be yourself.

When Darcie said, "how dreary to be a part of the majority," she modulated her voice almost as if to mute her statement, to phrase it as a question, to evade finality. Although Darcie and Jennifer ostensibly were commenting about gender, the intensity of their voices derived from issues that seemed unsafe to refer to directly. The identities to which they referred had outsider status, but only certain ways of being an outsider could be named in this classroom, in which there were few students of color and issues such as sexual abuse were invisible. As it was, much of the class remained silent in the face of what Nancy said that day.

Nancy's journal entry is a brilliant example of how the two languages of experience and theory can be brought together to reveal not only what a student knows but her evolving sense of who she is. As Nancy coupled the Ardeners' concept of a mute culture within a dominant culture with Dickinson's poetry, she evoked the themes of silence and voice, visibility and invisibility, to connect their theory to her reflections on her identity and experience as a woman. Nancy's interpretation of Dickinson as "a nobody knowing she's different from the dominant culture," became Jennifer's, Darcie's, and the entire group's language as well. Names such as "wife" came to represent others within the mute culture; to escape naming is both to remain a nobody and to remain free. These are the costs and benefits of invisibility in a society that portrays one's identity as an inferior one.

Berkson paved the way for the recovery of Nancy's voice and insights by selecting particular texts, by asking students to write about a previous discussion of Dickinson's poetry, and by allowing Nancy's journal to guide the classroom discourse. It is noteworthy that her own voice was relatively silent in this discussion as she let in disruptive voices, the voices from the "wild zone."

In her journal entry, Nancy's "silly example" of Hayley Mills, a prototypical blond American teenager of the sixties, evokes a rite of passage in which she tried to imitate the dominant culture's stereotype of "woman." The powerful metaphors she uses to depict her emergence from "ignorant bliss," the enforced pain of her awakening, the inability to face "yourself backwards," all suggest the second rite of passage she experienced as a Japanese-American woman who recognizes the harm of modeling herself on a trite stereotype of American femininity.

Her journal also suggests difficulties with articulating multiple constructions of identity. Even though Nancy might have been thinking of ethnicity as well as gender in her interpretation, there is no explicit mention of the former. In this class, not unlike Beverly Clark's, racism as one source of outsider status remained an unspoken term, partly because Nancy's attitudes toward her ethnicity were not as consciously defined as Michelle Barnett's. We later asked Nancy if her journal entry related to her personal experience. She said:

> I don't think there's a way you could be able to think about that sort of a concept of culture if you have not felt like you've lived it . . . thinking in terms of race, even thinking about different kinds of minority perspectives, I guess, things like that, I think I've started to look more into experience instead of just thinking about these theories. . . . I think that is something that sort of came out of this class.
>
> I really have grown up in this community where we are the only Japanese people, and since we never had really any Japanese commu-

nity I was never aware of that aspect in myself. Which doesn't mean that that didn't have any influence on my interactions, it just meant that I was not aware of that as influencing. Everybody is blond and tall . . . and then there was us.

Contributing to Nancy's reticence in class were, most likely, the same tensions Michelle alluded to in dialogues about racism and ethnicity among whites and people of color. When Nancy wrote, "It would split your heart" to try to believe in Hayley Mills again, she is suggesting that the pain of confronting both sexism and racism at that moment might have been too much.

Her students were all affected by Berkson's emphasis on journals as sources of knowledge in this classroom. While some students contributed frequently and consistently, the more silent ones such as Nancy spoke more after they read from their journals. It was as though they had indeed recovered their voices. Furthermore, male students became more conscious of power relations in the classroom and learned to listen. Daniel Ritter[*] spoke in his interview about the importance of hearing female voices, of finding out how "women feel about these texts":

> I could read Dickinson a thousand times and probably never relate to that because it just would never make an impression on me, but having the girls in that class interested in that particular topic—"How does that relate to me as a woman?"—then I sit back and think that's a really good question. Although I'm male I can learn how women react to women's texts, as opposed to maybe the way I react to it or Dorothy reacts to it.

Nancy's voice from the margins placed Daniel and the other men in the role of listener. This dialogue, as well as the one that follows about the process of "naming," illustrates the multiple ways that naming functions: it can be a personal affirmation, a group affirmation, an acknowledgment or rejection of dominant culture categories, a constraint, or a liberation. In naming oneself, one may also be naming, or categorizing, another. Such issues often create difficult challenges in the evolution of more multiple and inclusive classroom communities of discourse.

Our next example of the exploration of identity in the classroom is taken from Grey Osterud's class, Feminism in Historical Perspective/Feminist Theory, which is the final course in the Gender Studies program at Lewis and

Clark. This course is designed to use feminist theory to bridge the traditional disciplines included in the Gender Studies program, and to help students develop a more comprehensive understanding of the gender system. Faculty members assume that this interdisciplinary course is more directly political than the discipline-based courses. In Osterud's words, students should leave the course knowing "what an adequate theory looks like, what kind of theory they want, what is it they want to do, and what kind of theory is going to help them figure out how to do it."[13]

Students met in small groups during the first half of each three-hour seminar and then as a full group of thirty students (six of whom were men and three of whom were students of color) for the remainder of the class. The text considered in the full-group discussion one day, led by Dana Matts*, a European American student, was British historian Sheila Rowbotham's *Women's Consciousness, Man's World*. Cheryl Ibabao, a Filipina-American student from San Francisco who told us that she wished "we could have read at least one Asian woman," criticized Rowbotham for not taking racism into account:

> That part at the end made me think about the critiques of the feminist movement in the United States by women of color. Most of the feminist literature that I've come across doesn't say a hell of a lot about racism.

In the discussion that followed about how ethnicity and racism are related to identity formation and creation of a more inclusive feminist theory, the students of color, in particular, attempted to transform the classroom discourse to include themselves. They were struggling to see what would happen if they were able to give a name to their ethnic identities, as the standpoint from which to develop more inclusive feminist theories. Because this meant examining painful aspects of our culture, the discussion was awkward and hesitant, creating frequent openings for people to say anything. Much like the class in which Nancy Ichimura read her journal, the majority of students seemed stunned by the provocative topic and remained silent.

Ron Underwood picked up on Cheryl's critique by saying that feminist theorists co-opted the "methods of liberation movements—they got the paradigm and painted it white." When Margaret Collins, a white student who described herself as thirsting for theory after studying with Laurie Finke, wondered aloud whether it was fair to criticize Rowbotham's book for not dealing with racism, Osterud reminded them of the tensions between the range of personal voices and the voice of theory:

If you're going to base a feminist theory on subjective experience and you don't include the diversity . . . you're going to end up with an exclusive view. . . , you're going to end up with a false "we" from which some people's subjectivity is absolutely excluded.

The class continued to discuss the question of how to include different perspectives without losing the focus of a coherent theory about women. Dana then turned their attention to the demands and risks of creating a "minority" group identity within a hostile majority culture. Echoing a common mainstream view, she implied that constructing an alternative group identity could only be negative: "Is that necessary or is it better not to even develop a distinct group [identity] which is totally ridiculous to me, generalizing yourself as a group reinforces the whole thing." Supported by Ned Sharp, who emphasized the need to "draw power from somewhere," Ron Underwood, in language reminiscent of Nancy's evocation of the mute culture, reiterated Osterud's view that traditional theory is flawed because it doesn't take enough experience into account.

In a way, to get at the center you have rings of light, to bring to light what is marginal and spread it. And the only way to do that, being a woman or being a Black person whose experience is marginalized, you've got to talk about that experience, you have to establish some kind of identity.

Cecelia Mueller*, who is white, next asked how Black "have-nots" could "gain strength as individuals trying to deal with white people," in an indirect acknowledgment of racism. Cheryl and Ron took up her question to explore the necessity for people of color to form an identity in opposition to the dominant culture. But they also understand, like Nancy's "nobody," that visibility is dangerous:

CHERYL: But they all have to form an identity first . . . but in a lot of ways it doesn't exist, in that it is so threatened given . . .

RON: I think it's dangerous to form, the question of whether we have the wherewithall to form groups without first knowing who you are.

NED: But if identity, if group consciousness, is necessary for you to acquire an identity, then you are caught in a vicious circle.

RON: Caught in the loop again.

After a few more comments, Beth Sanchez, who described herself as "mixed Latina and Native American," responded and a dialogue ensued:

BETH: And sometimes I think about marginal people just sort of floating around, not really being able to name what is going on, not really knowing your identity. It's just knowing that for some reason they're not up there with the rest of society and that just finding names and creating an identity through naming together required a huge effort.

RON: It's a good thing for a while, it's a good springboard but I don't think you can really carry it with you. If you carry it with you, you're just carrying with you those same notions of those distinctions between me or we, me and them, or me and you, or us and them. The celebration of difference gets you into a a different bind.

BETH: (*a few minutes later*) I think one thing interesting about learning political language that the mainstream culture understands [is] so that by learning it you can as an oppressed group be validated. But once you learn that language, or learn how to communicate, then I think it is necessary to go back to your own language, your own identity, your own culture, and I guess they sort of . . . they, we, marginal people face sort of a problem, on the one hand, to be autonomous and form an identity and reevaluate it, on the other hand, be able to communicate to. . .

RON: So there will always be a double consciousness, sisters under the veil.

Cheryl asserted that theory is of little value to a single Black mother whose family is barely surviving, and that "action and theory go hand in hand." She then returned to her original point (over Ron's protestations that bell hooks writes theory) that most feminist theory is written by white women "with their ideologies and their values." But Ron protested:

But that's how language is used to oppress people. People close the doors and talk about all this stuff, and I'm saying that theory provides a key to that door, and theory also presents a way of changing meaning, changing the way things are.

A few minutes later, Osterud herself followed up on Cheryl's call for a theory of social action, and on Ron's assertion that theory can "change meaning" and "the way things are":

But there are two kind of theory here. I mean theory can be used to critique dominant ideology, to pull apart and to make visible the deep structures that are often invisible. Theory can also be created from action, through people's experience of their oppression in the aims of their movement. People can make theory, which is about what they are doing. . . .

This discussion dramatizes the tensions inherent in the interplay of personal voice, the languages of theory and experience, and the construction of multiple identities. It shows what can happen when personal narratives of racial and gender oppression and invisibility emerge into public discourse and intersect in the classroom. As Ron, Cheryl, Beth, and Grey Osterud imply, linking their own experiences with a broader discourse would not only bridge the languages of theory and experience for them, but yield new and alternative theories, expressed in yet different language and geared toward action and social change. They wanted to look in the mirror of their education and see themselves for the first time. The sense of position that they sought as a result of this process was balanced by the risks of such identification. It could be used against them by making them "the other"; it could enforce stereotypes and objectify them, as both Ron and Michelle feared.

Although these students wanted to move *beyond* the level of personal experience so that they would have a chance to fashion a public voice and identity based on their ethnicity, white students generally resisted this movement toward theorizing the experiences of students of color. In response to a draft of this chapter, Osterud described this process in a letter to us:

[Among the] tactics that white students adopted in trying to avoid confronting their own position as whites . . . they repeatedly objectified, generalized about, and posited the unknowability of the "other." The students of color spent time and energy trying to head off these tactics. . . . They did not, with the exception of a few striking, isolated moments, feel safe in speaking personally to voice their most painful experiences as people of color.

In fact these people of color did not want to share their personal experiences of race with white students—at least not in class—nor did they want their point of view reduced to a personal matter. The idea that Beth, Ron, and Cheryl all advocated, that people of color need to define their own group identities, represents their longing for such an opportunity as well as their political position on developing coalitions that accommodate difference and promote equality.[14]

112

Although some white students struggled with racism, others wanted to hear from the students of color only the private and individualized voices that they used to describe themselves. At the same time, they also wanted to push for a general theory of gender that would unite all women, or all oppressed people, without having to pay attention to particular forms of oppression, most specifically racism, that would disrupt that unity. As Dana put it, "all kinds of different colored people and different sexes can get together as individuals to share their program." Like male students' resistance to explorations of gender relations, white students' resistance to theorizing their "whiteness"—to being caught in the racial matrix—hampered the students of color in their aim of articulating their ethnic identities.

Osterud herself broke her customary classroom reticence that day. She said later:

> [During the discussion of Rowbotham's book] . . . when a few minority students were trying to raise the issue of race, I found myself violating the cardinal rules of feminist pedagogy. I got angry and argued with the class; I think I told one student that she was wrong and another that her position was morally indefensible;. . . I behaved in a manner that we might usually term authoritarian, and I was glad that, as a teacher, I had some power to support the minority students' right to be heard. It felt wonderful to get the issue out into the open, with all the conflicting feelings involved.
>
> . . . I felt that night that all those things which I stand for, and which are validated by the structure of the course, were being used to say that the race issue was not crucial or to make excuses for people. I always try to cut the ground out from under that.

For this teacher, democratic classroom processes were inadequate to cope with the issues raised by students of color. Democratic processes often allow white students to hide behind their experiences without exploring the larger social contexts that shape the lives of students of color. However, this class illustrates how learning continues after the class discussion ends. Osterud told us later that students kept talking about the class, frequently returning to what Cheryl or Ron or Beth had said. She concluded that students understood and remembered the discussion in a number of different ways. It had become a critical shared experience that shaped future thinking and discussions.

TENSIONS AMONG RACE AND GENDER, FEMALE AND MALE STUDENTS

Osterud herself was acutely aware of the difficulties of attending to differences of ethnicity and gender in classes where the longing for feminist "sisterhood" prevailed. As she told us:

> I do believe also that there is a kind of false unity that sometimes we strive for in our classes. . . . People talking together is one thing but a total coming together is something else. That's one of the things that I have been cautious of for really a very, very long time. . . . I never believed that all women shared some kind of identity that was in any way essential, on the basis of which you could build sisterhood.

Where there was interracial communication, it was because, as Osterud put it, of the "determined yet patient" efforts of students of color.

In her interview with us, Cheryl Ibabao criticized the false separation in white feminist theory of ethnicity from gender. Speaking of the discussion of Rowbotham's book that had taken place the night before, Cheryl said that it didn't surprise her that, at this predominantly "all-white" institution, people weren't "really dealing with the issue of racism":

> I didn't really feel like I could stand with anybody. I felt that Grey was supportive of me last night, but when she mentioned a minority woman, it was to say we are going to read bell hooks next week.

Lamenting the focus on "black" and "white" America, and the absence in the curriculum of texts by Asian or Asian-American women, she attributed this in part to Osterud's lack of familiarity with Japanese, or Korean, or Mexican authors. Her way of articulating her cultural identity in the course was to do a paper about the Filipino women in her family, all of whom had immigrated from the Philippines and many of whom were physicians.

Beth Sanchez also laid claim to a more inclusive theory, arguing that "as students of feminism, we have every right to define it ourselves." But she also worried that academic language, in particular, was a medium that obscured her freedom of expression. It was her view that when gender and ethnicity and racism are brought into the classroom there is "the urge to raise it up to a scholarly level and it's . . . limiting . . . to stay within the academic words, phrases, and expressions." It was important for her that "a lot of things that are conscious but can't be formed into the academic lingo . . . come out."

Like Cheryl, Beth felt culturally alienated and conspicuous on campus. She also knew from personal experience that if she and Cheryl hadn't been there, these issues might not have been raised in the classroom. Both these young women, in articulating their voices in this class explicitly as women of color, were trying to make their peers understand that their lives raised broader conceptual issues for feminism, precisely because their experiences were "different" from those of whites on *more* than a personal level. However, as Beth put it, "this gender thing is more than just a classroom issue; it's real and it operates in my personal world, in the world."

In sharp contrast to the white students' yearning for personal meaning, these young women faced a more complex task. In order to claim both their cultural and gender identities, they had to educate white students about themselves, which meant trying to get them to see culture and ethnicity and racism as part of their identities as well. At Spelman and San Francisco State, female students were also acutely aware of racism and ethnicity as integral parts of their collective and individual voices; and they expressed themselves as women of color without this sense of embattlement and frustration.

Ron Underwood combined an acute awareness of his own identity as an African-American male with a sense of responsibility for helping his peers confront issues of ethnicity and gender. His egalitarianism with regard to gender, along with the experience of being a member of a racial minority in his native Colorado and at Lewis and Clark, had shown him the dangers, as well as the benefits, of ethnic and gender identities—"the bottles that people are trying to pour you into."

In Osterud's class, Ron saw his role as pushing the class to discuss racism, and he was very frustrated because the white students would not engage him in dialogues on the subject. He was disappointed, because he believed that white students were fearful of race and, perhaps, even of Black men like himself. Describing a discussion of *Ain't I a Woman? Black Women and Feminism,* a book by bell hooks, which took place a week after the critique of Rowbotham, he said:

> I just felt like they didn't do the book justice because they . . . objectified Black people. I think it's great when a student who is not Black is comfortable talking about it. Because I want as much discussion about bell hooks as possible, no matter what color people are . . . but the students saw Black, Black all over it, and you know that scared

them away. It seems as though the students want to use the class sometimes as a platform just to air their personal views, and sometimes I feel like when we're talking about Sheila Rowbotham or we're talking about bell hooks, and the discussion gets diverted to the Bill Cosby show or something they, you know. . .

But Ron's obvious frustration with what he experienced as white students' naïveté and trivializations of Black experience did not silence him. Like many of the other males, he obviously felt comfortable shaping the discourse, and saw himself and Osterud as responsible authorities on issues of race. His balanced comments in discussion reflected the way he perceived his role in class:

> When I get into these classes, I hate feeling clipped and I feel like sometimes you have to compromise one part to get another part and that balance is something that takes up a lot of energy . . . trying to figure out when to say something and when not to say something or when to try to illuminate somebody else's point and when not to.

In this context, how did white students interpret the struggles for identity, voice, and theory on the part of students of color? Kris Lacher was an art major very involved in feminist politics and cultural expression. Reflecting the individualism that Osterud and Ron found problematic in discussions of ethnicity and racism, she understood that "what makes this class very different from my others is that the learning comes from me." Despite this position, she supported Cheryl Ibabao and felt that "people were ignoring the plea that was made to look at racism." Kris believed that Margaret's theorizing, which was similar to that of Ned and Ralph in Laurie Finke's class, was no less reflective of her particular perspective than a simple narrative based on personal experience would have been.

Another student, Laurie Lester*, understood that Osterud wanted the students in the class "to be able to think theoretically. . . . I think she wants to show that theory and personal experience can be bridged." Referring to a small group discussion following the class in which the Rowbotham book was criticized, she saw "some tension in the class because there are so many different orientations in that class to the topics. And there is some sense that there are students who are threatening enough [to others] that not everything can get spoken." Nevertheless, she observed, students in Osterud's class really talked to each other.

SEXUALITY AND THE CLASSROOM

The silencing of personal voices in college classrooms also involves repression of the topic of sexuality as yet another "unspeakable thing unspoken," dredged up from the culture's bywaters. Traditional academic discourse has interpreted sexuality from a masculine and heterosexual point of view, suppressing the personal, the feminine, and the homosexual.

The capacity for expression and communication of sexuality is especially important for the construction of a comfortable sexual identity. If you have named who you are and what you have gone through in a setting of support, then you can place your personal experiences in a broader, theoretical context, explore their meanings, and approach the world with more confidence as a result.

Since almost half the professors we observed brought up sexual issues explicitly in the classroom, we saw a wide range of conversations. One frequently encountered theme, illustrated in Bev Clark's class, concerns the tension between the female undergraduates' desire for heterosexual fulfillment in relation to men (with homosexuality seldom mentioned) and the narrative of woman as sexual victim often encountered in feminist theoretical work. Another issue concerns the defensive self-consciousness of male students when issues of sexual exploitation are raised; for example, Ted Michelini used the image of "a rape or an attack" to illustrate his feeling of being more closely identified with the oppressor than the victim during discussions in Osterud's class, and being frightened by that.

Some conservatively raised students in these classes also had problems with the explicit discussion of sexual issues. But most female students expressed relief and enthusiasm about speaking out. For a few, giving voice to abusive experiences was transformative. Laurie Lester, a senior at Lewis and Clark, described a personal journey from silence to the voice of experience to the articulation of wider social implications that helped her to make sense of her experiences.

When I was eighteen I was sexually assaulted and . . . one reason it took me so long to get into Gender Studies was that I didn't want to have to deal with that. It eventually came to the point, really with the help of friends, where I could deal with it and then started discovering that this has a political context to it, and my interest just blossomed everywhere.

Because gender studies classes were such "an incredible personal and political consciousness raising" for Laurie, she could finally go to her family and "start asking them why things are the way they are with that family. It's actually gotten to the point now where it's very positive." One of the things she wanted to take up with her family was her father's upward mobility through the military, his marriage to a middle-class white woman, and his denial of ties to his father, who is a Northwest Indian.

For Wendy Johnson at Spelman, a discussion of the meaning of "domination" led to a personal revelation about being raped that had profound consequences for her identity as a Black woman.

> We were talking about domination and Dr. Phillips . . . turned around to go to the board and wrote "domination" in her little empathic way. She started writing and I said, "Wait, I have to say this." My body was shaking . . . I started talking about feeling dominated, how this man could come with knives, guns and you feel this domination because you couldn't do anything . . . I have been denying myself. I have been so damn busy trying to make everyone else happy that I am not even making myself happy. Talk about domination.

The course enabled her to face the pain of her own experience by demonstrating that she could share it with others, that her personal story, although especially traumatic, was part of a larger history of oppression. Wendy learned about the historical position of Black women "at the bottom of the barrel" in white, male-supremacist society, as well as about distortions in mainstream accounts of Black culture: "We've always been heads of households since slavery . . . it's not necessarily that there is something wrong with Black women in households, it's just that we are still being compared to what is called normal for white America." Support from the class gave her the inner strength to embrace a unique self:

> I look at Black women, for us to even be here is something so special in that it shows a strength that not even Schwarzenegger can deal with. We have been oppressed, depressed, repressed for so long: How is it that we can still stand up and say, no, you can't overlook us. . .

COMMUNICATION, DISCLOSURE, AND SILENCE

The main objectives of Carla Trujillo's course, Women in Groups, at San Francisco State University, were to understand the personal and political dynamics of an all-female group and to bring students' voices into relation with each other and with major themes in the field. Central to the class was understanding how their diversities "add to the knowledge of women working together in groups to build a sense of community." This all-female group of twenty-three students was ethnically diverse, consisting of several Asians, Asian-Americans, and African-Americans, one Latina, and a majority of European Americans. Trujillo focused on the theme of voice, "getting used to hearing your own voice," because "oftentimes women of color are not allowed to hear our own voices or our voices aren't heard."

Trujillo's interest in pedagogy stems from her own experience with teachers who had low expectations for Latina students and failed to "validate their existence." She is also interested in students who, because of their class or ethnicity, enter the university without standard English skills.[15] She recalls how she overcame her lack of preparation at the University of California at Davis:

> The first couple of years were rough. That was part of my struggle at Davis. I remember taking notes and I'd look over and whoever was sitting next to me ... was taking much more detailed notes, and would pick up things that I would miss. And I'd say, "I know I'm not stupid, what is going on here?"

The classroom discussion that we describe centers around a piece by Adrienne Rich, "Women and Honor: Some Notes on Lying,"[16] which the class had read. Trujillo organized the discussion around a series of questions she had framed in advance, for example, "How is the concept of trust perceived differently by women and men?" and "Why do we lie?" The discussion wound its way through a series of topics suggested by Rich's essay, such as how power relations affect our ability to tell the truth. Laurel Clinch*, who admitted to being "raised in a very abusive situation," said that Rich's essay reminded her that "I lied to myself to survive, so when you're trying to come out of that it is very difficult to tell the truth to other people." After several other students admitted to the contexts in which they lied, Helen Valance*, a European American student in her late twenties, commented that this discussion on lying was not enlightening her very much. She proposed, instead, that the dynamics of the class group would be more interesting to explore.

Adhering to her feminist ideal "to try to do a lot of self-examination, to try to be fair and honest, not only with your students but with yourself," Trujillo said to Helen: "Well, do you want to start? Do you want to give an example and start?" Helen responded that she would find it more interesting to talk about the group dynamics in the class than "what happens to me outside." Teresa Glen* picked up from there:

> I have an example that's personal [and] really illustrates one lie or holding back truths to protect yourself. . . . I was incested by my father while I was growing up and I never told anybody for, like, six years after I left my house. And I realized that the reason I haven't is because I held a lot of shame.
>
> But what happens when you tell the truth is you find out that there are so many other people that have the same experience and they can help you and you get much closer relationships with them. I'm sure that a lot of people [here] have a lot of personal things and I was just flipping back and forth about whether I even wanted to bring this up in here because everyone else is like, "Well, at work I lie about this," it's like big fucking deal, (*laughter*) everybody lies about one thing, hiding it, or another.

Helen's response to this confession was "Thanks for sharing that," signaling a dismissal: such revelations were not what she had in mind. But a second student picked up the topic: "I think that a lot of the reason people bring in work and stuff like that is that most things dealing with lying are such a personal issue—most of the things that I lie about have affected me so hard personally that it's hard to share." In response, Teresa replied: "But don't you think it hurts more to hold it in and not tell anybody? I found that I would ask other people what was wrong and I was always, like, the counselor, 'Tell me, I've got so much on my shoulders that I'm not telling anybody else, I might as well take care of yours too.'"

Illustrating how "speakability" spreads, Laurel joined the conversation:

> I just want to specifically address the point and say that I am also an incest survivor and I appreciate you sharing that. And in that particular situation, I think the point is about being honest with yourself and what you said about shame. It's about being able to say that, and it's more important that I say that than you hear that, and the point is that I need to say it. It's important to recognize your purposes. . .

It seemed as though the two incest survivors emboldened each another to speak. Although incest was an unspoken, suppressed theme in several classrooms, Trujillo created a supportive climate for these revelations. The concept of disclosure as an integral part of healing was also prominent in the culture when we visited Trujillo's class in 1991.

Trujillo continued throughout the rest of the discussion to return to Helen's issues, encouraging her to be more specific. Helen continued to resist specificity, saying at one point: "No, things have come and gone for me here, and I mean, they're already done." Trujillo replied:

> Part of what we're trying to do is integrate the academic and the personal in this class as much as possible. It's not always easy and you certainly have instances where errors or omissions can occur in either case. But certainly, as an instructor for this course, one of my goals is to continue that kind of work from within yourself with the academic stuff that we read.

In her interview, Trujillo reflected not only on the "difficult dialogues" introduced into the classroom, but the challenges involved in helping students develop a voice that others could hear. What she wished she had done in this particular class was to validate all of the students who struggled with disclosing private experiences in public:

> I knew Helen was in a delicate position from talking to her. . . . The two incest survivors had their shit a lot more together than Helen. . . . What I should have done was . . . validate what [the two] did but I don't think I did it enough. I feel bad about that. I didn't know how to do that and not lose Helen because she was in such a tremendously difficult place . . . If I had it to do over again, I would have still tried to listen, to not write Helen off. . . . the thing I had to keep focusing on was not on me but on Helen so I don't lose her . . . I would have stayed longer with [the survivors] and really tried to emphasize the point they were making about how it relates to honesty and truth, and then come back to Helen.

Only later did Helen tell us in an interview that, in her opinion, the course had not always adequately taken up student remarks about racism and ethnicity, class and gender differences. For example, she cited her own "heightened awareness of my own prejudices and my own feelings of separateness . . . really noticing my fears coming up around Black women and the distances that I'd put between myself and women of different colors." Helen thought that Trujillo invited students to raise their own concerns, but didn't spend enough time exploring their group processes. As she put it, "People kind of put it out there and it kind of just floats away."

Although a number of exercises and readings in the course addressed group-process issues, during the three weeks we visited Trujillo and her students, not enough attention was paid to either resolving underlying tensions or pointing out the connections among them. Only the topic of incest allowed a discussion that connected personal revelations to the broader themes of lying, shame, disclosure, and healing. Trujillo was not an experienced teacher; and it may also be simpler to discuss sexual exploitation in a classroom than the more subtle dynamics of race and class within a heterogeneous group.

The problem may also stem from something more basic to the culture of feminist classrooms described by Alice Moore*, an African-American student who had taken many women's studies classes at both Indiana University and San Francisco State. One of Alice's quarrels with feminist pedagogy is that it assumes that everyone's opinion is valid, so that the feminist classroom becomes a safe space in which students can say "stupid things." Everywhere in the academy, including the feminist classroom, she felt that theory is separated from experience. While traditional professors exclude students' concerns, feminist professors tend to focus on experience at the expense of interpretation, so that classes tend to degenerate into therapy or consciousness-raising groups.[17]

Trujillo's "failure" to confront deeper classroom dynamics was something, Alice thought, that was not unique to Trujillo but intrinsic to academic culture. In fact, she might have been echoing Ron Underwood's, or Grey Osterud's, views that the culture of individual consciousness-raising was a barrier, in Ron's words, to "ripping apart the disguises" created by social constructions of gender and ethnicity.

All the same, Alice praised Trujillo for at least engaging in practical applications of theory. Even though she said it "drove her nuts" to work in groups, she acknowledged that one of Trujillo's primary goals was to have students understand how they functioned in groups. Other students also spoke enthusiastically of learning about group dynamics and how to express and value themselves as women. One of them was Hilary McDowell*, an Accounting major who described women's studies classes as teaching her not only about herself as an African-American, but also about "important white women, important Filipino and Asian women, and that women and people of other cultural groups have a place in this world." As she said:

I talk about it all the time. My mother is, like, "These have had to be the best courses you have ever taken," because I talk about them all the time. I was, like, "Mom! you just don't know." Carla encourages diversity and creativity. She wants to hear your side. She doesn't want you to say what she wants to hear. And I've said things in her class that I don't think I would have dared to say in any other class or maybe that I would have dared to say in any other company, and things that I've been proud of about my experiences being Black, being a Black woman.

AN OPEN DISCOURSE ON SEXUAL COMMUNICATION

For a second look at the treatment of issues of sexuality in the classroom, we turn to Bianca Cody Murphy's Human Sexuality course, taught, like Pat MacCorquodale's, to a coeducational class of more than one hundred undergraduates. Her main concern at Wheaton was in helping students, particularly female ones, become informed sexual agents. She wanted them to be able to give voice to their own sexual experiences while, at the same time, recognizing a variety of other experiences, attitudes, and values as legitimate. She pondered in her interview the relation between "experience" and knowledge as she saw it:

> I'm feeling that experience is not enough. But experience can stimulate one to gain knowledge. If we just tend to learn without experiencing things, or [on the other hand] if they didn't put their experiences into a larger framework, then I don't think they would be learning anything, so my task all along . . . is to go to where people are, to use what their experiences are, and then to encourage them to learn and broaden and expand their experiences *and* their knowledge.

Murphy often modeled her conviction that no student voices, no student questions, and, by extension, no student personal experiences are inappropriate. She told them that they were not going to limit themselves "to traditional views of sex, such as heterosexual sex. . . . It is very important that we recognize that there are no correct opinions or feelings. You can all have your individual opinion, and no one should try to change it, or tell you you are wrong about what you think. You can disagree about [their] information, but not about their opinions." In this large lecture class, the emphasis was on modeling and legitimating open discourse, not personal disclosure. Murphy set aside office hours for listening to students' personal concerns.

Because of the size of the class, student participation was carefully structured. On the first day of class, she placed the students in groups of five to discuss a true/false questionnaire on sexuality, demonstrating to them that they would be working together, that their knowledge was important, and that they knew both more and less than they thought. As a result of this strategy, most class sessions consisted of discussions woven through lecture material.

The following vignette is taken from a class on sexual communication: How can people talk to each other about such intimate and important things? Murphy began with a lecture about principles of communication.

One of the first things is how you initiate the conversation. Whether this is a conversation about sex or about doing the dishes, it is very important that the timing is right. . . . You want to do it when you have time together when you know that nothing will get in the way. . . . Some of you are looking at me like, "Are you kidding? Talk about my sex life with my partner?" Part of the reason you may be looking at me that way may be because in our society we don't talk about sex. We talked earlier about how, when we socialize, we know not to talk about sex, not to talk about our body parts. I think the main reason that people don't talk about sex is because they don't have the language to talk about it. The language that we have is basically either clinical, in which case we talk about intercourse, cunnilingus, fellatio, et cetera, et cetera, or it's street language.

Next she divided students into mixed-sex groups of five people in order to develop lists of words for sexual anatomy and activities, telling them to make sure that everyone knows what each word means and to "be aware of how you feel when you hear these words. Notice what words you would feel comfortable using . . . and be aware of how you feel when you hear other people using them. Think about if the phrase you hear has a positive or negative connotation."

In the group we observed, there was a sense of both embarrassment and relief as both men and women spoke up. When a male student said, "What's next? Words for sex. Ride, screw, score, tonsil hockey," and a female student inquired if the latter is oral sex, he replied: "It's supposed to be kissing."

Laughter and animation prevailed in all the groups in the room, as students discussed words like "prick" or "screw" or "score." The few unfamiliar words were defined.

When the groups broke up, Murphy told them to discuss their reactions to the exercise, and then asked: "What did you notice about the words for male and female anatomy? Were most of them negative?" The following conversation ensued:

MALE STUDENT: I think we have more derogatory words for female anatomy. More offensive words.

FEMALE STUDENT: The male descriptions sometimes have more power attached to them.

MURPHY: There is power with the male genitals and not with the female genitals. . . . When you think about it, the female genitals have words that are disgusting, bloody, and the males have power. And what about sexual activities? What did you notice about that?

FEMALE STUDENT: I would say that they were pretty impersonal.

MURPHY: Right. They're not talking about love and personal things. They're objectified.

FEMALE STUDENT: Sometimes they were about the things that men do to women. . . . Like slamming and things like that.

MURPHY: Right. These things have to do with violence. It's not just penetrating, it's slamming, boinking. So that is a problem. When we try to think about how we want to talk, we don't have a whole lot of words that we feel comfortable with. It's real important that you think about how you want to talk about it. So if you want to talk about oral sex, you have to decide what phrase to describe oral sex.

As the students in Human Sexuality became comfortable in talking about these issues, they learned to voice their own concerns and see a range of legitimate ways to think about sexuality. Kate Haigh, a sophomore, talked about how comfortable she felt with the way Murphy presented ideas and got the students to think and question:

> I think a problem with a lot of people [is] they don't feel they can say things to their lovers. . . . I think that people really aren't familiar with their sexuality and . . . why are women so gross and dirty that they have to clean themselves, and men are so afraid of menstruation. I see Bianca as kind of making women feel like these things are OK.

Murphy's concern for student involvement was not just a question of process; only if they were able to express them could students feel that their fears, questions, and hopes were legitimate and healthy. Another student, echoing Kate's reactions, spoke a truism about traditional-age students: "Sex is on everybody's mind and here's a class about it." Now that the school is coed, she believed that learning from other students was broadened by the "kinds of things each person brings to the class"

Sarah Lauriat, a junior with a minor in Women's Studies, noted the importance of the "acceptance of different lifestyles," and valued Murphy's practice of addressing the fact that not all couples are heterosexual. "You know, when they talk about partners they automatically assume that they are talking about a man and a woman, whereas she doesn't. . . . She'll talk about any kind of couple." Some explored the issue of sexual preference, Murphy's own included. Sarah said:

> A lot of my friends wonder and I want to say, "Hey, she's great as a person, you wouldn't know it, and even if you did it wouldn't matter." Because that's what that class is all about, accepting that and learning about it. Like, last night [watching a movie] I saw the first lesbian love scene I've ever seen.

In trying to step back from the various, even contradictory, expressions of voice in all these settings, it seems to us that all the students were figuring out "something else to be." Had Toni Morrison's Nel and Sula found themselves in one of these classrooms, they might have been able to fashion their voices, like these students, out of the ingredients at hand: the course materials, the emerging voices of other students and the teacher, and the possibilities and limitations in the setting. Had they been seated near Jayna Brown at San Francisco State, they might have been among the people on her side, sharing some cultural perspective with her. Had they looked into Adrienne Rich's "mirror" from any one of these classroom settings, they would surely have seen some reflection of themselves. But they also might have understood something else she had written, namely, that that there is "no 'the truth,' or 'a truth'—truth is not one thing, or even a system. It is an increasing complexity."[18]

CHAPTER FIVE

Authority

I don't believe that there are personal solutions. . . . I think there are structures that we are all in. I can declare my opposition, but that doesn't mean that students are going to respond to me as though I'm in opposition to them, especially when I'm wielding institutional authority, regardless of what I think about it. I can't get out of it. I'm in this position.

—Grey Osterud, personal correspondence

I feel that {Pat MacCorquodale} has to walk on eggshells in teaching the class. . . . If she had displayed a very feminist side to her personality, she wouldn't have gotten to where she is. If you're dealing in a man's world, or the university system, quite definitely a man's system, you have to play the man's game to reach a position of authority.

—Stephanie Jackter, University of Arizona

A CENTRAL CONCERN FOR the feminist professors whom we observed is the source of their authority with regard to their disciplines, their students, and the institutions in which they work. Traditionally, professorial authority comes from superior knowledge of the academic discipline; it is lodged in the hierarchical relationship of expert to teacher to student, and enforced institutionally by the power and duty to assign grades. The University of Arizona professors also observed its grounding in what Catharine MacKinnon calls "aperspectivity": "the traditionally-sanctioned intellectual assumption that distance assures more accurate access to and representation of 'truth,' that the scholar should or could remain neutral, . . . objective, and divorced from the subject in both senses of the phrase."[1]

Categories of authority are most rigid for feminist professors in research universities.[2] Their competence is defined hierarchically, in terms of their knowledge of a discipline, their ability to interpret this knowledge to colleagues and students, and their scholarly writing. The authors of *Changing Our Minds,* all feminist professors at the University of Arizona, pointed out the conundrum they faced as women seeking to redefine the sources of their academic authority. In challenging traditional standards on the basis of feminist thought, they risked encountering assumptions that prevented them from being taken seriously—stereotypic beliefs that women are emotional, incapable of imposing objective standards, and, worse yet, captives of a dogmatic feminist ideology.[3] Ruth Doell at San Francisco State, who had spent more years in higher education than our other informants, held that her female colleagues were forced to choose between becoming "masculinized," that is, behaving like males, or becoming sex objects. Noting that some senior faculty favored the young, blond women in the department, she said: "Women who stand up for their rights, who are strong, especially if they come out as feminists, are not well treated."

We saw the hierarchy of authority being determined differently in women's colleges, whose top administrators are women and whose mission emphasizes the education of female students. At Wheaton, more democratic and student-centered approaches to teaching grew out of the college's gender-balancing grant, and reflect the college's traditional commitment to educating women. At Spelman, among our informants at least, academic expertise seemed to be lodged in the larger learning community of black women. Students saw their professors as nurturing role models rather than distant authority figures. Johnnetta Cole was often referred to as "Sister President," and one of Mona Phillips's students likened her class to a family: "It's all of us on one level where we look to her as a big sister, which she can be because she is older and can tell us a little more."

The feminist professors we observed have sought alternative grounds for constructing their authority as teachers vis-à-vis both their students and colleagues. Despite institutional differences, they are all engaged in the challenging process of defining and claiming authoritative positions both as women and as academics, as well as resisting the androcentric standards of their professional socialization. Although, during the 1970s and early 1980s, many feminists viewed feminist pedagogy as an act of mutual consciousness-raising, in which the teacher could bypass the issue of her authority in the name of a common "sisterhood," most of our participants were able to avoid, or move beyond, this stage. They learned to define their authority in terms of their feminism by consciously positioning and modeling themselves as knowers and learners for their students. They see feminist scholarship, expertise in the discipline, and their own scholarly work as important not because they yield objective "truths," but because this knowledge has shaped their ongoing personal evolution. Like their students, they fashion multiple identities and grounds for authority, in terms of the contexts and demands of the communities they inhabit and to which they are responsible.

For example, Bev Clark's questioning of certain feminist theoretical approaches meant that she was not sure she was necessarily "ahead" of her students: "In this class, it's tempting to say [the students are going to be] at a certain level except that . . . that implies a kind of hierarchy and progression that I don't want to imply." Instead, she found new grounds for interpreting and shifting authority relationships with students. About Louise Bobosink, an older student attuned to the French theorists, she said, "The goal for Louise is to educate *me* a little bit more as to what she's thinking, so that if she is basically sympathetic to a French perspective [she can help me]": "Maybe Louise has been able to short-circuit [the early American approaches]; maybe she doesn't have to go through the whole American thing. Maybe she's just French. [Then] I find that in her journal she's quite literally [from] a French background." Louise forced Clark to criticize not only her own advanced knowledge, but even the criteria distinguishing between basic and advanced levels of knowledge upon which a teacher's authority is based.

Mona Phillips's rejection of mainstream sociological theory meant that the source of her authority shifted from scholarly expertise to identification with the broader African-American community:

I never saw another Black person as separate from me. . . . This doesn't mean that I'm any less objective. . . . I'm just saying that when I say "we" and I'm talking about low-income Black folks, I understand that my experience is the same yet different. I know that, but I can still say "we."

The rejection of a detached "aperspectivity" was particularly clear for us in the case of Chinosole and Angela Davis. Both understood early in life that the "truth" about their activism and connections to the African-American community enabled them to represent a range of perspectives shared by women of color within the university. Their playful course title, Wild Women in Music and Literature, expresses their view of the only way for women to "make it" in the secret male "treehouse" of academia: as Ida Cox said, "You never got nothing by being an angel child. . . . Wild women are the only kind that ever get by."

Once teachers begin to view their students also as possessors of authority, the process of knowledge construction changes. For example, Laurie Finke encouraged students to confront academic material on their own terms by asking their own questions. In such academic settings, students also may become authorities to each another. For example, at San Francisco State, Lori New Breast's position as a Native American female enabled her to use the Forty-Nine Songs to build cross-cultural feminist theory. Nancy Ichimura created a new interpretation of Emily Dickinson's poetry in Dorothy Berkson's class.

Finally feminist professors must negotiate authority issues in the institution as well as the classroom. The wish to be more democratic and student-centered creates tensions regarding one's responsibilities within a hierarchical institution. Finke noted that "efforts to promote non-authoritarian classroom environments have often ended up mystifying the very forms of authority they sought to exorcise."[4] The professor's responsibility to have the last word by evaluating students, after encouraging them to take on new responsibilities for their own learning, reveals this kind of contradiction.

To uncover diverse sources of authority for learning is to indicate what classrooms transformed by feminism might be like. It is clear, as Grey Osterud claims, that there are no personal solutions, but rather a need to examine the university's deepest cultural and epistemological assumptions concerning the origins and goals of knowledge. Reflecting the impact of feminism on her teaching at Lewis and Clark, Dorothy Berkson observed: "Once you get started on this, there is no end to where it takes you and how much you feel in total conflict with everything you've been taught, everything you've learned, all the things you've modeled yourself to do."

POSITIONING STUDENTS AS ACADEMIC AUTHORITIES

It is frequently claimed that of all the disciplines, science and mathematics have the least to do with gender. For many people, the sciences are the disciplines that set the standard for "objective" research, the fields that others emulate to achieve the status of a "true" academic discipline. During the past several decades, feminist scientists have been challenging the concept of scientific objectivity by raising questions about what scientific studies reveal about cultural values. They have asked, for instance, how the actual experiences of women, as compared to physicians' analyses, challenge traditional assumptions of the health care system. They have also asked how the gender of both the knower and those who are investigated might influence the choice of questions, hypotheses, subjects, experimental design, and theory formation in science.[5]

The two science professors we observed, Ruth Doell and Virginia Gazzam Anderson, found their feminism to be in conflict with much of what they had previously been taught. Doell brought credentials to San Francisco State that qualified her to be an authority in her discipline: a Ph.D. in Biochemistry from the University of California, Berkeley; teaching experience at Tufts University's medical school; and ten years as a Research Associate at Stanford. As far back as graduate school, she recalled being told by male professors: "I don't want women in my laboratory." Her Berkeley professor held the same view but conceded, "I need graduate students, so I'll take you."

Punished for her participation in the San Francisco State strike of 1967 by not being assigned most of her upper-division courses in microbiology, she did not become demoralized. Instead she became fascinated by interdisciplinary work, which seldom yields scholarly productivity in one's field. Her new interests led first to environmental studies, and later to the intersection of feminist philosophy and feminist biology. She began to question the value of biological research, particularly research on the kind of trivial topics that were fed by the need to "publish or perish" at San Francisco State during the 1970s.[6]

We observed Doell teaching The Genetic Revolution, a course that fulfills a general education requirement. The following discussion of her class demonstrates how she located the origins of her authority in her feminism, her long-term association with the biological community—"what scientists intend to do and think they do," and her publicly avowed social commitments. Seeking to make students authorities with regard to the social implications of science, Doell told us the course considered "the male dominance of women's reproductive lives, the male dominance of genetic engineering, the construction of science for the well-being of men, with no consideration for the well-being of society at large, or of women in particular."

A major part of the course focused on the biology of genetics, including reproductive technology. The class enrolled fifty-five students and met in a room that Doell described as "impossibly formal"; she stood on an elevated platform holding a lectern, a lab table, and a huge blackboard. Her class, one day, began with a lecture on sociobiology. Earlier in the term the students had read and discussed material dealing with the heritability of intelligence. Revealing her concern that students understand the ideological implications of the topic, she asked the class an important question, "whether you think that human sociobiology is science."

Two students responded. Barbara Bates was a returning student in her mid-forties. Studying to be a nurse, she had previously supported her husband through his doctoral work and was interested in women's health issues. Ted Donovan*, a traditional-age student, planned to be an elementary school teacher.

Barbara began by taking the position that sociobiology is *not* a science: "I mean the basis of science is following the observation, making notes, making hypotheses—all of that stuff that you find in the scientific method. [Sociobiology] doesn't follow it at all by any stretch of the imagination and you could not call it a real science on that basis." Ted added: "I think it's interesting theory, but it has no evidence to back it up—evidence that would take it [from] being an interesting theory to a science." He went on, under Doell's prodding, to say that "anything could become a science if you had evidence to back it up." But Doell argued against it, "just for the moment on the basis that the evidence has been looked for and looked for and looked for and has not shown up." Barbara, at this point, replied:

> I actually think I'd include it in the same category as creationism, that it's basically [starting with an idea] rather than looking at things and then developing a theory, and that is not science. Science is not based on making theories and then finding things to fit them. Science is the gathering of knowledge and then coming up with theories about the correlations between those events, but not making the theory first and then finding something to back it up.

Ted was uncomfortable here, recalling later that he wasn't trying to be "scientific," but just to clarify the facts. He felt that Doell was prejudiced against him because "she was on one track and I was on another." However, Barbara put her finger on the inductive nature of genuine scientific inquiry. Doell responded by modeling the position that she wanted these students to adopt, that deductive science—science at the service of ideology—is socially destructive:

> That's the point that I wanted to have raised. Remember when we were talking about the inheritance of intelligence? Underlying the whole notion of human sociobiology is an assumption of the inheritance of some human beings as superior to others, and that kind of ideological infiltration into the doing of science is contrary to what scientists intend to do and think they are doing. I think that people undertake this kind of work partly because it is very supportive of the status quo. Scientists build careers around their findings. . . . It is also

very good for maintaining the status quo with respect to the separation of classes, of races, and of sexes in the society. In the maintenance
of the hierarchy of power . . . because if intelligence and homosexuality and other kinds of behaviors are inherited, there is little we can do
in terms of social intervention or amelioration.

She then explained that "there *are* genetic influences upon certain aspects
of behavior." As an example, she described the effect of estrogen upon
women's moods, both in the menstrual cycle and after childbirth. "Those are
things I accept because of the inheritance of hormonal patterns, which is certainly something you can trace back to genes." But Barbara questioned this
idea: "You could say that even that's cultural, because those kinds of estrogen
mood swings happen primarily in Western culture"; and Doell agreed: "In
another environment, away from a hospital with supportive people around,
postpartum depression might never occur. That's a very good point." Ted
asked, "So you think it's just too vague to be scientific?" Doell responded:

I think human sociobiology is bad. . . . Sociobiological findings will
be used to the detriment . . . of social egalitarian progress. . . . I do
not believe we should undertake a pseudo- or non-science for those
purposes. I sometimes feel like I'm getting very dogmatic when I
make these statements, but I'm feeling more courageous because the
biological community is so strong. . . . *Science,* the premier scientific
journal in the United States, now claims editorially that the twin
studies of inheritance of intelligence are scientific fact. That kind of
statement cannot go unchallenged, because the vast community of
biologists do not agree with that.

While she ironically presented a strong, arguably even dogmatic, viewpoint
of her own in order to resist sociobiological dogma, Doell told us that "just
as feminism and sexism, together, have risen in my consciousness, the need
for presenting these ideas has overcome my reluctance to talk about issues
that are not considered proper in this course and in the science department."
Her stance of listening to and learning from students like Barbara, while
politely resisting Ted, was rooted in her feminist and social commitments.
As Barbara said:

I see her feminism reflected in her carefulness. . . . Early in the course
she critiqued the patriarchal assumption of the superiority of people

and used genetics to support [that idea]. She was very careful to show that taking that kind of absolute stand is crazy. [Because] of how she did it, it just started to ring bells. I felt like it's like the old underground where you link people and they quietly resist.

Partaking in such discussions of ideology and ethics in science, Doell said, students would often "sit enchanted at knowledge that they have not had presented to them any place else in their career." Nevertheless, sometimes a male student would say: "You should not present this material in class. It is destabilizing [to my ego], the idea that science could be unethical, that there could be sexism in society." But she wanted all students to be conscious of their own positions, particularly with regard to controversial topics like sociobiology. Ted understood this:

She's firmly against divorcing the study of science from how we see science. . . . She has a holistic approach to science and doesn't make it something that is just the pursuit of knowledge. She introduces social issues—that's the big difference in her class.

Doell also gave her students the tools of analysis, as Barbara noted:

It is interesting to see how the discussion changes because we have these tools to more clearly say what we want to say. . . . She's very clear in how she shows us what's going on so that we can think about it. The terms aren't piled on you. They're added gradually, so you can accommodate them. She is a very good teacher.

For Virginia Gazzam Anderson, the other scientist whom we observed, these tools were the means of empowering students to become scientists themselves. Anderson teaches Biological Literature, which is a class in scientific writing for biology majors, as well as courses in Science Education at Towson State University. Her academic specialty thus concerns the processes of science teaching rather than the content of science. Yet, because of her range of pedagogical experiments, her students often practice, as she put it, "real biology." She aims to "prepare them both to do the scientific thinking, and to exhibit the skills . . . to actually come up with some of the components of scientific writing." Much class time is therefore devoted to hands-on activities.[7] She told them: "What I'm looking for is that you can demonstrate the skills that are valued by scientists. Because when you get into a job, when you get into graduate school, they expect you to function as a junior member of the scientific community."

Anderson also sought to demystify the origins of scholarly and scientific authority, including her own. She divided the class into small working groups of four students, who consulted on problems and shared tasks both in and outside class. After introducing a problem, she would tell them to "build on that point with group work so [you] can refine it." By considering alternative means to solving problems, students could learn that knowledge can be collectively and democratically produced, rather than handed down authoritatively by a single expert. She wanted the class to become independent learners and give up the idea that "I'm supposed to do it the way Dr. Anderson said."

Regarding gender issues, the faculty development seminars at Towson encouraged her to think about the roles of women in science, gendered topics for scientific research, and the empowerment of women in her classroom. In one class, she had the students do a spontaneous writing exercise, called a "Free-write," to explore the question, "Why is less than 20 percent of the scientific community female? Is this nature or nurture?" She also made sure that males and females performed the same tasks in their groups. But she worried about sexist responses to her approaches: "I get the feeling that they think I am nurturing them because I am female." Therefore, she preferred "to use the coaching analogy instead, because it's a more male type of analogy." Reflecting the ambivalence of many feminist teachers, she feared that to couch her authority in primarily female terms was perhaps to minimize it.

We observed the Biological Literature course in the fall of 1989.[8] The class met in a large, sunny room furnished with several large tables at which the fifteen students sat in their small groups. The students were about half female, half male, all white, and mostly of traditional age, although a few were older. Unlike, for example, professors in the humanities such as Laurie Finke, Anderson was very directive; she initiated all the questions. In this vignette from the class, she presented a lab assignment that they were to critique by themselves at home. She used this method to introduce them to scientific procedures she wanted them to follow and, in this case, to the gender issues she wanted them to notice.

OK, this particular lab is supposed to help to understand animal behavior by viewing Siamese fighting fish—beta fish. [She asks a few more questions.] However, this laboratory experiment is a very interesting [one] because it needs some very important modification. In what important way does it not reach its objective? [We are] looking at patterns in betas, but what kind of betas? Male betas. . . . What they do is look at the behavior of male beta fish. Then they introduce a male beta fish to a male beta fish to see its signals. Then they introduce a female fish to the male fish to show its behavior. But what component of behavior is lacking in this study?

A male student responded, with what struck us as a very "male" question: "How quickly did the female recognize the male?" Anderson went on, with increased emphasis:

What else is it lacking? Female-to-female behavior. The point I want to make about the laboratory, is just like last time we were talking . . . sexual stereotyping makes females the victim in science, and therefore doesn't give the whole picture. . . . Whose behavior has been studied in the United States? The studies that are done are normally done on white middle-class males.

She then gave the class a take-home assignment to "modify the lab so that it really does what it is supposed to do, examine the behavior of betas." The next day, following a laboratory experiment by the students in small groups, she turned back to the problem of the Siamese fighting fish, the betas. First she asked about what was missing in the original lab, namely, the responses of female betas to the males and to each other. She then finished the class with a brief lecture on the exclusion of women in science, and the resulting impoverishment of scientific ideas.

If we continue to limit people to a male-dominated paradigm, then how do the women who enter this paradigm act? Like men. And when they do this, how can their diverse experience enrich the scientific community? It gets watered down, because the women that are bringing in different experiences that might be able to come up with new ideas are [limited by] the paradigms. So Rosalind Franklin [a scientist who did pathbreaking research on DNA but whose contributions were ignored] was probably in many cases trying to emulate her male colleagues. . . . But the real problem is that the paradigms tend to limit the way you look at things.

In the brief exchanges that we witnessed in class, we saw Anderson working to position her students as competent practicing scientists who are able to think creatively in groups and see alternative solutions to problems. She was equally concerned with their becoming familiar with conventional tools and skills of the scientific method that they would use in the working world outside, such as the rules of evidence, the importance of operational definitions, and the control of variables. She also wanted them to question the dominant structures of knowledge, which can limit scientific creativity as well as oppress women. Although males dominated the small groups, Anderson often called on females for reports.

Students viewed the course pragmatically, as did Anderson herself, as giving them necessary skills. Yet each student to whom we talked felt empowered and competent as a result of the course, specifically the group work. Tony, a junior who was unsure about where his interest in science would take him and worried because "you're a waste if you're not looking for a career," described his excitement about the course this way:

> You don't even realize you're being taught something, because most of the time is spent talking to somebody else in the class. So you are mainly just throwing ideas around and the next thing you know, "Hey, I just learned something," and you don't even realize it. Because rather than having her tell you what to do, she's letting you realize it among ourselves. She wants us to be able to write something that someone in the field could pick up and say, "This person is a biologist," not just "this person is a student."

Sarah Turner*, another junior, like many young women had been generally intimidated by science courses, having flunked out of a pre-med program at another university. She felt more relaxed in this class than in others because she easily could speak up in the small group. Therefore she could participate in a mutual learning process where people learned from each other's uncertainties, rather than being silenced by distant authority figures with the "right answer." "I don't talk in my other classes because it's scary," she said. "I feel shy." In Anderson's class, "if you're not sure about something and you get other peoples' ideas, then it might make you understand something more."

The students did not see gender as a central issue of the course. Their previous experiences seemed to dictate their responses to what Anderson was saying about women in science. Alex Costa*, whose awareness of sexism came from his family as well as a Women's Studies course, thought that she was trying to make people "aware of what they are doing," particularly with regard to sexist language. But Michael Rossi[*], who appreciated the course in general, was perhaps more representative of males in his reactions to her "consciousness-raising" initiatives:

> She said there's only 10 percent women in the engineering and science fields, I mean that's because they don't like that kind of job. . . . That's just the way men are, they like to figure things out, that's what appeals to them more, and that's what they major in. And women like children. . . . I know a lot of girls who are elementary school teachers or majoring in that.

Anderson tried to use her understanding of gender issues as a way to push at the traditional boundaries of scientific authority. But in her discussion of the limitations of scientific paradigms, as well as assignments such as the "free-write" on women in science, she seemed to be saying simply that if women—and their differences—were included in scientific thinking and practice, then science would be expanded and improved. She left untouched the structure of the scientific disciplines and the political and social uses to which they are put, and did not engage the broader views on gender differences held by students like Michael.

Both Towson and San Francisco State have many first-generation college students. The futures that Towson State students envisioned—working in research laboratories or becoming technicians, physical therapists, or biology teachers—were probably comparable to those of San Francisco State students. Thus it is instructive to compare the way Anderson and Doell each sought to position their students as independent authorities in their disciplines. Both teachers wanted to help their students to become scientists, and to use their introductory knowledge of science in the ways that they themselves did. Anderson's emphasis on job-oriented skills for her students fed into their own career orientations; as Alex put it, "you're a waste if you're not looking for a career." Doell, however, charged her students with her own sense of responsibility toward issues of social ethics and equity in science.

Our conclusion that Doell went further than Anderson in challenging the patriarchal premises of the discipline has perhaps to do with many factors: her more advanced scientific training, her history of political activism, and the highly politicized atmosphere at San Francisco State in comparison to the more conventional world of Towson State, where both professors and students were preoccupied with individual upward mobility. But it may also have to do with Anderson's understandable concern about status in her struggle to legitimize her own teaching as real science, in spite of the fact that her courses were in Science Education and not in Biology. Anderson's position, like that of professors at Arizona, shows that it is very difficult to challenge the androcentric basis of a discipline while you are trying to prove your own authority within it.

CHALLENGING PATRIARCHAL AUTHORITY

Of all the professors with whom we worked, Leslie Flemming had the most heightened consciousness of the uneasy relationship between her authority as a female and the prevalence of masculinized versions of authority at the University of Arizona. Male norms were taken for granted not only by her colleagues but by her students as well. She wrote: "I am aware that many students perceive female professors as less competent than male professors, even when both present the same material. For this reason, I have been very concerned, in my large classes at least, with maintaining an authoritative presence in the classroom."[9] Flemming described herself to us as much less diffident than she had been when she first started teaching. She humorously observed that her manner and even her dress—usually a dark suit—reflect this change: "I now engage in masculine gestures, put my hands in my pocket, and am no longer afraid of claiming physical space."

The women's studies seminar showed Flemming how women's experiences have been suppressed, and led her to understand that "mine are the experiences that have been left out of the dominant view of culture." The changes she experienced were, according to her account, largely attitudinal: a more positive acceptance of her marriage; a greater sense of personal self-confidence; more willingness to take risks; a deeper commitment to her research and teaching; and, as a result, "a real desire to serve as a role model for younger women and to make the climate of academe more hospitable to them."[10] Although she concluded that "the mainstreaming project validated everything I have done so far," some attitudes did not change:

> Although it was suggested that feminists ought somehow to teach in a less authoritarian manner than most men do, . . . a clear conception of what feminist pedagogy involves did not emerge. . . . Thus, despite exposure to feminist concerns, deep sympathy with the feminist cause, and significant changes in the content of my courses, my par-

ticipation in the mainstreaming project and exposure to women's materials has not resulted in any substantial change, for better or for worse, in my teaching style.[11]

Flemming's feeling of marginalization in the academy, and her internalization of the traditional norms of good teaching at Arizona, may have encouraged her to perceive feminist pedagogy in negative terms, as a "letting go" of authority, rather than as a positive inclusion of various student perspectives on course topics.

These issues were in play in the large lecture course, Oriental Humanities, a General Studies class we observed that enrolled over one hundred students. We were struck by the cultural diversity of the class, in which we could discern students of Asian, Middle Eastern, European, African-American, and Latino/Latina ancestry. The majority of students were of traditional age, but a few were older, and some students had transferred from a nearby community college. Reflecting her newly acquired gender consciousness, Flemming had revised her course to include domains in which women were actors. Her syllabus read:

The purpose of this course is to introduce you to the great humanistic traditions of India and the Islamic Middle East. Because we are essentially concerned with what it means to be human within these two traditions, we will not deal with theoretical or primarily social science issues (economics, politics, sociology, et cetera). Rather, we will deal primarily with religious, artistic, and literary expression of these two traditions.

Despite the large number of students enrolled in the class and her declared ambivalence about feminist pedagogy, Flemming posed questions that, in her words, "at least allow them to speak from their own experience." She tried to open up discourse, even though, she told us, students at Arizona rarely challenge professors,

These students don't question very much. The better of them respond to questions but they don't try to challenge back. . . . Very seldom will a student ask me, what do you think about this, or how do you make sense of thus and so? Or even, why is it important for us to study this stuff? Students are not going to ask that!

With this diverse group, Flemming framed discussion around their religious positions as Muslims and non-Muslims, to encourage self-conscious awareness of their own religious beliefs and to help them learn from each other. In a course in which the content differs so much from what most American students know, she sought to ensure that students had enough information to fashion an informed or sympathetic stance toward a vastly different worldview and to be conscious of the power relations implicit in their situation as First World observers of a Third World culture. She began with the following questions:

Let me put this question particularly to non-Muslims. I have a question for the Muslims as well. How do you respond to the two key claims of Muslims? The first one is the notion that Mohammed is . . . the last prophet and the conveyer of God's most final and most complete revelation. How do you respond to that idea? Depending on what your own religious identity is, there are a couple of implicit possibilities of response there. One would have to do with the view of Jesus. Another would have to do with your view of prophets since then, Joseph Smith, Bahai-ulla. Depending on, you know, what kind of prophets you've looked to since then. How do you respond to this notion that Mohammed is the last one, and that the revelation that he delivered is the most final and complete?

The non-Muslim students offered various responses. One female student thought it depressing that there could be no more revelations from God. A male pointed out, using the example of "being nice to your slaves," that there are "some things about the Koran that don't apply any more. I think it would be nice if he'd come down and tell us what applies now." Flemming noted that "slaves" could be "employees" in a modern setting. Several students then made objections to the Koran's dictates about particular aspects of social life, such as women being faithful to their husbands. Flemming responded:

One of the things that really makes the Koran different from the Christian Bible, and similar to the Hebrew Bible, is its specificity with respect to certain social codes. It has a lot of specific things to say about particular community issues and social codes. It talks about divorce, adultery, usury, inheritance, and so on. Whereas in the Bible you have practically no specificity with regard to social codes.

A female student resisted the idea that the Koran came directly from God. "If he wrote it himself, without being inspired by God, that would explain to me a lot of some of the stuff that he said, and how that was convenient to him. . . . I [just] don't believe with every bone in my body that that was given to him by God." Flemming replied to this comment as follows:

OK. Not being Muslim, one would not expect you to accept that. And that, of course, is the second question, because the other key claim in fact is that the Koran is in all its elements that final and complete revelation of God, and that's the other issue that a non-Muslim has to deal with, I think. . . . I suppose I ought to let the Muslims speak for themselves on this issue, but my understanding is, and you can correct me if I'm wrong, that growth and development then comes through the community. The community then speaks—for God.

A male student then asked about "the preferential treatment obviously given by [Islam] and a lot of other religions to a certain region or type of peoples. Why weren't [other] cultures in Africa or South America, why weren't they privy to some word of God?" Flemming pointed out the underlying structures of political power and influence that determine which are the "major" religions: "What you're really asking, I think, is how come the religious experiences of other cultures don't have the same validity as these particular ones that we've looked at." During this time, Flemming used her authority to guide the non-Muslim students toward a more contextual and contemporary understanding and acceptance of Muslim beliefs.

Flemming then turned to the Muslim students and asked: "How do you respond to these two claims, and to the things that you've heard said by the non-Muslims?" Maryam Kavoosi replied:

Islam says that Mohammed is the Master, but it doesn't say that that's the end, because I believe that there are some other people after Mohammed like the [direct] community today, a just community, and they developed twelve of them, right?

This response provoked a brief exchange with Flemming about the differences between Shiites and Sunnis. Flemming summed up by returning to her original question, concluding that "in other words even if Mohammed is the last of the prophets, God's guidance doesn't end with Mohammed." The discussion drew to a close with an impassioned narrative from Maryam, who rejected the two basic claims of Islam, but nevertheless valued Mohammed's opposition to female infanticide.

> In that time, the Arab community used to bury their daughters, because they were ashamed of having girls. So they needed someone to lead them, to take them out of the behavior they were in, and that's why, at that time, it was needed and Mohammed was the leader for the community. . . . Personally, I don't believe in any religion, but [I think] Mohammed was a good leader for the community because they believed in him as their ideal. But I don't believe you can apply these rules right now.

Flemming summed up: "So you've in effect rejected the basic Muslim claim, because you don't see those claims as binding on you. Is that right? OK, What about the rest of you?"

When a non-Muslim, white male student spoke up, Flemming said: "I want to hear particularly from the Muslims among us." But the bell rang and the class ended. Despite her strong efforts to bring these diverse perspectives together, she fell short in her attempt to give authority to the Muslim students in this discussion, in part, because she ran out of time. She drew on the experiences of different students, but failed to explore with them how their positions—as members of a particular culture or adherents to a particular religion—gave them particular kinds of authority and knowledge. As another informant suggested to us, the Muslim students who remained silent may have felt insecure about acknowledging aspects of their belief system in this public setting, perhaps fearing possible repercussions at home. Nevertheless, Flemming saw the need for Muslims to recognize their own expertise, and for non-Muslim students to be conscious of themselves as knowers in relation to the "other."

Flemming did not present her own knowledge as a narrative or as personal experience, but with much more objectivity. Reaching out creatively for the students' personal reactions, she did not share her own perspectives, nurtured by wide travel and deep reflection about cross-cultural religious issues. Perhaps she used her objective stance to assuage the students' insecurity—on the one hand, the non-Muslims unfamiliarity with the ideas of Islam and, on the other, the position of Muslims as a minority. Perhaps her expertise in a field initially unfamiliar to students placed her, like the scientists, at a further distance from students than the literature professors we observed, whose engagement with student responses may reflect that discipline's emphasis on interpretation. We also wonder to what extent Flemming's persistent feeling of marginality as a woman in the academy was a source of her failure to claim a different kind of authority. Did she regard her spirituality and her engagement with the feminist critique of religion as grounds for expertise equal to her knowledge of her discipline?[12]

Virginia Woolf saw teaching not as the practice of domination but rather, the "art of human intercourse; the art of understanding other people's lives and minds."[13] Flemming's class, more than any other we saw, represented the art of understanding non-Western cultures. Her self-consciousness about her legitimacy in the academy may have constricted her ability to see that by letting in student voices, she was letting go of dominance over the "Other," and so enacting the pedagogy that Woolf envisioned.

Flemming's goal in the Oriental Humanities class was, perhaps, to make the "strange, familiar" to the majority of her students. Kersti Yllo, a Sociology professor at Wheaton College, had the task of making the "familiar, strange" in a class she taught called Families in Transition. The grounds of authority for her were, therefore, very different. Because of her situation within the supportive atmosphere of Wheaton, she had the confidence to openly define herself as a feminist sociologist, who criticized the institutions of marriage and "compulsory heterosexuality" from a feminist position, and saw her authority in that light. But she was also caught up in one of those "structures we are all in," that of heterosexual privilege.

Yllo's research is in the field of family violence, a domain in which she sees herself consciously as a mediator among different groups and points of view. To her mind, male scholars dominate the field with their "objective" research, at the same time that they devalue subjective or experiential approaches to knowledge—what former battered women or activists in the field know.[14] Yllo said about her work:

> I ended up putting myself at the intersection of the mainstream researchers, the feminist researchers, writers, and activists, and now with this sabbatical (as a researcher at Children's Hospital), the clinicians. It's easy to get run over when you're standing in the middle of an intersection. But it's very exciting.

Yllo began her teaching career by working within traditional sociological paradigms. Remembering her first years, she said, "God, did I try to deliver a lot of stuff—most of it through lectures that could last an hour and twenty minutes to give an introduction to family sociology." As her confidence grew, she "covered less and less of the material," and worked with students to construct knowledge through discussions that drew upon their concerns. Along with exploring traditional models of the family, she examined lives out of the mainstream, "claiming a lot of emphasis on gay and lesbian sexuality and alternative lifestyles." Yllo wanted to awaken her students to a greater awareness of the ways gender dynamics work within our society, "not to change their minds but to do what they do more consciously. And to be more tolerant of other peoples' choices."

Families in Transition, which we observed in the fall of 1989, is an intermediate-level course that draws both Sociology majors and other students who are interested in the topic or the professor. The class enrolled about thirty-five female students, who, except for one African-American, were white. The class met in a small lecture hall with rows of raised seats. In spite of this formal setting, the atmosphere was relaxed, students spoke spontaneously, and there was typically a lot of teacher-student interaction. Yllo found most of the students in the class quite traditional, "which I like. It's hard because they have an idealized version [of the family] even when their own experience doesn't match up to it." She wanted them to construct their own definitions of the family, and, as she said, "I want to make sure the course works for the students who don't want to get married, have children. But it takes work to make that one of the choices."

The class had been engaged in an extended discussion of homosexuality, based on Adrienne Rich's insight that heterosexuality, as the societal norm, is socially constructed and "compulsory."[15] Yllo linked Rich's ideas to her own work on marital rape, which she described as a difficult issue for students:

> Making the transition from assumptions that we must be heterosexual—that compulsory element—to sexual coercion, which is material that I've never put together before. And it's also hard because it's negative. . . . You have to deal with difficult stuff. They participated in the discussion really well.

On this day, the class began with a "free-write" on the topic of "compulsory heterosexuality," in particular, forms of homophobia encountered by students. Yllo used this exercise to explore broader issues:

> Imagine a system, society, or culture where we could just choose to be sexual in whatever ways we wanted, where the whole diversity of sex-

ual choices would be celebrated. What would it be like if we didn't have that kind of compulsory aspect?

Students responded to this proposal in terms of their personal concerns: either they wanted to talk about their relationships and what conditions made for a good one, or they worried about the loss of a definitive sexual identity, a more abstract problem but still linked to issues in their own lives. In this discussion, as in Bev Clark's class in feminist literary criticism, we picked up a longing for connection, implicitly a heterosexual connection, and a resistance to Yllo's focus on the structural aspects of gender oppression. A student remarked:

> [Sexuality] wouldn't be discussed unless you had a relationship with someone—everyone would say well . . . I'm not only a heterosexual but I'm also a bisexual at some point. It just wouldn't be talked about at all unless you wanted your partner to understand you fully.

Other students worried about the fact that, as one put it, "the lines between male and female and all that would be blurred." Another said, "It's like having guy friends, just friends, and then one partner turning around and saying 'Well, I just want to change this a little bit.'" Yllo replied:

> But those kinds of changes happen now. He says, I really would like to see some other people now, not necessarily male people, but those changes happen. But you're right . . . that's why we have lots of social norms . . . but when we look at the other side of that—you know, when you have homosexual teachers that get run out of school, that just doesn't fit with, I mean if someone's scared that doesn't quite fit.

While engaging their concerns, Yllo was pushing students to see that social norms, while comfortable for some people, are harmful to those who don't conform to them. But comments by the next several students showed their confusion and their resistance to the idea of heterosexuality as "compulsory" and institutionalized. One said, "[The idea of] compulsory heterosexuality as a means of keeping male dominance . . . I don't know, maybe it's because I wasn't brought up in the same environment as my parents, it doesn't seem that it's such a big thing anymore." Another, expressing nostalgia for traditional roles and authority, said wistfully that she would "almost rather have my parents break in and say, okay you're going to get married, you're going to have children, not have something like this where there are too many things—"

A third student, however, praised Yllo's image of sexual diversity, because, as she put it, "It also opens up a communication line because the more you wonder, the more you have to talk about it, the more you have to say to someone, well, I'm basically heterosexual, how about you, and just like a pick-up line, you know—I just think it makes more open communication." Yet each of these students expressed a different form of resistance to what Yllo was trying to say: either by defending the status quo or the security of traditional ways, or by suggesting that the issues would be experienced, and could be resolved, on a strictly personal level. Nevertheless Yllo persevered:

> For you it might feel more comfortable to have the sense that your parents raised you and that you would get married and have children, but if deep down you felt that you were a lesbian and didn't want to get married to a man, that kind of rules and from parents would be excruciatingly painful, so you know it depends on whether it happens to fit what you would like for yourself, which makes it much harder for some people than for others, of course . . .

The class ended with a discussion about the place of marital rape in marriage. A student again resisted the idea of coercion as a major factor, saying, "I think of this whole thing as not—I don't see it as a matter of sex, whereas maybe there are problems in the relationship, but sex itself is not the issue." Yllo replied as follows:

> Right, absolutely, I mean that sort of consensual, intimate relationships that are part of most marriages, are sort of in a separate category—then you have the issue of coercion and violence; but then there are issues of degrees of coercion. . . . The question becomes at what point this becomes what you would call rape.

In this conversation, as in her research, Yllo attempted to interpret disparate viewpoints as they emerged and intersected in discussion. After this class she said to us:

> I love that class where we were talking about compulsory heterosexuality—because it's out there in terms of touchy subject matter, I mean

the whole time I feel this tension. . . . Something could come out that could be very difficult to handle. . . . So I like that kind of risky aspect, making them think about stuff that I'm pretty sure they haven't thought about before.

The entire class discussion illustrates the difficulty of talking about lesbianism or coercion in heterosexual relationships in a context, no matter how disputed, of "compulsory heterosexuality." The pervasive force of student yearnings for heterosexual connection and the students' focus on individual concerns meant that it was hard for them to hear Yllo's critique of traditional marriage, her concern to legitimize alternative lives, and her criticism of homophobia.

Yet their resistance may also have been related to how students viewed Yllo's authority to speak on these issues. She saw her consciousness-raising stance as viable in part because of her personal circumstances. She told us:

This course gets easier to teach, partially because I'm getting older. [It got easier] when I got married, when I had children because I share that with them. They know that I'm married, have two children, a raised ranch house, and a dog. I mean this woman is OK in very typical terms. It gives me the freedom to say much more critical things about the institution [of marriage]. I don't know, it just gives me some kind of credential, which is very weird. . . . If I were someone else I might teach the course entirely differently.

Although she often provided the class with amusing anecdotes about her family life, on the topic of marriage Yllo drew solely upon her research on marital rape, making sure that her scholarly expertise, and not her personal situation, gave her authority. But it did feel "weird" for us to think about the students' perceptions of *her* (perhaps in terms of "the consensual, intimate relationships that are part of most marriages) as opposed to her research. Yllo was emphatic that she did not "want students to feel like I'm the role model." Yet, although she continually deconstructed her own situation by offering an indictment of traditional norms, the students' expectations and assumptions worked against her. It is interesting in this regard to wonder if lesbian students—assuming that some percent of the class might have been lesbian—were silenced. The students who talked in class all assumed the perspectives of heterosexual females for whom lesbianism was a "difference" to be tolerated.

Students we talked to varied in their responses to this issue. One student echoed the "credential" of respectable married woman to which Yllo had referred. "I don't think she has ever said anything too radical. In the back of your mind you know that she's married and has two kids, and that is always there in everything she says." When pressed she went on, "She knows what she's talking about, [if she were divorced] I might be a little more suspicious of the course. I think the natural reaction would be well, what does she know, she can't even. . . " (Did she mean "hold a man"?) On the other hand, Kate Salmon a senior Sociology major, appreciated seeing Yllo "as a woman and a mother and a person," but questioned whether "that makes her any more credible to talk about a homosexual relationship or violence. I don't think it really matters too much."

Bianca Cody Murphy faced the other side of the same issue with regard to her personal authority. Although she wanted her students to know she was lesbian, she did not want them to think of her authority as a teacher as either deriving from *or* limited by her sexual position. She said in a 1992 interview:

> I have decided that my being a lesbian is public information, now, in a way that it has never been before, and that's fine with me. But that I am not going to speak as a lesbian, or as a heterosexual. Because heterosexuals *do* speak as heterosexuals [in that] their heterosexuality is assumed.
>
> My lesbianism is an integral part of who I am. . . . So it feels absolutely important to me that the students know who I am. . . . If my lesbianism is visible enough in the real world, it [can be] just assumed in the classroom, just as heterosexuality is assumed.

Murphy defined her authority around sexual affection in several ways. She described her training as a sex counselor, emphasizing, as did Yllo, her professional experience in the field. She once referred to her partner as "she" in an anecdote about buying car insurance. She had another lesbian talk to the class about lesbian life, "not as the authority, but as the example . . . the authority of experience." Then the students could ask the speaker, not Murphy, "how she came out to her parents, or how did she know she was a lesbian? Not information they need from me." Finally, in every discussion of sexual practices, "heterosexual" was considered one of several alternatives. Never was sex equated with heterosexual intercourse; its meanings were always multiple.

Yllo's and Murphy's students loved their classes for opening up their world to important issues in women's lives. As one student said about Yllo:

I love Kersti in class—she's terrific: she knows what she's talking about. A lot of the things we discussed—family, marriage, divorce, sex, heterosexuality, there's no right or wrong answer. You see, maybe there's another way of looking at it—expanding your own ideas and opening up your mind. I used to think that family violence only happened in poor uneducated families and now I see it happens across the board.

Because Yllo seemed open to their ideas, students could use her perspective to expand their own horizons.

Yet these two classes dealing with sexuality and the family remind us how the sources of feminist teachers' authority have become complex, especially as they have engaged personal issues in the classroom. Whereas the science professors wanted to help students become scientists, most of these students took courses with Murphy and Yllo for help with the "real life" topics of sexuality or the family. These two professors thus had to signify their authority through a complex balance of scholarly expertise and the circumstances of their personal lives. Feminist professors cannot simply become equals, or "sisters," to their students. The complex grounds for feminist authority lie in the intersection of personal identity and professorial and academic responsibilities. Although all of our informants revealed their *individual* concerns in class, it is difficult for some people to publicly acknowledge the power of their own *positions* in society and the academy. Yllo's candor was an important step. But given our pervasive heterosexual assumptions, she would have to go beyond the authority granted by her expertise—even within the emerging canon of feminist scholarship—and signify her own privileged position with regard to these themes.

By contrast, the system of "compulsory heterosexuality" made Murphy's "coming out" a political as well as a personal act. To name her lesbianism placed her within a category that she wanted both to affirm and to transcend. To the extent that heterosexuals affirm themselves as socially privileged, lesbians will be able to call attention to that privilege rather than remain fixed in their own marginal territory within "identity politics."

NARRATIVE AUTHORITY AND TEXTS

Bianca Cody Murphy, Kersti Yllo, and Leslie Flemming all intended to use their authority to model different ways of thinking about social issues. The following discussion from Dorothy Berkson's class at Lewis and Clark concerns, both in form and content, the empowerment of students as readers of literary texts. It demonstrates Berkson's inclusive and democratic view of her authority, as well as her excitement at "risking the act of interpretation" with her students.

During the class we observed in Berkson's course, Women Writers after 1800, the opening discussion featured two student journal entries dealing with the first three chapters of Charlotte Brontë's novel *Jane Eyre*. Anne Alley, a senior English major from Santa Fe, set the agenda in her journal entry by opening up the possibility of more than one reading of a text. "The most striking thing about reading *Jane Eyre*—it's my second time—as I open the book again I realize how much I've changed." In her journal entry, Anne compared Jane's alienation to Virginia Woolf's experience of "walking through Oxford, talking about how she didn't even have a letter of introduction to go to the library."

This comment led Berkson, a few minutes later, to return to Woolf's *A Room of One's Own,* observing: "When Woolf talks about Shakespeare's sister, she says that if she had been a writer her work would have been distorted and full of anger." This remark prompted a long discussion of Woolf's idea that because it is more detached and "universal," Shakespeare's work is superior to Brontë's. Berkson added:

I think she was saying that to develop a sense of self when all the forces of society are telling you you are a thing or a toad or less than fully human . . . , the kind of anger and the kind of energy that it requires to have any sense of self—that is going to show in the thing that is written. It's not going to have the kind of smooth, urbane quality that Shakespeare has.

In response to Anne's question, "And does that make it flawed or what?" Berkson replied:

Where you don't sense anger but a kind of ability to accept every point of view and perspective. Privilege is what produces that point of view, not exclusion. I think that's what she was saying. Is that what the rest of you are . . .

The idea that universality is a mark of privilege runs through much of our informants' thinking, although seldom has it been articulated as clearly as in this classroom. Typically, Berkson sought to involve other students in the discussion. The following exchange illustrates how she conveyed to the students that their ideas were contributing to the evolution of knowledge, making the learning process a collective enterprise.

FEMALE STUDENT: That's kind of what makes Shakespeare's work so great, is that he was detached and you couldn't, I think, you were saying something about you couldn't figure out who he was by reading his plays.

ANNE: And so that's what makes his work better than a work by Jane Eyre [*sic*]?

BERKSON: I would say that literary critics throughout the ages have tended to say, "Yes, that makes one better than the other." I'd say that maybe we ought to keep an open mind about that.

Anne disagreed with the critics, and Berkson encouraged her to elaborate:

> That is such an inside academic's idea. She's on the outside looking in and she's still holding that [idea]; that was such a disappointment to me.

In *A Room of One's Own,* Woolf judged Shakespeare to be superior to Brontë because of his detached position. She writes about Brontë: "She will never get her genius expressed whole and entire. Her books will be deformed and twisted. She will write in a rage where she should write calmly. She will write foolishly where she should write wisely . . . write of herself where she should write of her characters. She is at war with her lot. How could she help but die young, cramped and thwarted?"[16]

Berkson pointed out, in defense of Woolf, that she was writing in 1920, and "you wonder what it cost her as a writer to accept a patriarchal view of good literature." As if to demonstrate the group's resistance to a universalized perspective, she then turned back to Anne's original idea about the possibility of different readings of a single text:

> You mentioned, Anne, that you felt different reading the book when you were a child and when you were an adult, and I think that's an interesting issue. . . . It also points to certain things about reading literature. I believe that there is no one *Jane Eyre.* . . . All you have to do is read a book at different moments in your life to know it feels like you're reading a different book. . . . Did you feel you were missing something reading it this time, or did you just feel like you were adding something to your experience before?

As in the class discussion of Nancy Ichimura's journal, Berkson is reenacting mastery as interpretation and widening the sources of authority. The child's reading is as valid as an adult's, she implies; later readings may add something but also miss things that the child sees. Carole Reagan, a student for whom feminist perspectives "opened up other channels of my mind," made the point that "when you read things at that age, you really live them." Other women chimed in to give examples. Joy Engleman, a freshman, remembered "being horrified by Jane's childhood, especially the part about Lowood School." Another student described, to much laughter, going to the kitchen, like Jane, for bread and water. Another mentioned "people talking about you when you are right there, as if it didn't matter to your feelings." Others spoke of "being manipulated by adults and feeling alienated that way," or "feeling inconsequential, too, like it doesn't matter and you can be sent off to school or whatever."

Berkson then turned to other readings, deftly orchestrating the multiplicity of voices to include first-time readers of the novel as well as male students:

> The people who read it for the first time as adults, what is the experience of reading it for you? Did you identify with her, did the book catch you in that kind of emotional intensity if you've read it for the first time now? . . . Also I think that the experience of reading it for the men in the class is different than for the women, too. I mean it is bound to be.

After a short interlude, three of the male students joined the discussion to explore the issue of the character Jane Eyre as a child. As Daniel Ritter saw it, "It is important to understand this stuff, but she acts much differently than I can ever imagine a ten-year-old in any time acting." Bob Vaux, a senior Religion major, replied:

> Our society works to maintain the dependency of children and keep them young. So, for instance, we are not able to imagine a ten-year-old girl who reads about the history of Rome. . . . But maybe Brontë was stressing the untapped capabilities of the child, how we work to hold them down.

Jamil Mustafa pointed out that the Brontës were unusual: "I can see [them] doing this sort of thing." It is interesting that Daniel's comments were taken up by two other male students, and that they focused on the issue of Jane's veracity as a character, which the female students never questioned because they identified with her experience as a young girl. Berkson then gave a lecture that wove together student comments, aspects of her own childhood, and her knowledge of the Brontës and Victorian childhood:

> The Victorians had a very different conception of childhood than we do today. And they really did see children as little adults. . . . But I [agree with] Carole's point that a child who feels as lonely as Jane, who has no television, no friends, nothing to escape into, will probably as quickly as possible find the library. I grew up before television and I did a lot of reading as a very young child. . . . Jamil points out, we haven't talked about the Brontë family: Charlotte grew up in Yorkshire in a very lonely, isolated village. She was the daughter of the clergyman, which meant that they were anomalies in terms of their class and status. They didn't really have any peers in the town . . . . so there are some real differences in culture we have to keep in mind. But they were also gifted children, and she is writing about a child that we would think of as unusually gifted.

Berkson demonstrates here how different perspectives may interact when interpretive authority is lodged in many voices. Because this lecture represented her practice of teaching in response to student-generated concerns, we had concluded that Berkson lectured in response to what she decided students had to know in order for learning to progress. But it was not that simple, she told us; rather she always thought ahead about providing the theoretical knowledge needed by students to interact with the text, and brought it up at the appropriate time in the discussion.

In this discussion we saw Berkson and her students engaged in the interactive learning and knowledge construction that are a hallmark of her pedagogy. It juxtaposed the voices of adults and children, males and females, teacher and students, Charlotte Brontë and Virginia Woolf. It explicitly addressed the authority of different forms of knowing—Brontë's rage as well as Shakespeare's detachment. Her other topic, namely, the multiple readings of a single text, depending on one's age, circumstance, and gender, also elaborates this concept of the diverse origins of knowledge. Because the position of the reader influences the meaning of the text, each reading has its own validity. Berkson put it succinctly: "I believe that there is no one *Jane Eyre.*"

This theme of multiple readings also informed the discussion process. By evoking different perspectives, Berkson called for a connected communal learning that sharply contrasts with Anne's description of the traditional pedagogy to which she had been exposed:

> I went through years of school without saying a word because the professor would ask something, and I'd know what they wanted to hear, but I wouldn't tell him. I got to the point where I hated discussions because they would feed us these little things and they wanted us to snap . . . and I just wouldn't, and I'd spend so much time thinking, how can I not snap.

In Berkson's class, understanding is created in a community of discourse, not in the minds of competing individuals with differing levels of expertise. Because the sources of knowledge are recognized as multiple, authority is redefined as well. When Berkson said, "Did you feel like you were missing something, or . . . adding something?" she was giving validity to childhood readings as well as to those of an adult, and asserting that one's position as a reader, whether "calm" or "enraged," is an authentic source of interpretive authority.

OPENLY CHALLENGING THE PROFESSOR'S AUTHORITY

Among others, Stephanie Jackter and Leslie Flemming have noted that students often respect male professors more than they do females.[17] Adopting the psychoanalytical concept of transference, "the psychic interplay of desire and power among historically specific, gendered teachers and students," Laurie Finke observed that student attitudes toward teachers reenact previous relations with authority figures, especially parents.[18] The authority of male teachers, like the father's authority, may be more easily confronted overtly, and then negotiated, than the expectations placed on the mother figure for care and nurturance. Ned Sharp, for example, took courses with all three of the Lewis and Clark professors. Although he respected Finke for "divesting her power as a teacher," he also longed for teachers from whom he could learn through combative discourse. As he mentioned previously, "I think there's plenty of people . . . who would like to have an out-and-out debate. And would like to argue with an authoritative voice."

Our classrooms are arenas in which we can view the effects of such unsettling transformations in teacher-student relationships. As the Lewis and

Clark professors, in particular, struggled to place students at the center of classroom discourse, they faced complex new challenges, such as how to enable students to set their own agendas and become independent learners, while preventing the class from being dominated by a small number of students who, by virtue of their intellectual sophistication and maturity, familiarity with the material, among other factors, wielded more authority than their peers. In the courses taught by Grey Osterud and Dorothy Berkson, these challenges led to open resistance to the way the class was being run.

Osterud's class in Feminism in Historical Perspective/Feminist Theory represented a wide range of student skills and sophistication. Ned Sharp and Margaret Collins, for example, had taken Laurie Finke's course in Feminist Theory and they and Ron Underwood were all knowledgeable in theory and history. But others, such as Calvin Smiley*, a sophomore Biology major, felt excluded, as he noted in his journal one day regarding a discussion of Margaret Fuller's *Women and Economics*:

> Today's big group discussion . . . seemed very intellectual to me and I felt stupid. I didn't really understand what everyone was talking about most of the time and I kept thinking I had read the wrong book or that I was in the wrong class. [When] I feel that way I sit silently and hope class will end soon.

It was Beth Sanchez, also a sophomore, who broke this silence. One day she complained openly that no one spoke during discussions but "this select group of people." Like Calvin, she was floundering because she didn't understand the material or its context and assumed that "everyone (else) understood. . . . I remember specifically saying in class that I feel like I'm learning what a pine and oak and maple is without knowing what a tree is." Other students added that by the time they were able even to formulate questions about a topic, the class had moved on to a new text.

Osterud understood the situation, particularly the skewed authority of students from Finke's class, and told us it was "in violation of feminist classroom processes and had to be stopped."

> I could see it, but I could not do anything about it. Maybe some teachers could if they are authoritarian but I knew that anything I did that was directive would defeat the whole purpose. . . . They had to realize there was a problem and . . . break open the process.

She waited for more than a week for students to clarify the problem themselves and come up with a solution together. Although she then offered some suggestions about class structure and the course readings, she insisted that the students take collective responsibility for the class as a whole. In this course, students met in small groups for part of the class and then as a full group of thirty students (see chapter 4). They agreed to select report topics for the small groups and the subsequent agenda for the large one, and to choose a student to chair the large-group discussion each day. Osterud argued that this new responsibility would allow the entire class to respond to students' needs, and enable them to look to each other rather than to her for feedback. Later she told us that this repositioning of her authority would, as she put it, "free me from the role of orchestral conductor to become an 'expert participant'":

> I could try to clarify matters or pull things together instead of elicit-
> ing the expression of opposite points of view or setting up controver-
> sies as I'd been doing.

The following full-group discussion, on ethnicity and culture, race and identity, which is described in chapter 4, was initiated and developed by students, without much input from Osterud.

As she told us, Osterud seeks to share her authority by distancing herself from any "superior" knowledge and, as she describes it here, contextualizing her own role. But she also sees how many factors complicate this process, echoing Finke's notion of psychological "transference" and pointing to the constraints of grades:

> I'm not going to try to pretend that what I'm projecting is truth or
> what history says or anything that comes from the discipline. So I try
> to separate, in other words, myself as a person with certain convictions
> from this role that I inhabit and that is reinforced by the structures of
> everything we do here. I have certain kinds of power which I don't
> think I should have, but I do. I don't try to pretend I don't. . . . I give
> grades. Students treat me in ways [based not on] who I am and what I
> think about authority, but on who they are and what their experience
> with authority has been. I try to be conscious of that, if I can.

Nonetheless, Osterud's resistance to hierarchy in the classroom, and her commitment to feminist processes, spurred her to try "not ever to reinforce the kinds of structures that exist everywhere else in these students' lives, which make them passive and deprive them of authority." More than any of the professors whom we observed, she tried to foster an atmosphere in which teacher and student share, and assess, responsibility for what happens in class.

The "journal revolt" in Dorothy Berkson's classroom is another example of student attempts to impose their own authority in the classroom. One day Bob Vaux told Tetreault that he had just initiated a discussion with Berkson about the role of journal entries in the class as well as student dependence on the teacher. Berkson reported to us:

> [Bob] said I was controlling the class too much, I was doing this, I was doing that, da, da, da, da. So I said, "You know, I think you are right, and I have been feeling it the last week or so. And, what do you think we should do about it?"

Mariko Ihara*, a freshman who described herself as coming from a "traditional Japanese family, mixed with a lot of independent Western ideas," told us that some students were intimidated by others, as in Osterud's class:

> We talked about being comfortable in the class and . . . how some people were dominating and some were afraid to speak because they didn't think that what they had to say was . . . good enough, and they were insecure about that. And we were relying on Dorothy because— I mean it's not that we didn't have ideas—it's just that we weren't sure if it was all right to say them.

Berkson thought this challenge to her authority came from tensions between the collaborative, interactive, and informal types of knowledge created in journal entries and class discussions and the more competitive, public knowledge represented by formal, graded student papers. Also at issue was student responsibility for carrying out the agenda of reading their journals in class. Students like Mariko were reluctant journal readers because two of the male students, Bob Vaux and Jamil Mustafa, produced entries that set a "standard" that other students felt they should emulate. Berkson grasped this problem:

> The [others] got the idea that they were supposed to be doing what Jamil and Bob were doing . . . complete interpretations that didn't

leave anything for anybody to say. They were sort of closed systems. . . . whereas some of the other students would read their journals and there were a couple who would just ask questions. And I always praised [them] but I think that the students still thought they were meant to [write like] Jamil and Bob. And, of course, the way I evaluate papers reinforces that.

Berkson resolved the issue, on one level, by telling the class that while "everyone should write in their journals, because it is a way of engaging with the texts, we don't have to start [discussions] with them." In an interview she elaborated: "And so we decided that they could come in with just questions, rather than reading journal entries. . . . And things have gone better since." But she also sensed that the students needed to confront her, to find out it was okay to vent their anger "because they didn't all get 'A's." As she observed:

They're sensing that there's a discrepancy between the ideology being stated in the class and what's really going on in there. Absolutely right! When I have to put a grade on their paper, I become an authority figure and it isn't collaborative anymore. I think I'm coming to a point where I can see this as part of a process of breaking down authoritarian structures.

Acknowledging that she still expects students to write traditional papers taking an argument through its "development, proof, evidence, and conclusion," Berkson, like Osterud, felt stymied by the constraints of institutional authority. Nonetheless, these "revolts" marked real shifts in class structure, and we think it is significant that they happened at Lewis and Clark. It is hard to imagine such transformations taking place in the more formal and hierarchical environments of the University of Arizona or Towson State.

However, grading policies in every institution we visited revealed how intractable were the individualistic approaches to the evaluation of learning. One challenge to this framework was a collective mid-term evaluation that we observed at San Francisco State. In one class, Chinosole asked students to discuss in her absence their views of "the course, the students, and the teacher." They were asked, "What has been good and stimulating, has met or surpassed your expectations, about the course, the teacher? Given the objectives and limitations of this course, how could the course or the teacher be improved? What have you as students done well and what needs improvement?" At the same time, in another room, the professor responded to similar questions in writing: "What has been good and stimulating, met or surpassed my expectations about the students? How could they improve? What have I done well and what needs improvement?" When the class next met, they exchanged their answers. The rationale for this evaluation, according to Chinosole, lay in its relational aspects:

> The Women Studies program is committed to constant . . . evaluation of its courses, its students, and its teachers. Students and professors in a class are in a relationship to each other and to the work of this department. Good criticism is an act of love, concern, and appreciation. It means an effort to continue the relationship, not . . . to cut it off.

STUDENTS AS RECIPROCAL AUTHORITIES

Although she was heartened by our initial analysis of her teaching, Osterud disagreed with our view that her classroom represented an authentic sharing of authority with the students. Rather, she sees classrooms as reflecting deep societal inequalities, on the one hand, and individuals' unawareness of them on the other. As she wrote:

> I may have done better around authority than around race, but sharing authority with students who are predominantly white and who are unwilling to recognize their position and the different positions of others, or unable to develop a systemic analysis of racial inequality, leaves crucial problems unsolved. As a teacher, I want to create classrooms that prefigure the possibilities of emancipation. That means not only sharing authority with students and generating gender equality, but also . . . critically examining, . . . and opposing hierarchies of domination and subordination based on race, class, and culture.

Thinking about the struggles of these professors to share their authority with students has led us to ask on what grounds, once that authority is shared, students may become authorities for each other. Only the teacher possesses the formal authority of the scholarly "expert" and evaluator. Yet, the struggle to empower students risks reproducing in the classroom the societal "hierarchies of domination and subordination based on race, class, and culture" that make student members of dominant groups, by default, the authorities for other students. We have already observed the power of male students in this context. Beth Sanchez put the issue clearly when she said that she resisted authority "no matter who happens to present the more authoritative position, be it from more experience or better command of the language or understanding of the idea. [That's what I was] thinking when I [led the revolt]. . . . On the one hand, it is a negative thing because I have taken the authority to challenge the authority . . . and it's not easy because we've been socialized to not do that."

How, instead, may students become genuine resources for one another? The answer may be found partially in student relationships outside the classroom, particularly in the residential colleges where traditional-age students live. Osterud wrote us that "students' outside relationships invisibly but powerfully shaped their interactions in class. . . . Some sought to test or cement romantic heterosexual relationships; others sought to reinforce ties of friendship and political solidarity, both along and across gender lines. The gay and lesbian students all stayed in the closet, which was their position outside of class as well."

In Bianca Cody Murphy's class, male and female students listened intently to each other for clues about what the "other side" thought about sexuality and relationships. However, in all the classes we observed, with the exception of Carla Trujillo's, lesbian students remained "in the closet." Such silences also prevailed around other hidden forms of "difference," such as social class, preventing such marginalized students from asserting their authority in relation to others in the classroom. The students' sense of their own and each others' positions, and thus their authority, were ambiguous, particularly since many students were still working out "who they were" with regard to many aspects of their identity.

Yet, on the basis of our observations and reflection, it seems that female students often gain authority in these classrooms because of the way they use their personal, nonacademic experiences, inverting the usual, tacit grounds for authority accorded automatically to privileged males. For example, Nancy Ichimura and Anne Alley provided authoritative readings of texts because their academic environment, and particularly Berkson's class, granted authority to students who articulated their positions as consciously evolving learners. In Margaret Blanchard's class, Joan Hammond and Lillian Massey claimed authority because of their age. In Chinosole's and Angela Davis's class, the white women were apprentices who constructed multicultural knowledge by learning from women of color like Lori New Breast. For students, as for teachers, the positional dynamics of gender, culture, and race are factors in the construction of authority in the classroom.

While male students still tended to dominate discussions by expressing themselves freely in public and asserting universalized views, they learned to question their classroom relations with professors and students, especially at Lewis and Clark where they were challenged by feminist teachers. Ralph Goodman told us about his self-consciousness in feminist classes: "A lot of these classes I just shut my trap. . . . It's real easy to dominate, and I wouldn't want to do it. I mean, I walk on eggshells." Even though Dorothy Berkson felt as though she needed to check their behavior, Bob Vaux and Jamil Mustafa both spoke of learning from female students. Bob recalled that his first Gender Studies course included three senior women, whom he described as "seasoned veteran feminists who always talked." Rather than challenging them he wanted to "figure out a way to make each other a part of what we're doing because to me that's part of this transformative process of getting away from just a certain few doing the leading. . . . I think you have to be able to listen to people trying to learn."

Recognizing the importance of mutual give-and-take in learning, Jamil also sought to grant fellow students authority: "If I have questions on the material or . . . if I haven't worked out my own interpretation, I definitely want some feedback from people, and so I will introduce my ideas just to bounce them off some other people."

Ned Sharp, one of the most vocal males, recalled that in one of the small-group discussions he once felt that the earth was sinking under him. In frustration, he turned to a female student and said, "I can't express myself, but I think you're wrong and I want to tell you five reasons why you're wrong because that's the source of my frustration." When she learned about this remark from a female student, Osterud talked to Ned. He later told us of the profound effect the course had on his self-concept, equilibrium, and attitudes toward authority:

> I'd almost been pulled out of that group for really seriously hampering other people's experience—and I just had to completely reshift. . . . The level of personalization around here . . . enforces the self-consciousness that pervades this entire environment. I haven't figured out how to have a unified self. I mean I don't have a body of work or a body of knowl-edge or a philosophy that's going to see me from situation to situation to situation. And it necessitates behaving differently from teacher to

teacher. . . . I haven't suffered criticism in a long time with my new attitude. . . . If I were to try to be combative as one of only six males in a
class on feminism, [then] I . . . replicate the problems of authority unin-
tentionally. And I don't want to set up that kind of situation.

Even though he did not want to "replicate" problems of authority, Ned
spoke of his struggle for a unified self, coming from a "body of knowledge or
a philosophy that's going to see me from situation to situation." However, in
this feminist classroom, he encountered a powerful challenge to the concept
of authoritative, universal knowledge, specifically its conventional role of
conveying autonomy and identity, a clear mirror image of themselves, to
members of privileged groups. In constructing novel interpretations from
the viewpoints of those "selves" that are fragmented or repressed by traditional "bodies of knowledge or philosophy," these classrooms demonstrate
the capacity to give voice to multiple sources of learning in a context in
which students and teachers share authority by mutual consent.

The disequilibrium felt by Ned and other students with various kinds of
privilege is part of the decentering they feel as a result of this process, which
marks a shift away from a universalized, autonomous "self" to the need to
construct a specific identity positioned in relation to others. He is becoming,
as he says, literally more "self-conscious," as a man privileged in relation to
women, for example. Ned's comments show that until professors and students explicitly define themselves as differentially positioned by the hierarchies of knowledge, power, and achievement in the academy, then the hopes
of authentically challenging traditional hierarchies, or imagining the possibility of genuine social change, will be dim. We agree with Grey Osterud
that delineating these positions, and constructing knowledge that recognizes
their relationships, is the first necessary step to shaping a classroom that lib-
erates the various people who share it. This vision of the classroom takes us
back to Adrienne Rich's mirror image with which we introduced this book.
It is only through the reflections of positioned teachers and students that we
can construct a mirror in which every student appears, a mirror that dimin-
ishes psychic disequilibrium and fragmentation and makes them believe that
their education was "made for them."

CHAPTER SIX

Positionality

─────────────────────────────────

What we need is a description that is not based on categories but . . . on positionality, on relations. . . . No group is in and of itself oppressed or marginal. It's only in relation to something else. So that, for instance, we can say women are marginal compared to men. But Black women are marginal compared to white, middle-class women. "What is perceived as marginal at any given time depends on the position one occupies."

—Laurie Finke, Lewis and Clark College

The positional definition of "woman" makes her identity relative to a constantly shifting context, to a . . . network of elements involving other people, economic conditions, cultural and political institutions and ideologies, and so on. If it is possible to identify women by their position within this network of relations, then it becomes possible to ground a feminist argument for women . . . on the claim that their position within this network lacks power and mobility and requires radical change.

—Linda Alcoff, "Cultural Feminism versus Post-Structuralism"

THE HEATED ARGUMENT, in chapter 3, among Laurie Finke's students about whether to define "woman" in terms of gender or class showed us both the impossibility of determining "primary oppressions" as well as the limitations of social analysis based on abstract concepts of gender, sexuality, ethnicity, race, or class. Finke's comments in this course in Literary Theory introduced us to the idea of *positionality,* in which people are defined not in terms of fixed identities, but by their location within shifting networks of relationships, which can be analyzed and changed.

Seeing "woman" in terms of her multiple positions opens up a view of the classroom as an important example of Linda Alcoff's "constantly shifting context," in which a critique of "woman's place" in this network of relations becomes the basis for a "feminist argument for women."[1] By highlighting consciously gendered perspectives in their classrooms, feminist professors emphasized the role of multiple viewpoints in the construction of knowledge, which also resulted in new relationships among themselves, their disciplines, and their students. As researchers, we, too, had to realign ourselves constantly to these shifting contexts, gradually abandoning our own universalizing of gender, race, culture, and class for more fluid appraisals of their dynamics in different contexts.

The particular form of knowledge that emerged in each classroom was specific to each context and to what the different class participants brought to it, illustrating Jill Tarule's insight that knowledge is not produced in individual minds, but in communities of knowers.[2] Sometimes class discussions explicitly focused on positional aspects of knowledge and power, as when Grey Osterud's students wrestled with racism and identity, or Lori New Breast placed Native American oral traditions within a larger historical context.

As we compared the classes we observed, we saw that dynamics of position shaped the particular forms that mastery, voice, and authority took in each classroom. Spelman teachers and students constructed their knowledge in opposition to "white social science" from their collectively realized positions as African-American women, demonstrating that mastery is positional, cast either explicitly or implicitly in relation to other forms of knowledge.[3] Wheaton students and professors often framed their knowledge oppositionally as well, in terms of a common female stand against patriarchy.

The construction of voice is also partly a function of position. Students fashion themselves in terms of their awareness of others in their particular classroom and institution, and in terms of their individual or group relation to the dominant culture. The multiethnic environment at San Francisco State University elicited a politically defined self-consciousness about personal attributes—"I am a woman of color"—that differed even from that at Spelman, where students spoke usually of their identities as African-American women vis-à-vis whites. Michelle Barnett's silence about race at Wheaton, Marta Thomas's silence about social class at Spelman, the male students' emerging consciousness of their own gender at Lewis and Clark, among other examples, all reflected the role of specific contexts in shaping voice and identity.

A positional perspective also illuminates the "constantly shifting context" of professional authority, and the relational aspects of authority among professors and students. These feminist teachers tended to make their authority positional, rather than externally imposed, by grounding it in personal experience, knowledge, and situation. Kersti Yllo explicitly placed herself as a heterosexual white woman interpreting more radical lives to her students. Ruth Doell asserted her authority as inherent in her practice of science, making it available to students by demystifying it. Dorothy Berkson, Chinosole, and Bev Clark, among others, shared authority with students by having new interpretations of texts originate in their questions.

Because these professors viewed mastery, voice, and authority as relational and evolving rather than dependent on a fixed view of society and peoples' place in it, their classrooms became places in which both students and professors could see "that their position lacks power and ability and requires radical change." As groups attempted to communicate across race, class, and gender lines, we saw how both classroom diversity and positional awareness led to radical changes in images of the "other" and of American society, as well as to the construction of knowledge from multiple positions and sources.

IMAGES OF THE OTHER:
DEALING WITH DIFFERENCE

For many of our participants, the retrieval of knowledge from the "bywaters of the culture" allowed them to explore a world in which women were at the center, and in which men, for the first time, were positioned as the "Other." This was particularly pronounced in the predominantly European American all-female classrooms where no "Other" was present to speak. In Margaret Blanchard's class one day, for example, students contrasted male and female views of time throughout history, and one of them pointed out, to affirmative murmurs, that "actually the whole system, our whole world, is set up by men, which is totally against our natural flow." Blanchard referred to cultural archetypes, including the goddess, explaining that goddess imagery is:

. . . an attempt to give us some prototypes or images of ourselves as women that are positive, to counter the negative images of women. Virginia Woolf said, as women we are supposed to be mirrors to reflect men at twice their natural size (*laughter*). And I think to counter that we need images of ourselves at twice their natural size. We need images that show us as powerful spiritually, in terms that are female.

While the construction of a female community was especially pronounced in Blanchard's class, it also took place in classrooms such as Bev

Clark's at Wheaton. Students' isolation from males in a single-sex environment made them worry that feminism would create even more separation, particularly as they confronted sexism in the academic disciplines and in society for the first time. Their ambivalence toward the "absent presence" of men came up in Clark's class during the discussion of "Little Red Riding Hood" where Elisabeth Stitt and Michelle Barnett, among others, worried about the "differences between men and women building up barriers."

But if this unified, static approach to gender, sexism, and feminism often positioned men, albeit uncomfortably, as the "Other" in Clark's class, it also became a means of identifying with all other women, even women who were markedly different in experience and background from those present. To see how this process worked, we turn to a discussion of Toni Morrison's *Sula,* which was launched with a journal entry by Louise Bobosink, a twenty-eight-year-old Political Science major. Approaching *Sula* as a narrative of patriarchy, rather than racism, she searched for commonalities between white and Black women by exploring one issue of positionality and knowing, namely, how can white and African-American, lesbian and straight, readers and writers of texts communicate with each other?[4] She had written in her journal:

> Barbara Smith [a Black feminist critic] says, "Writing about Black women writers from a feminist perspective and about Black lesbian writers from any perspective at all [is] something dangerous."
> . . . Perhaps it would be less presumptuous and less offensive for the white woman critic to try to comprehend the "feminist" or "lesbian" issues within Black women's literature. These ideas and issues may prove to be starting points for Black and white women to understand and interpret each other's literature more intelligently. . . .
>
> One of the issues that Toni Morrison's *Sula* explores is the value system imposed on women by patriarchy and the conflicts between women that arise when women defy these value systems. . . . While white women can never expect to express a total understanding of the Black woman's experience, they can express concern and understanding in those areas of Black women's lives and literature that parallel their own.

In proposing that lesbianism and feminism can help white readers to understand African-American women's literature, Louise explicitly positioned students with regard to their similarities to Sula and Nel given by gender, in effect ignoring Barbara Smith's warning about such identifications. Taking up one of Louise's suggested points of departure, the class entered into a long discussion of lesbianism in the novel. As Martha Johnson put it, "Sula says that no man could ever be the perfect companion, and maybe there is that—that struggle between being heterosexual and lesbian in the relationship between Nel and Sula." When Clark asked, "Is this a lesbian novel," Liz replied, "It depends—I mean if you use [Adrienne] Rich's lesbian continuum, yes. But . . . there wasn't that physical, genital contact, to my knowledge." And yet, as Liz herself said a few minutes later, it is a profoundly sexual novel: "I would prefer to say it was bisexual rather than on the lesbian continuum. Because it is . . . everything is so sexual, everything that she describes is sensual."

Another journal entry provoked Clark to wonder if the student implied that Sula and Nel's lesbianism is of the experimental kind that adolescent girls "go through before they reach their 'natural heterosexuality'"; as the discussion proceeded she warned the class that this interpretation implies that lesbianism is simply a phase of immaturity. The students, however, seemed to position themselves as somewhat uneasy heterosexual observers of one kind of "difference" they felt, but could accept, in Morrison's characters.

However, it was not until much later that the issue of race was raised for the first time, as part of the discussion of Sula's character. In remarks evocative of her use of her own discomfort to push the analysis, as she had done in the discussion of "Little Red Riding Hood," Clark remarked:

I'd like to come back to some points of discomfort for me. . . . I want to admire Sula, but look what she does—she watches her mother burn, she sleeps with her best friend's husband, she sends her grandmother off to an old folks' home. . . . Sula keeps doing these things that make me uncomfortable, things about her I don't like.

The class turned to debate whether Sula was "acting like a man," and Michelle Barnett, the sole African-American student, finally broke in to capture a main theme of Morrison's novel: because "they were neither white nor male, . . . they had set about creating something else to be."[5] Michelle grapples with Morrison's idea in her comment:

I think that's a problem because a lot of times we're talking about how they're not men and they're not white, like you know here they are, they're stuck being Black women, you know, this horrible fate, and I think that Sula tried so hard to be a man. . . . I don't know, she really has masculine qualities to me, and—it's as if she can't accept herself the way she is. But society's not going to accept her the way she's trying to be.

Michelle was the first person to mention race. (This was the course in which she had held back during the semester from raising the topic of race, only to do so in this, the last class.) Clark took up the Michelle's views, acknowledging how "tricky, scary, and difficult" it is for white middle-class feminists "to talk about Black women's writing, especially when they're writing about a community that's not particularly middle class. . . " She then challenged the students to confront racial difference for the first time, rather than hiding behind their similarities to African-American women. She elaborated on this perspective in replying to Michelle:

> But that's not the whole story. And it's important to keep in mind that racism and sexism are not neat little separate packages, and now we're going to attend to sexism and then later we'll attend to racism. . . . It's a burden to be a woman, you know, and you know racism maybe makes it twice as large, and if you're also working class . . . that makes it three times as large. . . . In ways that may not be expectable, a Black woman is going to feel an allegiance to women, and an allegiance to Blacks, that often those two are going to clash, and sometimes she's going to feel an allegiance to both simultaneously. . . .
>
> And I've sometimes had the sense in reading some Black women's work . . . that there are certain aspects of these works that in a way seem kind of male identified, (maybe because of) an allegiance to blackness. . . . Violence is something that in some Black women's writing is more acceptable. . . . It makes me really uncomfortable—I don't want violence to be acceptable. But how can white women be sensitive to women of other races if we don't try to at least raise the possibility of different attitudes toward things that we thought it wasn't possible to have different attitudes toward?

Michelle's incisive remarks about Sula—she "stands alone in a society where everyone is against her," is "stuck" in "this horrible fate," "can't accept herself," "society's not going to accept her"—were a call to ponder how the dominant culture's view of the "Other," in this instance, a fictional Black women, stunted Sula's life. In her courageous response, Clark struggled for a way to mark and appreciate that her own attitudes, not Morrison's, might be the "different ones" that ought to be examined. She was also working against suppressing the discussion of race, which so often occurs in a culture "seething with my presence," as Toni Morrison put it.[6] But no students explored this idea further in the discussion.

While both Louise and Bev Clark positioned themselves explicitly as white women, Clark reflected the dominant culture's bifurcation of African-American women by contrasting their allegiance to women on the one hand and to Blacks on the other. This separation of the woman from the color, to paraphrase Chinosole, most likely reinforced the white students' views of gender, race, and sexual affection as fixed and separate categories of identity, even though Clark emphasized that they interacted and were not "additive quantities." Clark's characterizing certain aspects of Black women's writing as "male identified" and linked to "violence" reflected many white attitudes about African-American culture. The idea that an illuminating *feminist* perspective could also be forged from "Blackness"—because Sula was a *Black* woman—was ignored, except by Michelle, a Black student.

This discussion, which took place in 1987, illustrates how "difference" often was constructed within white feminist theory, which focused on gender as the major issue and subordinated race, class, and sexual orientation to the primacy of gender oppression (while ignoring white women's skin privilege on other accounts). Implicit in their discussion of Sula and Nel, the class assumed commonalities of gender experience among all women that left uncomplicated, and slid over, differences among white women and between white and Black women. Some of these connections were not so much commonalities as they were instances of framing African-American or lesbian experience in "white" or heterosexual terms in order to understand them. This class discussion also illustrates the problematic contexts in which many white feminists work. The racial insulation of their classrooms, as well as the enforced silence of many lesbian students, means that gender is often discussed apart from the racial, class, and sexual dynamics that give it more complex meaning.

In the following vignette from one of Mona Phillips's classes, however, we encounter a context in which gender and race together framed the discussion and analysis. One day Angela Waters mentioned that a novel they had just read, Gloria Naylor's *The Women of Brewster Place,* had been on television.[7]

Phillips used this occasion to argue that the television production was a "women's story" that ignored the "overlapping circles" of culture, class, and gender analysis present in the novel. Referring to the formulation of her Spelman colleague Gloria Wade-Gayles, she reminded the class that "Naylor's book recognizes—all right, here we go—the dark enclosure within the narrow space, she never lets you forget the narrow space." This distinctly positional metaphor of the constricted life of Black *women* organized their thinking.[8] As Phillips explained:

> And what you see in a televised version, you miss Naylor's, you miss the voice, you miss the language she uses, but you realize how inadequate it is to just apply gender analysis to Black women's lives. You cannot, you cannot do it and end up making some sense.

The students complained about the television show's "terrible stereotypes of Black women" and also its ignoring the victimization of Black men in our society. Finally Wendy Johnson pointed out the media's role in shaping the social construction of the positions of Blacks and whites:

> Well then what about the institutional constraints? Now I don't know what station this was on—it wasn't by any chance NBC? [It was on ABC] . . . I always hear people talk about NBC as the Negro Broadcasting Company (*laughter*), because they always tend to try, well this is a stereotype, they try to cater to Black struggles, but it's not necessarily that realistic, because we go from "Good Times" to "Cosby," and there is no middle. You know, it's just so *extreme,* you're either at the very end or the very top, and I started thinking about how they're trying to do this carefully for white people, you know what I'm saying? It frustrates me how . . . Oh, God!

Throughout this discussion, Phillips and her students refused the separation of race and gender and the accommodation of their oppression to gender alone. Their keen perceptions of this "network of relations" in their lives was summed up by Phillips: "You realize how inadequate it is just to apply a gender analysis to Black women's lives." Rather than simply men, whites were the "Other" in this classroom, and gender dynamics within the Black community were seen as part of a larger struggle.

Sometime later a student asked, "Can we discuss the Hammonds case?" This was a case in the Atlanta press involving a Black male called Hammonds suspected of raping and then murdering a white female. The ensuing discussion included comments that mixed horror at the rape with sympathy for the position of Black men. For example, Angela remarked: "I sympathize with [Hammonds's victim] and all that she had to go through, and if there were other victims that would just totally influence me—I don't understand how someone could brutalize . . . " However, Kristin Lane* later replied, to appreciative laughter, that "the system is set up so tightly, of course they would have been in jail because every Black man has to be in jail at least once." Toward the end of class, Wendy Johnson made a point about the way in which even sexual abuse is a racial issue. Having recently "come out" to the class as a rape victim, she pointed out that her own assailant had been given a lesser sentence than he would have gotten if his victim had been white:

> I was thinking about what happened to me. . . . We're talking about two Black men. So why is it that the Black man can do it to a Black woman and he gets fifty-five years whereas a Black man kills a white woman and it's death! . . . I saw some other trials of Black men who had raped white women, you know, kind of the same line, they were getting, they would get a life sentence!

Her story is a powerful instance of the ways in which racial factors position societal attitudes toward sexual crimes.

Across Atlanta at Emory University, we observed Gloria Wade-Gayles, who was then on leave from Spelman as a visiting professor, struggling with images of the "Other" in a very different context. The physical location of Emory is different from Spelman; rather than a poor urban neighborhood, Emory is surrounded by an affluent one, and the campus is on a grand scale, with magnificent trees and buildings and beautiful landscaping. Its research orientation and predominantly white and coeducational student body and faculty also contrast to Spelman.[9]

Wade-Gayles decided to become a professor because, as she put it, "I come from a family of teachers; I come from a race of teachers. Being a teacher in the Black community was a real privilege, an honor." She saw the liberation of African-Americans, and women in particular, as her main teaching goal. "Black women have a greater need to understand how special we are. For whites—you need to understand what you can do working in this world as a white American, one who can make a difference—but no one has to tell you that you're special." She wants all her students to become self-sufficient and self-aware, through a process of emotional as well as intellectual growth. The essence of this process is the undoing of the pernicious stereotypes in our society that keep people divided, insecure, and powerless.

The spatial imagery that Wade-Gayles used in her book to describe Black women—the "dark enclosure within the narrow space"—which was used also by Mona Phillips, evokes an understanding of the meaning of position in the creation of consciousness. She saw it as imperative that students communicate with each other across racial and gender lines, so that students who come from different perspectives can share in creating a common knowledge: "If their energy isn't there, if their honesty, their ideas, their feelings aren't there, we're going to miss something."

Although a numerical minority at Emory, African-Americans were in the majority in the course on Images of Women in Literature, which included a heterogeneous mixture of Black and white, male and female students.[10] The class met in a small lecture room that Wade-Gayles organized in an informal half-circle, about two rows deep. The white students usually sat along the perimeter, although not together. Wade-Gayles told them, "Who you sit next to is important, because you pick up the energy of someone who is sitting to your right or left, and you share your energy." Twice, while we were there, she asked students to change their seats by saying, "Change energy"; the white females then came closer to the center and were more intermingled with their Black classmates. This energy of which she spoke indeed charged her classroom: we had a sense of ideas sparked, emotions touched, and connections made concerning issues that truly mattered to them all. It was as though you could almost feel the group's "growing pains," the emotional and intellectual growth Wade-Gayles had set as a goal for her students.

The course syllabus consisted mainly of novels by African-American authors, male and female. In fact, William Faulkner's *The Sound and the Fury*, the text under discussion in the classes we describe, was the only work by a white novelist.[11] In the initial class we visited, Wade-Gayles worked with students to make the transition from studying *Clotel* by William Wells Brown to *The Sound and the Fury*—in the words of one African-American male student, "from a Black perspective on women to a white male perspective on women."[12] The class's comparison of the two novels opened up discussion on the roles of mammies and mistresses that Black women historically have been forced to play in relation to white women and men. Discussion began with an exchange between Wade-Gayles and Blanche Burch, an African-American woman who was the only older student in the class:

WADE-GAYLES: So mammies are asexual and the Jezebel uses sex. Can the two come together?

BLANCHE: No. Mammies are not supposed to be attractive enough to have men, they just devote their life to raising white women's children.

WADE-GAYLES: It's white *women's* children. Notice what she said, white women's children. What's wrong with that? We've been in this class for almost half a semester. What's wrong with that?

A male student observed that "the children belong to the woman and not the man." Shortly thereafter, Wade-Gayles turned to stereotypical images of white and Black women as preparation for a discussion of the female characters in the novel who themselves were powerful representations of black and white womanhood. Reminiscent of Bianca Cody Murphy's efforts concerning sexual terminology, she asked students to name and work through emotionally charged stereotypical language as a way of initiating a new level of communication. In a highly charged atmosphere, with the white women looking very uncomfortable and Black women calling out all of the adjectives except "selfish," Wade-Gayles created two columns on the blackboard, as follows:

African American Women   *White Women*
Outspoken, Enduring, Strong,   Quiet, Fragile, Selfish
Caring, Resentful

In response to this labeling, one of the white students, Sarina Stelmack, a senior English major whose family background was Southern, said, "I think this is getting kind of silly." A few minutes later she added: "Excuse me. I just don't like having to say that white women are this and African-American women are this. Why divide us? I mean why can't we all be women?" After a chorus of African-American female students replied, "Because we're not," an African-American male student, echoing the students of color in Osterud's class and elsewhere, argued for keeping their culture separate until its perspectives are clearly articulated: "The reason why it has to be separate [is that] a lot of people don't think African-Americans have a culture, whereas the Chinese have. People think it's just Black and white, but we do have a culture of our own."

Interspersed with the class's list making were not only cautions against generalizing the "Other," but also resistance to the idea of reducing identity in terms of race or gender. An African-American woman observed: "A lot of people think almost all of us are the same. As long as you recognize the differences then that's fine, and don't pool us all together." Sarina responded: "I'm just as different from white women as I am from Black women. I mean, I know lots of dependent Black women and I know lots of strong white women. I mean it's just . . . we're all different."

When one person spoke of white women as "beautiful" and Black women as "ugly," upsetting the students, Wade-Gayles explained the psychological and social processes she wanted to elicit in the students, stressing the importance of speaking their minds so that stereotypical assumptions can be named and confronted:

> The problem is that the culture tells you these things again and again and you internalize them, and you make an effort to find the cases that support what you've been programmed to believe. Liberation is liberation of the mind. You liberate your mind. Then you change society. But you can't liberate your mind until you examine honestly what has been put in your mind.

The difficulties inherent in this process of publicly confronting stereotypes emerge in the following exchange involving Wade-Gayles and two African-American students, Kathy Kennedy* and Eugene Williams:

KATHY: I can understand how you want us to tell you what's on our minds, and how we think about things, but it's hard to discuss sometimes with the group when there are Blacks and whites . . .

WADE-GAYLES: Well, I expect a class full of young scholars. . . . The atmosphere that was created in the class from the very beginning was to help us to talk about men, and, man, did the men get upset! (*Laughter*) And we're not going to grow, racially, unless we talk to one another.

KATHY: I'm just saying it hardly ever happens that this stuff we're discussing comes out. The friends I listen to, they won't say they hear, "Black men are muggers." There's something they're not saying.

EUGENE: It doesn't behoove me to be honest, actually (*much laughter*). At Emory University, as a Black student, a lot of time it doesn't beehove me to be honest. Every single day we think about the relationships between Blacks and whites.

WADE-GAYLES: I didn't say that there wasn't a problem, I said *you* have a problem. If you compromise your intellectual integrity, it's your problem. It's not the university's problem, it's your problem. And unless you are intellectually honest, you are robbing other groups of the opportunity to be honest with you, for you to be educated by them and for you to educate them. It is *silence,* not communication, that is the problem.

Even though this highly charged topic was explored on a rudimentary level by having students call out their stereotypical notions of Black and white women, the discussion indicates how one teacher attempted to illuminate and transform what we think we know about the "Other" and ourselves.

The students we interviewed showed a fascinating range of responses to being confronted with these issues; responses that were related to their emerging awareness that racial and gender identities conceal positional relationships of inequality. Although Sarina resisted being categorized herself as a white woman, this resistance may have been the catalyst that started to break down her own categorical thinking. She told us, in an interview, that she had learned a lot about Black and white positions from the class. "I thought we all thought alike, but it seems like a lot of Black people think differently than I do." She also saw that this was in large part a result of racism: "I mean they always were working towards equality . . . but there's so much racism that, just with things they see every day, they look at things a different way." Her burgeoning awareness of race may also have been related to a recognition of her unequal relationship with her boyfriend, and her feeling that Wade-Gayles was empowering her to do something about it: "Like, if my boyfriend says things, I'll often comment. . . . I use Dr. Wade-Gayles as my scapegoat, I say she would shoot you."

Mark Adams*, who was usually the only white male to attend the class sessions we observed, told us that he had a sense of having learned more about sexism than racism in the class. But he saw that the teacher might have different goals for him than for the Black women in the class; he was struggling with a new sense of having a specific position in society. As he put it:

> It seems like she's teaching on more than one level. She's teaching me just to open my eyes, but with Blanche it's totally different because Blanche *has* open eyes. I mean Blanche and myself, two exact opposites. I would see things one way, the way a white male would see them.

Mark found the discussions particularly valuable because they occurred in a context of diverse perspectives, sexual as well as racial. The ability of these Black and white students to understand some aspects of gender inequality may have helped them all to confront the tremendous barrier of racism by articulating their positions across racial lines as well.

Blanche Burch, who was studying for her B.A. and a nursing degree while she worked as a secretary at the medical school, was acutely aware of sexual inequalities. Asked whether she believed that male students could learn from the class, she remarked:

> I really don't think most can change because they are men, they are white and Black men but they are still men. The dogs are going to be the dogs. Maybe they are little puppies now, but they are going to grow up to be canines. And this class is not going to change that.

Michael Cash*, an African-American male who wanted to be a doctor, had a view of Emory and of this course that was different from Kathy's or Eugene's. Michael felt Emory to be "quite Black. . . . I like the school, I like the friends I have, I like the atmosphere." In spite of his relative optimism and sense of belonging, Michael described the unsettling feeling of being shifted, in his own position, from oppressed to oppressor:

> I've learned much about the ways we, in our subtle ways, perpetuate our sexism. It's good for me to step back and look at [oppression] in another instance because usually I'm always looking at it from a racist standpoint. . . . I am a male, so in some ways I feel the oppressor category, and it is a strange feeling. . . . I've never developed a lot of the views she says men have.

The discussion that took place in Gloria Wade-Gayles's class, more than any other we observed, made us aware that a classroom is not an isolated laboratory that can be analyzed for its pedagogy or its treatment of the "Other," but rather a place embedded in a web of social relations. Kathy's and Eugene's discouragement indicate that it is not enough to bring heterogeneous groups of students together and get them to talk to each other. During 1990, the year we visited, Emory was a racially charged environment, in part because of an ugly racial incident that caused a young African-American woman to leave the university. In this environment, African-American students were in great need of support; even though they were the numerical majority in Wade-Gayles's course, they were a marginalized group in the university. They could not walk away from the class, as the white students could, and forget about racial tensions; as Eugene said, they had to think about the relations between Black and whites every single day. We worried, therefore, about the differential impact of these discussions on the students as well as the likelihood that white students were not as affected by displays of prejudice and narrow-mindedness as Black students.

———

Comparing these three classrooms, we can see how the participants' involvement in the societal power relations of racism and sexism resulted in widely different positions from which to construct knowledge. Despite Bev Clark's efforts, her students considered gender the primary category of oppression, tending in this process to erase racial difference rather than confront it. They could not envision their own positions in society as shaped by their whiteness, or by their commonality with white men. In contrast, Mona Phillips's students were struggling for a common front with Black men against racism. The erasure of race was not a choice for Phillips's students, who, like all people of color in this society, are rarely permitted a sense of "aperspectivity," especially concerning issues of race. These students engaged the issues of both race and gender as they thought about relationships between men and women. Not surprisingly, in this classroom solidarity with Black men in common opposition to racism was held in complex balance with the struggle against sexism within the Black community. Finally, Gloria Wade-Gayles showed us that a heterogeneous classroom can also be a place in which to initiate an exploration of the tense relation between racism and sexism in our society.

PICTURES OF AMERICAN SOCIETY: THE ROLE OF SOCIAL CLASS

Our next set of vignettes juxtaposes classes at Towson State University, Lewis and Clark, and Spelman College to illustrate how students' social-class positions shape their thinking about American society. While most of our analyses have focused on gender and race, issues of social class are equally important to the construction of knowledge in the classroom. Unlike gender and race, lower social-class origins can be denied and disguised, a process that is a major component in realizing "the American Dream" of upward mobility. Moreover, class is not so much an "unspeakable thing unspoken" as it is a sometimes anomalous form of positionality, since most white Americans see themselves as middle class in any case. Confounding class and race, they tend to view people of color as the "underclass."

Higher education is often regarded as a crucial way-station to "the American Dream." First-generation college students, particularly in relatively privileged institutions, often face a loss of innocence about their parents' social-class status. They may feel inadequate about the quality of their clothes, or hear denigrating remarks about working-class occupations or recreational habits.[13] How, then, do social-class position and awareness function in the college classroom? Can professors and students step outside the prevailing network of class relations, whose inequalities are more pronounced outside the university? Are students with lower social-class origins perhaps more open about their experiences of class in institutions where most students and faculty share their backgrounds? What new insights do we gain into positionality if we consider social class an important factor in Alcoff's "network of relations"?

To illustrate our theme, we first look at an Honors Freshman Writing course taught by K Edgington, who, because of her institutional marginality as a long-time lecturer at Towson State, was highly conscious of signs of insecurity among Towson students. As she observed:

When they are leaving high school they are leaving their hometown identity. So they are in a state of "Who am I?" And what they have are these sororities and fraternities. Some of the younger students, especially young women, are coming to classes dressed alike. They are all wearing their hair in pony tails this semester. That's how intense the need to belong. So they are in a very vulnerable state.

Edgington saw herself as responsible for raising controversial social issues, if necessary in her lectures, and helping students to work them through. "I want my students to think and I want to change the world as a general goal. Education is my way of doing that." She saw her own students, predominantly white and female, as more socially conscious and feminist than most students at Towson. Most of her course readings focused on the theme of gender and other forms of oppression. She explained to us why she selected these works:

I [look for] texts that enable me to do the individual and society; class, race, and sex are issues that are very important to them. [But] students [say that] "there is no class in America," "women won the war for equality," and "racism ended with Martin Luther King". . . . Other people say I'm a pessimist but I see nothing wrong with a reading list that is scary, nothing wrong with scaring the shit out of these kids.

In the class we observed, students had begun to read *The Women of Brewster Place*. The group of five males and six females, all white and traditional-age freshmen, met in a small seminar room. Edgington stood in front of the room; the students sat scattered in two rows before her. To introduce students to the multiple oppressions of class, race, and gender suffered by the women in the novel, she asked them to discuss their ideas about social class: "Have any of you read any books that talked about class?"

Although she framed the question around books rather than personal anecdotes, students answered initially in terms of their own experiences and seemed to interpret social class, and upward mobility, mainly as a matter of rising income. One student contrasted rich people who "can afford to do what they want" with those who have only a "moderate" amount of money, who "cannot just go crazy; they are saving up and investing." Another described his mother's remarriage: "She and my stepfather have risen in class [because] he combined his stuff with ours. We have luxuries . . . and their standard of living has risen considerably."

While agreeing with the students that "income is a major determinant of class, often related to education," Edgington pushed them to consider more structural issues, asking "Is there class mobility?" Most of the students quickly answered, "sure," but several male students began to explore the underlying rigidities of class. Chuck Sawyer observed:

> I just think that a lot of old snobbery exists between old money and new money. . . . I could become rich tomorrow, but because I don't come from a rich family I could not be in that upper class. Class isn't what I determine myself to be, but what someone else makes it, and that's the problem with it. It doesn't matter how good your standard of living is, some people may just see you as classless, because their standards aren't . . .

Feeling personally objectified by stereotypic notions of class, he sought to reframe class not as a fixed social category but as a position. The next speaker, Mark Carpenter*, echoed this theme, drawing on his own experience:

> I knew a group of guys and they were all middle class to lower class, what we consider lower class, and then one of the guys that was an

upper-class person, all of the other friends still think he's lower class, no matter how much money or what class everyone else puts him in, they still see him as one of the guys, who's now turned snobby because he thinks he's high class, but he'll still be in that same class as them.

These students seemed to want to talk about their own positions within social-class networks, but lacked the language to do so. Edgington responded by contrasting the Protestant work ethic, that "through one's own efforts, given equal opportunity, native abilities and good character will rise," with "hidden biases which reflect tastes, education, culture." On reading our early version of this discussion, she told us that she was trying to get at hidden assumptions here, how class, race, and gender differences are unconsciously constructed in our culture.

However, the ensuing discussion underlined the difficulties of laying bare these assumptions, demonstrating how obfuscations regarding social-class position were tied to assumptions about race and gender as well. Edgington next asked the class, "What about racism?" and, in particular, "What about Affirmative Action? Does that help?" A student named Martin O'Brien* responded on the assumption of another stereotype, possibly based on his equation of Blacks with the underclass, that minorities who get ahead are not qualified:

It's really like a slap in the face. You've got the job just because you're Black or Asian, they're not saying you got the job because you're better or more qualified. We need your minority groups because our supervisor is going to come down on us.

Underlying this comment probably was the student's feeling that Affirmative Action is a personal threat to his own mobility. Admitting that "that's certainly one of the side effects, that Blacks who are [in] professional schools . . . have been regarded as supported because of Affirmative Action," Edgington nevertheless sought to persuade the students that Affirmative Action was a justified response to racism. "Affirmative Action is necessary in order to create enough chances for talented Black people." After citing the example of women's former exclusion from medical schools, she turned to Towson State, pointing out the lack of talented Black people as a result of past discrimination:

So, Black students come to Towson, they find that there are two Black faculty members in the English Department, that affects them too. A school like Towson has to compete with much more prestigious schools, with a limited number of Black applicants. . . . I think Towson has had difficulty recruiting Black students. This doesn't mean that there aren't intelligent Black students here, but I find that often the good Black students that I have in English are ones that didn't start off at Towson at the beginning of the year. They were someplace else. Economics is a factor . . .

What was the subtext here about *white* students? How did these students feel about their own situation at Towson compared to "intelligent Black students here"? Towson pulls students typically from the top half of their high school class, so it is not particularly selective compared, for example, to the University of Maryland at College Park. On the other hand, this was an Honors class, so that these students presumably felt secure about their own intelligence. Yet Edgington's efforts to help her white students understand the positions of Black students were foiled by their own class insecurities, and the ways in which their own racial attitudes obscured those insecurities, even to themselves. They were able to displace their feelings of class inferiority onto a resentment against Blacks for taking unfair advantage. The next remark, from a student named Paul Krysiak, reveals some aspects of this resentment:

It's interesting how distinctions can separate people on campus from each other. . . . I was at a convenience store and I heard two Black students talking; they were looking to reopen a Black sorority that had been closed after two years; so that's even more separation. But you know, maybe they don't feel comfortable in Greek organizations that we have now and they want their own.

In replying to this student, Edgington focused on Towson's homogeneity, which for her symbolized the uneasiness of the school's position, as well as the community's general discomfort with both poor people and the topic of racism.

The idea is to create a positive image of Blacks on campus, to become a sorority or a fraternity member. . . . But anyway, class issues are divisive in some ways. There's a homogeneity if you look at Towson. . . . We have moved into a range where our standards overlap with a lot of very good schools, and expensive private schools. . . . There are some very rich people and some poor people here, but you have a homogeneity here . . .

Chuck Sawyer responded with an anecdote about class:

A friend of mine, a blue-collar worker, started at Loyola and did not do very well, didn't fit in. All the kids there are rich, a lot of them have their own cars, and for him being rich was having your own car. He's from a big Catholic family where his father might make $35,000 a year, they're not poor, but there are lots of kids. And they can't afford . . . Chuck can't afford college and the car. So he's an example.

These stories reflect the students' economic pressures as well as status anxiety, two factors that probably strongly underlie their attitudes about African-Americans. They also express the students' sense of the importance of money and possessions in measuring status. Acknowledging how students were affected by this form of class oppression, Edgington pointed out that "for some students not being able to join a fraternity or a sorority because of money makes them feel like outsiders." She then turned the discussion to gender discrimination and, in a final remark, sought again to help her students confront racial issues:

The consciousness level in the United States has been raised, where we're much more highly aware of gender issues. Whereas race, white people don't often think of racial identity in terms of their own identity, what it means to be a white person. . . . The minority races are much more conscious of who they are. That's not true for whites in America, that the first thing you identify with as "who are you?" is white.

The difficulty of discussing the connections between social class and race overshadowed the class's discussion of *The Women of Brewster Place* the next day. Edgington was constrained from fully exploring its context because of her struggle with student attitudes and, as she later put it, her reluctance to alienate and antagonize the group. For example, she tried to have the students understand why Eugene, a male character who leaves his wife and child, would do such a thing, raising the issue of Aid to Families with Dependent Children (AFDC). A female student named Vera Randall*, expressed a typical point of view:

> I know a little bit about it. My mother works in an inner-city school and I know that they get a little money for each child. . . . Some of them will have kids just to get money, or if they have a teenager that is going to have a kid they won't get mad about it because that means there is going to be more money that is coming into the house.

Edgington countered with a long history of AFDC, placing the issue of welfare in the context of the poor economic prospects of Black men, who don't earn enough to support their families. "Which is the problem we have today," she pointed out, "people who work but can't make enough to live. Because of racism, which was excluding Blacks from jobs and training programs and education."

Edgington's agenda was to find out what the students thought about race, social class, and gender, and to set them "straight" about these categories as causes of discrimination. Yet this unusually candid discussion struck us as representative of the difficulties faced by white professors who try to scratch the surface of white students' internalization of the race and class biases of American culture. These students were enacting the profound anxiety experienced by upwardly mobile white people, whose uneasy class status heightens their distrust of upwardly mobile people of color as a threat to themselves. Furthermore, rising unemployment and poverty among whites due to the recession has exacerbated such insecurities and fears.

In her trenchant comments on reading our initial analysis of this class, Grey Osterud pointed out as well that for these students to confront the pain of class inferiority, in the face of a still pervasive ideology of classlessness, could be likened to Black students trying to talk about their oppression in the absence of a theory of racism. The group could not work through the complex interrelations of race, gender, and class inequalities that undergirded their individual positions.

Their confounding of white with "middle class" and Black with "poor" meant that these students could not see themselves positionally, either as economically disadvantaged or racially privileged. They were left with the uneasy, acknowledged feeling that their own or their families' futures were at stake. Most likely, they entered and left the class with a picture of society that was drawn from personal experience, organized largely in terms of money and status, and based on an ideology of individualism, upward (and downward) mobility, and an unquestioned acceptance of the rigid and hierarchical demands of the American dream.

Although the students to whom we talked in Edgington's class, particularly the women, appreciated her feminism, her focus on women's issues, and the informal atmosphere of the class, female students were silent on that first day, perhaps reflecting Edgington's lack of focus on gender in that discussion. This may also reflect social-class factors, since some feminist professors hold that female students from less privileged backgrounds tend to speak less often in class than their middle-class counterparts.[14]

Paul Krysiak understood that Edgington also wanted the students to engage with broad social issues. Reflecting on Edgington's political commitments, he said that she used her beliefs "to provoke something, I suppose, . . . and that's what I appreciate about the class. . . . She eggs us on, because I guess I'm the kind of person that if someone tells me something can't be done, I'm going to say I'm going to prove you wrong." However, like many male students, he felt that the discussions fell short:

> I want to be taken on a bit more. . . . I can't have the greatest understanding of my own views unless I know what someone else's views are. [Unfortunately] some people don't want to get out of their shells; there are people who would just rather be in the little discussions and never have to deal with something huge, never have to deal with a great issue.

Paul here seemed to be responding to the group's failure to deal explicitly with the deeper personal, social, and structural issues that were raised.

Because we were so struck by this discussion at Towson, we were drawn to look through our transcripts for other impressions of social class in American society. In sharp contrast to the concrete and anecdotal approach of Edgington's students, Grey Osterud's class at Lewis and Clark College, on Feminism in Historical Perspective, considered quite abstract and utopian views of society. This was due, no doubt, in part to the fact that Edgington's students were freshmen and those who dominated Osterud's class were mostly juniors and seniors.[15] But it was also due to the different social-class makeup of the institutions, which positioned most students at Lewis and Clark differently toward capitalism. The college, a more expensive school than Towson, draws many students from middle-class populations of the Northwest; about half are from Oregon, where there is little factory work and virtually no industrial working class. However, the more privileged students from California as well as prep-school graduates from the East seem largely responsible for the dominant student culture.[16]

Osterud's students all wanted to use "theory as a way of changing meaning, changing the way things are," in Ron Underwood's formulation. But, inhabiting a kind of personal classlessness, they seldom applied stories of their own social-class experience to the construction of theory. In the following discussion, their "universal" viewpoint, analytical and thoughtful but abstract, does not reflect explicitly positioned differences of race and class, either in society or among the students themselves. Gender differences were certainly apparent, but they, too, were not explicitly noted.

As we take up the discussion, the class was speculating about the changes required in our gender system before an ideal society could be created. Kris Lacher, who wrote about Mary Wollstonecraft in a journal entry, placed the blame on capitalism, arguing that to improve gender relations "you have to get rid of capitalism first of all."[17] Another female student, Linda Brinkley*, picked up on this idea:

> I think capitalism really encourages the dualism. Men have been taken out into the public sphere to produce a surplus that is profitable and women are producing without wages. Production for use. Or if they are in the public sphere, they are used to promote capitalism. They're being paid less.

The discussion continued, with, for example, Cheryl Ibabao noting that the competitive qualities of capitalism lead to the belief that "We're No. 1!" A male student's reluctance to give up his "belief in individualism or freedom of choice" then generated a debate, from which this excerpt is taken, that posed individualism against community:

ROBERT LAURENT*: [There is] something in me that is sort of a Horatio Alger kind of thing of being able to do as much as you can . . . people should be able to get as much as they want. Or get what they want without taking away from somebody else.

NAN WHITE*: For me we have to change the whole, our whole worldview, . . . it's so unfair because we want more and we're all sharing this planet. And if you have a little bit more, you're taking it away from somebody else. So we have to create something so we don't . . .

MAGGIE GILBERT*: What needs to take place is transformation within the individual first. And until that happens, until each person learns how to transform within themselves . . . it's a process of education and I don't think that you can bring in capitalism, socialism, communism until people transform themselves.

Throughout the discussion only two students spoke explicitly about "everyday social realities" or the material conditions of peoples' lives. Except for Osterud, who supported these students, the rest of the class ignored them, perhaps because it would have thrown them back on their own class privilege. Following are the students' remarks and Osterud's comment:

DANA MATTS: I don't see in this system how most people have a choice anyway. I only think a very small percentage of people in this system have a choice. I think most people are forced to do the work that they have to do to survive.

LINDA: You know, having the need of mother's paid leave. I think it's really essential that fathers get leave too, and that's where it all starts in child raising, and that if children have both a female and a male role to identify with they will grow up being able to accept both of the two . . . typically male and female characteristics and that will possibly lead toward changes.

OSTERUD: So you want to talk about how not to just create change within existing individuals but to have people grow up in a different way?

Perhaps in response to these ideas, Beth Sanchez, alluding to a theoretical analysis of capitalism prominent in many classes at Lewis and Clark, described a burgeoning positional understanding:

Do you remember when Gilman says that people don't notice their own trappings because they are accustomed to them, they don't see them? And I think in a way we can stand back and look at it, at society from a different way, just because we're here at this college being exposed to these ideas; and if we weren't, we probably wouldn't realize it; and that most of society doesn't, and therefore while we may be able to change individually, people are affected by structures.

A few days later, Ron Underwood used a discussion of the work of bell hooks to link race to capitalism. Ron reminded this predominantly white group of students that race matters as they generalized about American capitalism and gender roles.

bell [hooks] makes the point that capitalism doesn't have an effect on the Black family because of the nature of [capitalism]. A lot of people believe in capitalism as the accumulation of material goods and nice objects. And bell makes the point of saying that Black people don't make enough money to accumulate objects. They barely have money to live on, so capitalism as an indicator of success, or making women dependent, that doesn't really apply to Black people.

Although Osterud pushed consistently for a theory of action rather than critique, and for attention to everyday realities, Lewis and Clark students had a much keener sense of their own experiences in relation to gender than in relation to class or race dynamics. Like Nancy Ichimura, very few students could feel safe in expressing their most painful experiences as women of color. We later learned that Maggie Gilbert, who was employed in the lumber mills while she worked on a Master of Arts in Teaching degree and searched for a teaching job, also could not voice her pain. Her insistence on "transformation within the individual" was not about upward mobility, but about women in her family, married to abusive alcoholic men, who needed to change their personal lives. As a union member, she indeed had a positive sense of class identity, but she concealed her personal experiences of gender oppression.

Nevertheless, few Lewis and Clark students made use of stories of their own experiences in examining their positions within the social-class structure. This avoidance may have partly reflected the culture of Lewis and Clark, a culture that encourages, through a large number of student trips abroad, often to Third World countries, a comparative contemplation of American society in general. This internationalist approach to knowledge and culture reflects a prevalent professorial attitude toward capitalism that many students come to share. Osterud explained:

> The students saw capitalism as a system that exploited everyone, not just the "working class"; they felt the alienation, commodification, depersonalization, et cetera, that accompany contemporary capitalism, regardless of their class position. Students from upper-middle-class backgrounds felt little "guilt" about that position of "privilege," since they had a strong cultural critique of their own situation and the system that produced it and saw themselves as political allies of the majority of economically exploited people.

But this theoretical critique of capitalism also allowed students to keep their own social-class position at arm's length. Again, according to Osterud, they also did not see race as a category that defined them, but rather "they conceptualized racial inequality primarily in global terms, as having to do with the relationships between the predominantly rich, white United States and the predominantly poor, nonwhite Third World." Their resistance to Ron Underwood's view of the position of Black people in America reflects their different relation to poor Blacks, as they tended to view racism abstractly as another function of capitalism.

Ron's posture toward other African-Americans as well as toward white Americans provides an interesting illustration of the workings of race and class among more affluent African-Americans. Ron's social-class position was higher than that of some of his white peers; both his father, who was a scientist, and his mother, who had been a teacher, believed that educated African-Americans had an obligation to "uplift the race."[18] His assertion at one point that Blacks would always be "working on the lowest rung" reflects not only his frustration with the attitudes of white students, but also his feeling of responsibility to educate his peers, to use his social-class position to improve the lot of his people. Like Mona Phillips, Ron, too, "never saw himself as different from other Blacks."

Comparing the two classes taught by Edgington and Osterud led us to speculate on the role of their two institutions in creating the pictures of society reflected in these discussions. The discussion of social class at Towson State seemed mired in students' anxieties about their own socioeconomic status. Osterud's students, who criticized capitalist consumerism, could be imagined looking down on the Towson students for being concerned with material rewards. In comparison to Towson students, those at Lewis and Clark took a much broader view, drawing on ideological constructs to name and analyze oppressions of race, class, and gender. However, far fewer Lewis and Clark students seemed to position themselves personally within the class structure, which, as Osterud noted, was one way of remaining comfortable with their own class privilege.

It is as if the students who really need the "class analysis" provided by the study of capitalism, namely, those at Towson, cannot get it, while those at Lewis and Clark lack the narratives of personal experience required to apply their theories to the reformulation of social issues in their daily lives. Again, we see the need to combine theory and experience in providing students with useful knowledge about society and their own positions in it.

Images of American society were also the theme of the last class we observed in Mona Phillips's Sociology of Women course. Phillips had asked students how they could bring the ideas of liberation they had learned from thinkers like W. E. B. DuBois out of the classroom. In response, the students talked about how "the system" held them back.

Angela Waters called for a nonviolent restructuring of the system that would begin with a policy of economic separatism for Black people. The group then went on to discuss the seductiveness of the dominant American material culture, as reflected in the following comments.

FIRST STUDENT: Basically it's the principles of Kwanza, we talk about collective work and responsibility, and economic support and unity, that's basically what it comes down to.

PHILLIPS: Let's look at it in the most micro-level way. What kinds of things would we have to change?

SECOND STUDENT: Restructuring our minds, the things that we think are exciting, our whole society, using those words; those aren't our words. Wearing those clothes; those aren't our clothes. If I could live in the ghetto with my little kids as long as they're healthy, and be a school teacher and teach my Black children about their people, then I'm rich. But nobody sees that, not even our own people.

With their image of an idyllic place for themselves and their Black children, they seemed to extend their own position of relative privilege beyond Spelman's gate into the world of the housing project outside. We saw here the evolution of a collective knowledge that was able to draw on personal stories to forge a theoretical stance. The social agenda is much clearer for the students in this class than for those we observed at Towson or Lewis and Clark.

Nevertheless, implicit in all three discussions is the vexing issue of what their knowledge, their education, will be for. The Towson students imply that education is a rung on an individual ladder of opportunity that will lead to an improvement in their social-class status and material conditions. The Spelman students articulate an ambivalence about education, opportunity, and affluence, in relation to both the white-dominated "system" and the rest of the African-American community. They know that the ladder of opportunity is not equally accessible to all who compete for a place on it, and so they make the case for economic separatism. They evoke both a sense of a larger community and an uncertainty about how to relate to it. The Lewis and Clark students take an even broader, and with the exception of Ron Underwood, an even less grounded view. Beth seems to suggest that the aim of education is societal understanding, but what to do with this understanding is left poignantly unclear.

THE CONSTRUCTION OF KNOWLEDGE
FROM MULTIPLE POSITIONS

In both Gloria Wade-Gayles's course in Images of Women in Literature at Emory University and the course called Wild Women in Music and Literature taught by Chinosole and Angela Davis at San Francisco State, we observe how knowledge is constructed in an academic environment that explicitly calls attention to multiple, juxtaposed positions with regard to race, class, and gender. Does combining heterogeneous groups of students enhance their sense of their own positions? Can such combinations foster a discourse grounded in a variety of experiences and lead to more complex theories of society?

For us, the diverse positioning of students in Wade-Gayles's course as members of racial, gender, and social-class groups created a unique and evolving reading of *The Sound and the Fury,* as did the diversity of positions in the discussion of *Jane Eyre* in Dorothy Berkson's class. At the start of class, Wade-Gayles reminded students of their assignment to write a letter to one of the characters in the novel. Citing Dilsey as an example, the "mammy" figure, she went on.

When you write this paper, please note that you must have quotes from the book, you must have specific details on the book. You're not just writing to someone who happened to have the name Dilsey, you're writing to a mammy, which is Faulkner's Dilsey. You must go into the book.

Wade-Gayles initiated the discussion by asking: "What do you want to say to Dilsey?" Immediately, a Black female student spoke from the position of Black children whose mothers must take care of white children: "It doesn't seem she cares about her own children as much as she does about Quentin" (the Compson son). This comment spurred the following responses shaped by the students' positions as Black and white males and females. With the exception of Mark Adams* and Amy Richter, the speakers here are African-American.

NICOLE CARTER: I think she's just trying to survive in the situation that she lives in because slavery was not so far removed from her own life. And maybe she doesn't want to get too attached, maybe they'll get rid of her kids. She still has this mind set that is not very different from the situation they went through in slavery . . .

EUGENE WILLIAMS: Mine is more of a defense and an attack. A defense in that even though it was the 1920s, she did have that mind set that . . . goes from generation to generation, so the time we are dealing with is something like slavery. Look at what it did to African-American lives. You really can't put a time limit on that. But the attack is that she totally forgot about the nurturing of her children . . .

MICHAEL CASH: I agree with him in the sense that I felt that she didn't love her children. In fact, I would go as far as to say that she more or less did not give them a stable beginning whatsoever, she criticized everything they did . . .

NICOLE: It's not her fault that she has to take care of those children!

EUGENE: It seems to me that she doesn't spend enough time nurturing her children. Regardless of what the social constraints are or whatever, she's a Mom, and she could nurture them in some way.

NICOLE: I think that we're putting a lot of pressure on Dilsey. . . . You just cannot necessarily assume that she is automatically, by nature, a nurturing, caring woman for all her children. And just because she has kids it doesn't mean that she has to treat them that way. I mean we're imposing a lot of qualities on her that aren't in the book . . .

EUGENE: It is obvious that she has the capability to nurture. Why couldn't she do it with her own children?

MARK ADAMS: It seems like it's more of a job, though, isn't it? Wouldn't it be her job to do that? It would be like any other job, when you leave, when the job's over, you're not necessarily like what you were on the job.

JAMES ISLER: But that's the thing—it's not just a job!

AMY RICHTER: I think the character of Dilsey fulfills a stereotype of the Black mammy and serves the purpose that Faulkner wanted it to serve. . . . It's not like we go into Dilsey's mind and go in her house and see what she's like with her children. It's a very one-sided portrayal of her and her family, and I don't feel I have the information to sit there and judge what her family is like and how she is with her family.

There followed more discussion of Dilsey's relationship with the Compsons, during which Wade-Gayles pointed out that Faulkner created Dilsey as "the moral conscience of the novel," but that "she is also a stereotype."

EUGENE: I think that Faulkner thinks she's positive, but she's positive for white people. And it really upsets me, that I get the impression that Faulkner thinks he's doing us a favor by showing a positive—when she's not really being positive for us! I wish she could be positive for us, not for them, 'cause they have their own family—their mother and their daddy.

WADE-GAYLES: She's positive. I mean, be honest, I mean, give Faulkner credit. The negative images are the images of the white people! I mean give him credit. . . . She's the moral conscience of this novel, and we, the readers, are supposed to say this is positive. You would be surprised at the volumes that have been written on this novel, on this character. She is the image of mammy that Americans have. . . . When we read *The Bluest Eye,* looking at Mrs. Fisher, we're going to examine the mammy image in the Black woman's novel and see the difference.

Eugene then brought up the issue of class divisions within the Black community by telling about the hostility he felt when he encountered Black maids in the homes of wealthy Black friends. Remarking that a number of African-American scholars have written about the phenomenon of psychological enslavement, Wade-Gayles continued:

> If I were to say to you that the way that Faulkner has defined mammy and the way you've analyzed . . . it, if I were to say to you in various ways we as African-Americans have some mammyism in us—would I make you angry?

In this context, Wade-Gayles asked for a definition of "mammyism," to which James replied: "It might equate to subjugation, a putting away of yourself, a loss of some of your self-respect, a willingness to put all the things like condescending statements made towards Black folks." After a few more student remarks, Wade-Gayles further attempted to place the Dilsey figure as a specifically *Black* woman:

> How many feel better about Dilsey because we've had this discussion? . . . Then let's not get upset with Faulkner! I mean if there are . . . if Dilseys exist, if there are real Dilseys then it's not just this woman. This is an excellent novel, this is a picture of reality. I'd like you to raise your hands: how many of you believe there are women like this? How many of you believe that in order to be a Dilsey—and this is going to be crazy—How many of you believe that in order to be a Dilsey, you must be . . . [She writes "Black" on the board]

This question about "mammyism" being about blacks draws two white students, Carla Reed* and Amy Richter, back into the discussion.

CARLA: You know you were talking about how she has resentment? I worked for three summers in a resort, and I served food to very very rich people and I also felt that resentment, and I can understand both sides of it. Because I did go to high school with them and worked for them in the summer, and I can totally . . .

EUGENE: I have to ask what are the contexts in society where a white person would be relegated to that role?

MICHAEL: I would say I agree with her; I don't think race is conscious here because I've been in situations where I was in a Black school and there have been Black people behind the counter and you get the same resentment.

WADE-GAYLES: That's still race—that's race. That's race and class, isn't it? That's race and class. I asked this question for a reason, and the reason is that I want you to be sensitive to the issue of class here. Yes.

AMY: I don't think that that subservience has anything to do with race, I mean it has to do with her position.

EUGENE: I think it's a race thing, because I feel from my experiences that out of all the minorities in America, Blacks as a whole are the least accepting of each other in many instances.

After a heated argument among Eugene and a few of the other Black students about whether Blacks or other minority groups have been more divided among themselves, Wade-Gayles reminded the African-American students that their posture toward one another was not all that different from their position toward Dilsey: in both instances, they blamed the victim.

While we do not know the particular childhood histories of these Black students, their identification with Dilsey's children appears to be shaped by their personal experience in some profound way. Wade-Gayles told us later that Eugene would not have expressed his anger so forcefully in a homogeneous class of African-Americans, but that his anger and pain came out because "he knows Dilsey; he has Dilseys in his family." The reason why Dilsey was so objectionable to the African-American students was not so much because her portrayal in the novel seemed to them to contradict stereotypic notions of women as nurturing; rather, it was because of the whole history of the merging of femaleness and racial identification in slavery.

It seems clear from the white students' comments that this discussion was not about their mothers or their childhood relationships. They saw Dilsey as either a literary character or as "just doing her job." Perhaps because she felt less personally involved with the situation, Amy saw Dilsey as a fictional character created by Faulkner, but also as a stereotype. Her reading of the text was the most distanced and literary of all the students. Mark said to us that "in Faulkner's mind he is writing something positive about Black people. . . . I sort of get the impression that he is being a caring white Southerner. But, like, when the Black men and women read the book they see it as this guy, some racist."

When Eugene opened up the idea of reading the novel from the position of a Black reader—"she's not positive for us"—he labeled Faulkner as a white author, a position that he felt ignored him as a reader. Wade-Gayles asked him and the other students to step beyond their particular positions in order to understand Faulkner's, so that they could perceive the dynamics of racism and sexism from the perspective of the society that he depicts. (In the novel both Dilsey and her son, Luster, provide the only nurturing love for a very dysfunctional white family.)

This turning of position, this playing with perspective, can be seen on the part of both Wade-Gayles and the students. For example, by relating to Dilsey, and identifying Dilsey with slavery and its pernicious legacy throughout history, the students identified as historically particular subjects. Eugene's question—"I have to ask what are the contexts in society where a white person would be delegated to that role?"—speaks volumes for the positionality of race. Implicit in Eugene's and the other students' reactions to Dilsey is a discourse about homes that are headed by women in the Black community. It is a context in which the absence of the mother often meant the absence of both parents in the household. The whole discussion reminded us of Laurie Finke's observation about "the psychic interplay of desire and power among historically specific, gendered teachers and students." It evoked very emotional, and yet very different, responses in students, depending on, for instance, how much time their mothers had had to care for them, or the pain they might have experienced as children of domestics.

This portrait of Dilsey illustrates how Wade-Gayles worked to empower her students to deal with the internalized and externalized oppressions they faced and needed to overcome. She and the African-American students were drawing on allusions that encompassed much more than this particular text. She used the idea of the mammy to explore students' ambivalence about their own positions within the Black community, and to show them all, particularly the Black students, their unconscious attitudes of class privilege. It is as though Wade-Gayles was suggesting that students will never be in a position to promote racial change until they understand these structures.

Wade-Gayles's success in sensitizing students to the racism, sexism, and class divisions in American society, and to their own positions concerning these structures, depended not only on her teaching but on the unusual mix of students in the class. Maybe *none* of the students were used to thinking of themselves in terms of the ways in which they had been privileged; certainly Michael found the focus on sexism eye opening, and Sarina Stelmack was shocked to find out that these Black women did not think women were all alike.

Mark Adams's elaboration in an interview with Maher of what it means for him to *be* a white male showed us the complex way in which his position was bound up with and expressive of his sense of entitlement, a combined entitlement of gender, race, and class that was still only partially conscious to him:

> Never in my life have I ever been ashamed of being an upper-class white male. . . . I sometimes feel that what I say in that class means nothing. . . . And other times I feel like it is real important, *because I don't have anything to gain by it,* having Black and white, you know, being equal, so to speak.
>
> I feel like if it happens, I'll still have a good life, a profitable life. And if women stay home or not, you know like men want them to have. . . . Obviously I can gain, like mankind gains, or womankind, but personally I don't have to deal with that. I'm an upper-class white male; I'm the boss. . . . If you're born and you could have your choice of what you wanted to be, white male would probably be the choice, because that's the best thing to be.

The knot of race remained more difficult for everyone to untie than did those of gender and class. Because of her experience as an African-American woman, Blanche was less optimistic about addressing racism than sexism. In her view, whites "aren't willing to develop relationships with Blacks," and "even though gender, sex, and race come together in the classroom," white students were going to leave "without having the information," in other words, without gaining a sense of Black people's position in society: "I feel like they are still going to do whatever it is they were going to do before they took this class." Kathy Kennedy credited Wade-Gayles's class with her own emergence as a proud "African-American woman," and emphasized in her interview the role of both men and women in discussing sexism in public. Yet she was much more guarded in her assessment of Black-white relationships.

It's so hard because toes are constantly being stepped on. People get offended, and then they become defensive, and then before you know it's almost like an argument . . . it's like Dr. Gayles says, even though they're assumptions they're up there, you just know.

One wonders if she and Blanche would have been more optimistic if they had perceived the changes in Sarina quoted above.

At San Francisco State University the participants in the Wild Women in Music and Literature class lost no opportunity to emphasize the constructed, or "fashioned," nature of their knowledge, its positional grounding on the margins of the dominant culture, and its usefulness for social projects and social change. As we have mentioned, this self-consciousness was due, in large part, to the overt struggles over the curriculum and other issues at San Francisco State, where, in Women Studies, students and faculty saw their education as a political struggle for meaning and power.

Chinosole once said, "Black feminist theory is a radical point of departure for many other related theories, nationally and internationally." The following vignette from her class illustrates the explanatory powers of Black feminist theory. It is about the myths of identity that were constructed to enslave Black people, the "characters which African people presented to the slave master," and the social consequences of language and meaning. Angela Davis introduced the theme by discussing a passage from Zora Neale Hurston's *Of Mules and Men*.[19]

This is Hurston's description of Black people. She says: "They are most reluctant at times to reveal that which the soul lives by. And the Negro, in spite of his open face laughter, his seemly acquiescence, is particularly evasive. The Negro offers a feather-bed resistance, the theory behind these tactics. The white man is always trying to nose into somebody else's business. All right, I'll set something outside of the door of my mind for him to play with and handle. He can read my writing but he sure can't read my mind. I'll put this play toy in his hand and he will seize it and go away. Then I will say my saying and sing my song."

Hurston suggests that when we think about racist stereotypes, we also have to give ourselves credit for being shrewd and smart enough to project those characters . . . as a means of creating a shield behind which we could then do the work that we really needed to do.

The two professors and their students then talked about the concept in African-American culture of "the trickster": a figure, as in many other cultures, who resists the oppressor through camouflage, trickery, and manipulation, such as the Uncle Tom who actually helped many slaves to escape. The following exchange shows them exploring the effects of such stereotypes from a Black perspective:

BEATRICE GORDON: Was the danger that there came a point where we began to believe in our own tricks? As if that oral history did not get passed down quick enough or often enough for us to understand that this is what we're doing and not to believe that that is what we are.

DAVIS: Oh sure. Maybe that's why the artist Bettye Saar, for example, put a shotgun in Aunt Jemima's hands in one of her installation pieces.[20]

JAYNA BROWN: We're talking about the trickster, but then also the stereotypes of the Jezebel and the mammy. Sometimes I kind of wonder if there was any truth in that? I mean what did the mammy do?

DAVIS: Mammy had the closest contact with the slaveholder's family. She could, for example, steal books so that members of the slave community could learn how to read and write; she could put poison in the master's food, . . . There's a whole range of resistance that she was able to accomplish that no one else could.

CHINOSOLE: We studied that in *Incidents in the Life of a Slave Girl*.

MARISSA NORBERT*: The historical accounts being put out by white racists, Eurocentric historical documents that say "Mammy she was a good old girl"—what's that one, *Gone with the Wind*—we have all these stories that [are] from their perspective and not our perspective. I have such a problem thinking that we would just believe our own tricks.

The group then went on to explore the loss of African-American consciousness and its relation to broader issues of class, culture, and identity:

DAVIS: Isn't some of this about people who move into the middle classes often severing cultural connections with those whom they left behind and therefore not . . . teaching their children about the symbolic meaning of the devil, the rabbit, and other figures so that their children are no longer in possession of the knowledge required to understand their own culture. They begin to take literally things that they should be able to analyze in a much more complex, metaphorical way.

ANOTHER STUDENT: It's that we had to survive as house slaves and field slaves. . . . Another way to survive is as an assimilated slave these days and that while I may have begun to adopt certain characteristics that the master was going to beat the shit out of me if I didn't [do those things] . . . I became accustomed to them, but deep down inside, in my baby toe, or in my soul, I still remember and I still know. I just don't have those opportunities to express it, and if I do express it I'll be penalized.

MARISSA: I was listening to someone say, "We should have a period of mourning, ten years easily, for being in slavery." Just think of what a massive reality that is and we never really have mourned it. This country has never really set aside space to say, "Oh my God, what a thing to do to a people."

BEATRICE GORDON: We had a conversation last night, and it was a big struggle for all of us. Ultimately this feeling came into the room and we were talking about things like not knowing your language. You have this memory and not being able to express those memories, not having the language that would capture concepts that are necessary for survival. And . . . the pain was so deep that we had to leave it because it was too much and we didn't know how to handle it, you know? But we know, we feel it.

Beatrice's reference to "not knowing your language" and "not being able to express memories," as well as the other student's comment on the failure of books written by Europeans to capture Black experience, were calls to construct the knowledge that Blacks need to reclaim their culture. These remarks also suggest how difficult it is to build an oppositional knowledge, and highlight these students' appreciation of their own positions. The content of this course lent itself to building theory from unexpected places. There were times when we, as white women, and perhaps also the white students in the class, felt we were hearing what "the soul lives by."

This discussion, like similar classes at Emory and Spelman, evokes Johnnetta Cole's assertion that "we can never understand America, nor can we ever understand Black Americans, until we confront slavery."[21] As at Emory and Spelman, these students and teachers were exploring issues raised by the position of African-Americans—both male and female—within the dominant culture. They also explicitly confronted the process of knowledge construction through language—the language of oppression, often written, and the language of resistance, often oral, repressed but emerging into consciousness through the learning process taking place in classes like this one. The students in "Wild Women" also explored class divisions within the African-American community, to a greater extent than at any other institution we visited. We wondered whether class issues are repressed, especially at the liberal arts colleges, because, despite the presence of many students who receive financial aid, the dominant culture is middle- to upper-middle-class, leading students from different backgrounds to keep silent?[22]

In sum, exploring the meanings of positionality in heterogeneous classrooms at Emory and San Francisco State, or Lewis and Clark, or in Bianca Cody Murphy's class at Wheaton, entails basic challenges to our conventional notions of communication and knowledge construction. In these groups, we saw how knowledge could emerge from the acknowledgment of deep positional differences. The layers of language, emotion, and conflicting meaning implicit in different positions can be plumbed, raised to the surface, and explored. Although this is hard to do when the group is heterogeneous, it is perhaps impossible when the group is, on the surface, homogeneous, because then the lines of divergence, of difference, tend to be repressed or smoothed away.

CHAPTER SEVEN

Toward Positional Pedagogies

When those who have the power to name and to socially construct reality choose not to see you or hear you, whether you are dark-skinned, old, disabled, female, or speak with a different accent or dialect than theirs, when someone with the authority of a teacher, say, describes the world and you are not in it, there is a moment of psychic disequilibrium, as if you looked into a mirror and saw nothing.

—Adrienne Rich

So {I tell my Sociology of Women class} the way I look at the "beauty myth" is about trying to look into a mirror and trying to see yourself. In a very systematic way thinking about those sociocultural corporate entities that keep you from seeing and appreciating who you are—your face, your breasts, everything. And then we move on from there to how to wipe the mirror clean. Not with Windex, which involves buying something already packaged, but with vinegar and water, which is something that your mother told you will cut through the dirt in a real special way.

—Mona Phillips, interview

WE INTRODUCED THIS BOOK by quoting Adrienne Rich, who describes the "moment of psychic disequilibrium, as if you looked into a mirror and saw nothing," that comes "when those who have the power to name and socially construct reality," those with the authority of a teacher, say, "choose not to see you or hear you." The image of holding up a mirror to reflect the relationships among teaching, learning, and self-knowledges indicates the importance of the choices that teachers make. When they represent and express the world of "sociocultural corporate entities," they may inflict on many students the invisibility, loss, and denial of which Adrienne Rich speaks. Instead, Mona Phillips speaks as a teacher who creates a discourse of family and community. By "wiping the mirror clean," that is, recovering a language used by mothers and not "packaged" by the culture, she helps students place themselves in a new context in which they can see and appreciate themselves whole. Phillips said later on:

What we want to do is free up our third eye. We are always doing, but we are always looking at what we are doing. You go from the center out. For me, it goes back to wanting them to know some very basic things. Like who they are. And there's so much that works against that. It's not just a matter of hair and skin color and nose shape. It's how knowledge is constructed, and if you go through that construction without the use of that third eye it makes you uncomfortable with yourself if you aren't conscious that there is a particular structure involved.

What do "hair and skin color and nose shape" have to do with how knowledge is constructed? What is this "third eye"? To us, it represents a form of knowing based on an understanding, as Phillips put it, of those "particular structures," such as racism or sexism, that, for these young female students, control their sense of themselves. Categories of physical attractiveness categorize and demean all young women, as Naomi Wolf's *The Beauty Myth* explores in detail, but particularly young women of color.[1] Until they understand the structures of meaning and value behind those categories, they will not be able to reconstruct the world or their place in it. The "third eye" is a form of theorizing, but rather than reflecting either a universalized mode of thought—thinking about thinking—or one that is personal or psychological, Phillips gives this way of knowing a positional cast: you have to go from the "center out" by first knowing the place where you are.

Positionality, as we learned in chapter 6, is this kind of "metaknowledge," locating the self in relation to others within social structures, such as the classroom, that re-create and mediate those relationships. As Carmen Luke explains, "the key for theorists and for feminist teachers [is to locate] perspective, experience, and knowledge in historical, political, and cultural contexts."[2] The meanings people create about aspects of themselves, like gender, cultural identification, and class position, vary widely in different classrooms. Although these meanings are in constant flux, they nevertheless reflect the unequal power relations that govern the society outside the classroom. For example, the empowerment of African-American women in Phillips's class reflects their situation in the world outside even as they are learning to resist it. Moreover, the degree of positional awareness itself often reflects societal power relationships, to the degree that people in positions of privilege, such as Mark, a student in Gloria Wade-Gayles's class, are likely to resist the awareness that their individual perspectives are shaped by the social positions they occupy.

In *all* classrooms, positionalities are at work. Teachers and students may assume, aspire to, and/or directly challenge and undermine the social structures they inhabit, but they cannot completely step outside them. Yet, if the classroom setting can help students to understand the workings of positional dynamics in their lives, to see them through their "third eye," then they can begin to challenge them and to create change.

Looking back at the book, we decided to focus this chapter on glimpses of, and barriers to, classroom constructions of this form of knowledge, that is, "pedagogies of positionality." The classrooms we visited all represent differing degrees of positional knowledge since they are all examples of more or less explicit encounters between the "voices from the bywaters" expressed by marginal lives and the worldviews of the dominant culture. For this reason, teachers and students in these classrooms were taught to be aware of their own viewpoints as partial and oppositional in some way, rather than representing uniquely individual perspectives or universalized searches for "truth." Like many others, Ted Michelini, a student at Lewis and Clark, conveyed the power of learning in such a context, in this instance, through the lens of gender analyses. He put it as follows:

> I find that in classes where gender is explored, it's sort of as if you admit that you're walking in quicksand and stop gazing at the sky. . . . You're a human being and you are set in this matrix. You have to deal with some of your foundations before you can jet on [to] the impersonal and large and oceanic.

Ted saw that the exploration of gender meant placing himself within a relational matrix—surroundings that shifted like "quicksand"—rather than in the "impersonal" and "oceanic" world of abstract thought.

Insights such as this demonstrate how some students come to understand themselves as "situated knowers," in Donna Haraway's terminology.[3] However, such grounded understanding of social structures is often hampered by the complex workings of these same structures in the university. Institutional and classroom hierarchies and the narrow perspectives of the academic disciplines, as well as the limitations of dominant cultural ideologies, all hinder its realization. The impersonality of some academic environments make it impossible for students to get to know each other and thus to speak from a shared context. The decline in community outside of the university, related to the increasing individualism and fragmentation of our entire society, is also a factor. To reframe people's pervasive individualism requires group solidarity and consciousness, a specific sense of common location that is both historical and cultural. Although some members of dominant groups, such as Ted and many of the other male students at Lewis and Clark, began to view themselves as privileged for the first time in their lives, positional consciousness most often emerges in people who are in marginal situations, as part of their resistance to attempts by dominant groups to treat them either as "people like us" or to categorize them as the "Other."

Indeed, reading the transcripts of our classroom visits, Grey Osterud commented to us that to "figure out [positional approaches] would mean observing practice which nobody's doing yet." We seldom witnessed discussions in which all the participants seemed to understand, in Osterud's terminology, that their "identity is not, in fact, individual but is embedded in a community of discourse."[4]

SOME VIEWS OF POSITIONAL PEDAGOGIES

A few of the classroom discussions we observed did offer glimpses of such understanding at work. One example might be from Bianca Cody Murphy's Human Sexuality class. In an early exploration of the ways descriptive language is embedded in social power relations, her students analyzed the words used for male and female sexual organs in order to understand how these terms enact male power and female victimization. Margaret Blanchard used her own menopause to help students understand how an experience may be narrated and understood in terms of different language and descriptive lenses. The older women in her class, in particular, came up with novel personal perspectives to illustrate her point. What is interesting about these classroom examples, indeed, is that in these instances teachers were reinterpreting categories of biological sex—typically seen as the most "natural" and least "social" kinds of difference—to demonstrate the social construction and significance of gender meanings.

Another example of conscious positioning comes from Leslie Flemming's class, where she began to explore some meanings of contemporary Islamic thought by explicitly juxtaposing the perspectives of Muslims and non-Muslims. Gloria Wade-Gayles at Emory pushed both Black and white students to confront aspects of their racial and sexual position by examining their relationship to Dilsey, a fictional character through whom William Faulkner explored the tangled knots of these relationships. A somewhat more elaborate instance of constructing knowledge positionally is found in Chinosole and Angela Davis's course on "Wild Women," in their discussion of the complex differences among African-American responses to the legacies of slavery. Speaking of middle-class Blacks, Davis noted:

> People sever connections with those whom they left behind and therefore ... their children are no longer in possession of the language required to understand their own culture, so they begin to take literally things that they should be able to analyze in a much more complex, metaphorical way.

Beatrice Gordon, a student, echoed the importance of symbolic and interpretive understandings when she said, "[It's about] not being able to express those memories, not having the language that would capture concepts that are necessary for survival."

This kind of knowledge is theoretical, based on the dynamic evolution of a group's consciousness, not individual or merely "experiential." It is constructed within circumstances of oppression and resistance, and must be continually and consciously rediscovered and remade, since assimilated groups have lost "the language required to understand their own culture." The high degree of positional consciousness reflected in this discussion was possible, and necessary, partially because of the highly politicized diversity at State. Students and faculty of color saw an acute need to re-create knowledge and history for their own communities.

We also saw the burgeoning of positional consciousness in those discussions in which students expressed contrasting, or opposite, points of view. In her course, Women Writers. After 1800, depicted in chapter 5, Dorothy Berkson prodded her students to explicate their readings of *Jane Eyre* from their standpoints as women and men, adults and children, observing, "I believe there is no one *Jane Eyre*."

> Did [those] who read it for the first time as adults, did you identify with her, did the book catch you in that kind of emotional intensity if you've read it for the first time now? ... The experience of reading it for the men in the class is different than for the women in the class too. I mean it is bound to be.

While the female students remembered identifying with Jane, even starting diets of bread and water, Bob Vaux transformed his own identification into a statement about the general powerlessness of children, noting that "our society works to maintain the dependency of children and keep them young." The reactions of male students reflected the universalizing perspective often associated with more privileged groups, which, nevertheless, could be also viewed as an emerging positional analysis. The confidence with which students expressed their own readings reflected the atmosphere of the class in which Berkson's emphasis on their written journal entries decentered her own authority. As she put it in a recent interview with us, the issue is "how can I position myself and the students in the classroom so that we are both agents of interpretation?"

A particularly vivid example of the emergence of new interpretations from student writing is given by Nancy Ichimura, whose journal entry exploring Emily Dickinson's poetry in Berkson's class triggered a deeper interpretation of the roles of women's positions, their silences, and the use of Dickinson language in relation to understanding and transforming their identities.

> You could call yourself a wife and the admiring bog says lovely, yes. You could call yourself a spinster even, and the bog would still admire you because you fit. But what if you don't want to be any of these things? Well, then you stay a nobody.

Nancy's emerging sense of the ways stereotypical categorizing can erase the self, and the development of her own conscious position in opposition to that way of being, is seen in her choice of the image that, from her perspective as a Japanese-American young women, would now "strike her dead":

> It's like watching a Walt Disney movie as a child where Hayley Mills and these other girls dance and primp before a party singing "Femininity," how being a woman is all about looking pretty and smiling pretty and acting stupid to attract men. But once you realize how this vision has warped you, it would split your heart to try and believe that again.

As in their discussion of *Jane Eyre,* the students in this class situated themselves not only as individual readers but in terms of their different positions. Berkson's class enabled students, such as Daniel Ritter, to see himself as a male reader, to say that he could learn not a single "best" interpretation but rather "how women react to women's texts as opposed to the way I react to it or Dorothy reacts to it or something like that."

The need to construct and reconstruct racial and ethnic identities and their relation to feminist theory, formed the basis of the discussion in Grey Osterud's class, described in chapter 4. The students of color strove, like Nancy, to define their own group identities in relation to the structures they found oppressive in the dominant culture. Yet, they also faced the constraints—and ultimate impossibility—of stabilizing those identities. They were learning that identities had to be constructed, and continually reconstructed, rather than "found" or discovered. Wrestling with these issues revealed to them that their own experiences, their sense of themselves, could be consciously theorized and shaped through language. As Beth Sanchez remarked:

> I think one thing interesting about learning political language that the mainstream culture understands is so that you can as an oppressed group be validated. But once you learn that language, or learn how to communicate, then I think it is necessary to go back to your own language, your own identity, your own culture.

As Ron Underwood put it, "So there will always be a double consciousness, sisters under the veil."

At the end of the class, after discussing the potential and actual role of feminist theory in peoples' lives, Ron concluded:

> But that's the whole point, that's how language is used to oppress people. People close the doors and talk about all this stuff, and I'm saying that theory provides a key to that door, and theory also presents a way of changing meaning, changing semantically, changing the way things are.

These students of color sought to articulate their longings for power and agency by making their stories intelligible not only as individuals with personal "experiences," but also theoretically, as members of particular groups. Yet, they did not want to be trapped within those groups. When we had first examined this discussion, we did not notice that Ron's focus on the uses of language for both celebration and repression was a positional statement about the constructed, and contested, nature of group identities, as well as a statement about the power of classroom knowledge to reconstruct the "real world." Theories may be deployed to close the doors on people, or to actually "change the way things are." It is noteworthy that Grey Osterud said almost nothing during this discussion, except, in a few important instances, to encourage the students of color. This shows the degree to which students can explore theoretical issues, given responsibility and encouragement by the teacher.

The courses taught by Osterud and by Chinosole and Angela Davis directly addressed the idea that voice and experience fashion, and are fashioned by, theoretical frameworks, and that language is a key element in the process. Not incidently, such classroom discourses also demonstrate that classrooms may be sites not only of the enactment of feminist pedagogies, but also of the development of feminist theory. In class discourse, positions are not always fixed, as the claims to identity sometimes seem to be, but rather relational. Openly positional classroom discourse represents an important arena in which a variety of complex relationships can be renegotiated and transformed.

THE EPISTEMOLOGIES OF ACADEMIC DISCIPLINES AND INSTITUTIONS

In many classrooms, we observed, the "mirror" of education did not so much make students invisible to themselves as it created oddly fragmented pictures of the world and their places in it. From the perspective of our pedagogy of positionality, we begin to see how positional understandings are discouraged or blocked in the academic environment. In most institutions the academic disciplines, as traditionally formulated, still hold sway as modes of structuring and transmitting knowledge as well as repositories of the accumulated wisdom of trained scholars, even though they now include the contributions of some feminists and other "minorities." Women's Studies and related departments such as Ethnic or Black Studies are often seen as "add-ons," whose existence is necessitated by the failure of other departments to incorporate their challenge to mainstream views. For this reason, separate programs such as Women's Studies are retained in many institutions as a way to serve some of their constituencies, namely, female students.

The continuing need for Women's Studies thus highlights the continuing absence of women from mainstream disciplines. As Mona Phillips said to her students, "We create the knowledge, and just because our creations are not in the places where knowledge is held, which is in textbooks, that doesn't mean we didn't do it." Feminist scholars have shown that their interpretations of the world are more inclusive, and therefore more accurate, even by conventional standards, than traditional views.[5] But while we have described our participants working to promote such new perspectives, consciously positional approaches to academic disciplines are a more difficult task. They entail a critical examination of the differential grounds for the scholar's, the teacher's, and the students' knowledge and authority, in order to put them all into relation with one another. Some of our professors teach within disciplines, and in institutions, with hierarchical structures that are especially resistant to student contributions, in particular, as sources of knowledge or interpretation.

One place to examine these academic constraints is in Pat McCorquodale's course, The Sociology of Sexuality, at the University of Arizona, where the traditional hierarchy of knowledge transmission and acquisition was more firmly lodged than in the other places we visited. She wanted to show the students, she told us, that the interpretation of facts might vary—"very contradictory positions might be supported with the same set of, 'quote,' facts"—and that generalizations are made from individual experiences, so that "if there's enough individual experience that contradicts the categories, then the categories need to be changed." However, the history and structure of sociology, which foregrounds "the facts" from some peoples' perspectives and not others, remained unexplored in her classroom.

Other classes that we observed also testified to the power of the positivist methodologies of the traditional disciplines to shape what counts as knowledge, so that discussion of its sources and purposes is avoided and students' questions remain relatively marginal to the process of its construction. Kersti Yllo used the tools of the field of sociology to expose women's experiences of marital violence, and edited a book that presents innovative feminist research methodologies.[6] She wanted her course in sociology to help students expand their tolerance of other lifestyles. But like MacCorquodale, she considered the outcomes of sociological research methods as relatively unproblematic in her undergraduate courses, suggesting that *imagined* alternatives to the status quo were a matter of getting the research right, getting "good" research, rather than critiquing the structure of academic research itself. In this context she observed:

> We don't know exactly what proportion of us would be gay or straight if there were no pressure on us; the estimate found that 10 percent of the population is gay or lesbian but we don't know exactly, not much good research in that area.

As another example, Virginia Gazzam Anderson opened up scientific writing and research to the claims of feminist scientists for equal information about females, but she was situationally unable to challenge the positivist scientific paradigm in which her students had to be trained in order to become employed.

We can further reveal some disciplinary barriers to positional knowing by reconsidering the separation of generalized theory from narratives of personal experience that we explored in chapter 4. As we saw through our "glimpses," positional knowing operates by critiquing the *relationships* between particular stories and broader interpretive frameworks. But in many disciplines, generalized and abstract knowledge, emerging from the persistent search for universal "truths," is placed *in opposition* to narrative approaches that are seen as individualized, particular, less "true." While traditional disciplines have made the stories of privileged males the basis of human experience and female stories the particular exceptions, the persistent search for all-inclusive theories itself perpetuates these distinctions.

Thus, in Laurie Finke's course in Literary Theory, Ned Sharp and Ralph Goodman were searching for some general framework for linking gender and class oppressions. They opposed Jill Marts's arguments based on her experiences in the workplace. Although these male students were arguing from their own positions, they were able to adopt the universalized discourse of Marxist theory to disguise their standpoints. When Ralph asserted that "gender is defined by economics," Jill retorted: "You argue that it's power and acquisition, but the fact of the matter is, *a high majority of women are making less money* [italics added]." Ned's response was to replace the particular experiences of women with an abstract category: "If you look at gender you will see all women as being oppressed." Such abstractions strip away peoples' actual positions, either disguising them as theory, as males have been accustomed to do, or adding them on as "personal experiences" on the margins of "real knowledge," an approach often taken by females. In fact, Jill was unable to express her work experiences within the abstract terminology set by the debate over whether gender or class was "the primary oppression." Even though Finke here acted to introduce the theory of positionality, the theoretical level at which the discussion was pitched militated against the students' placing their own lives within the abstract structures they discussed.

Gender differences in reaction to a course topic also occurred in Dorothy Berkson's course on women writers. However, Berkson explicitly marked these differences in interpretation, laid them to reading "as males" and "as females," and gave them equal weight. Was she able to do this partly because literature was the subject and discipline, of her course, as opposed to literary theory, which was Finke's topic? As many feminist scholars have remarked, the field of literature has been more hospitable to alternative analyses and interpretations because it is not a positivist, generalizing discipline in the same way that, for example, sociology and biology are. It rather depends on unique and particular events and creations rendered through narrative as well as more "objective" forms.[7] This factor helped make Bev Clark's, Berkson's, and Chinosole's and Angela Davis's literature courses places in which students could express explicitly positional readings of texts, as, for example, Nancy Ichimura's connection of Emily Dickinson's poems to her own history of silencing, or Michelle Barnett's rueful remark in Clark's class about reading as a man, reading as a woman, and then reading as a feminist "after I took this class."

However, tapping personal or individual responses to intellectual or literary themes is no more a necessarily positional approach than it is an exclusively theoretical one. Dorothy Berkson told us recently that she wants students to interact constantly with the text, in part so that they will "understand the connection, which I think is particularly important in literature, between emotion and reason. Because literature is intended to work on the emotions. Yet the analysis of it is supposed to be, you know, emotionless." To *connect* reason and emotion is the crucial task. Returning to the text means that students can find the places that generated emotional responses in them, and then reapproach them from an analytical perspective. To have students react to intellectual and artistic material, without exploring the grounds of their reactions in their own positions, is to leave learning at a personalized and subjective level. Chantal Tetreault learned, from studying classrooms for her senior thesis, that students become authorities for each other only to the extent that they are "explicit about themselves as social and political actors with respect to a text or an issue."[8]

Besides the disciplines, the structure of academic institutions acts to restrain positional knowing. At research universities like Arizona, academic status derives from scholarly expertise in the discipline, and the norms of "good teaching" presume hierarchical arrangements of knowledge and authority. Thus, feminist teachers must assert not only scholarly expertise equal to their male colleagues, but also the same kind of authority as their male colleagues in the classroom, even if they are also trying to enlist their students in more democratic modes of interaction. Leslie Flemming and Pat MacCorquodale shared similar feelings of needing to prove themselves as authority figures, learning to "put their hands in their pockets" and stride across the platform, as Flemming put it.

The particular status of our professors in these institutions determined, to a large extent, how much they felt they could challenge the power arrangements in their settings as they affected the production of classroom knowledge. At San Francisco State University, for example, the Women Studies program functioned as a democratic enclave and home for the students of color who felt undermined by the Eurocentric, top-down lecture style of the rest of the institution. As Jilchristina Vest saw it, "The more I learn [that way] the more dysfunctional I get . . . because I couldn't relate it to anything." The professors in Women Studies thus felt emboldened to critique the power relations of the institution as a whole.

At Towson State, both K Edgington and Margaret Blanchard worked along the edges of the English department, from which positions they were free to evolve their own idiosyncratic teaching methods. But as Sara Coulter explained, it was partly because of their marginal status as instructors in fields like writing, that teach skills rather than content, that they did not feel, as Coulter herself did, the pressure to "cover" the material, or to transmit academic content in a conventional way.

Furthermore, the current financial crisis in most universities means larger classes, usually organized around a lecture format, which works against the kinds of interactive teaching required for exploring different positions around a topic. Leslie Flemming and Bianca Cody Murphy, among many others, were constrained, at least partially, by the large size of their Oriental Humanities and Human Sexuality courses from examining in greater detail the different perspectives on the issues they raised. In Flemming's course, Women in South Asia, which enrolled only seven students, she was able to more fully explore her own history as a student of Eastern religions.[9]

At the liberal arts colleges, the hierarchy of knowledge was less overt, and our teacher informants saw as their responsibility the initiation of their students as equal participants into the concerns of the discipline that they shared. Kersti Yllo, for example, had several students who told us that she had helped them to "think like sociologists" and to consider sociology as a career. This student centered institutional epistemology led to different standards of good teaching. Student questions, like those originated by their professors, were often taken seriously as a source of classroom knowledge. And yet the cultures of teaching at liberal arts colleges may also vary. For example, Laurie Finke compared Lewis and Clark to Kenyon College, where she recently became Director of Women's and Gender Studies:

I spent eight years at Lewis and Clark . . . and my teaching methods sort of merged with the teaching culture of the school so that students knew who I was, knew what to expect. And then to come to a new place where that's not true. And it's often very difficult [here] to get students to engage in interactive sorts of things because they feel forced to. . . . Because it's not a part of the teaching culture.

The professors at Lewis and Clark, Wheaton, and Spelman were also more comfortable with personalizing their authority. Bev Clark, for example, shared with her students the enthusiasm for American literature that she owed to feminism, along with her discomfort with the French literary critics, in order to encourage her students in their own critical processes. At San Francisco State Angela Davis and Chinosole spoke openly to the students about their political histories and commitments.

To deal with their own knowledge positionally was easier for most of these teachers than to question the grounds for their authority to evaluate students. As we will explore next in chapter 8, several of them have since begun to discuss these issues openly with students, exploring the kinds of responsibility and authority that belong to teacher and student. However, the teacher's authority, in the best of situations, is a paradoxical and conflicted issue, because it also represents the teacher's standards for excellence and the different kinds and levels of progress and achievement desired for students. Mona Phillips, for example, "is still firm on deadlines"; Dorothy Berkson sets the format for reading texts and says, "I want you to follow this approach."

Unfortunately, the most frequently used tool for the assessment of student progress is the grading system, which represents an institutional normative demand that students be held up to certain a priori standards of achievement and treated as isolated individuals who take their places along a unidimensional, hierarchical continuum. Grades cannot assess learning situations when students may be learning different things, or learning as a group and not as individuals, or learning from each other and not only from the teacher. Individual grading ignores the social and community contexts— both within and outside the classroom—that leave individuals positioned differently in regard to the production of knowledge. The practice of group evaluation of teachers and students by each other, undertaken by some of the Women Studies teachers at San Francisco State, is perhaps one way to mark the shifting grounds of expertise in settings like the "Wild Women" course, where Lori New Breast, a student, was one of the most knowledgeable and authoritative voices heard.

Traditional classroom and grading structures give the teacher responsibility for transmitting the subject matter of a given field, even though she chooses the specific topics. We have come to wonder what new kinds of institutional and classroom arrangements would reflect the more interactive reconfigurations of knowledge and pedagogy that, we imply here, might be necessary to produce positional knowing. Some of our informants have begun to explore different ways of confronting these problems, as we will discuss in the next chapter.

SOCIAL STRUCTURES AND INSTITUTIONAL SEGREGATION

Educational settings reflect, as much as they might try to challenge, divisions within the society at large. Thus, from the perspective of positional pedagogies, more general and more disturbing than the hierarchies within institutions are the disparities *between* institutions that reflect our societal inequalities of social class, race, and gender. The different degree of intellectual agency offered to their students by small liberal arts institutions and large state universities also reflects the social position of their student bodies, in that the former charge higher tuitions and tend to represent more privileged sectors of the population. It has been Tetreault's experience, in moving from Lewis and Clark to California State University, Fullerton, that state universities, with much larger student-teacher ratios, offer more lecture courses, more multiple-choice examinations, and more textbooks, as well as less primary-source material, less student writing, and, overall, less attention to individual student learning.

Such divisions and differences among educational institutions have a long history in American education, where the promise and illusion of upward mobility has always been undercut by sharp interinstitutional limitations to equal opportunity. Moreover, these class divisions in American higher education are becoming greater. Tuitions at liberal arts colleges continue to rise while financial aid from all quarters has sharply fallen off, making it increasingly difficult for less affluent students to attend institutions like Lewis and Clark, Wheaton, and Spelman. The current financial crisis in public higher education often means for state university systems a decline in those elective courses that do not lead directly to credentials or a career. As Chinosole pointed out, the budget cuts in higher education in California and elsewhere have amounted to delivering "fast food learning," an "education on the cheap," to working-class students. Recently Ann Reynolds, the former Chancellor of the California State University system and currently Chancellor of the City University of New York, proposed the cancellation of 97 programs, mostly in the liberal arts and humanities, leaving in place the career and job-training programs that give urban students only limited upward mobility.[10]

One major factor, then, that constrains student understanding of their positions within an unequal social structure is the increasing segregation of our educational settings in terms of social class and material privilege. These institutional inequalities have racial and ethnic implications as well, since students of color tend to be less privileged than white students and are therefore less likely to be able to attend liberal arts colleges. Students we met who did attend, like Ron Underwood, or Cheryl Ibabao, or Nancy Ichimura at Lewis and Clark, or Michelle Barnett at Wheaton, or the Emory students in Gloria Wade-Gayles's class, seemed unusually conscious that their positions were anomalous even though their social-class backgrounds varied markedly. They knew about being a "nobody" or a "somebody," or having a "double consciousness, sisters under the veil."

However, reading what we say in chapter 6 about the emancipatory possibilities of positional pedagogies in classrooms with a diverse student body, some of our informants, Grey Osterud and Chinosole in particular, sharply warned us about being too optimistic about what the classroom can do. Relationships among different groups in heterogeneous classrooms reflect and often re-create the power relations and ideological frameworks of the dominant culture even while challenging them. Since these structures are not only middle class but, of course, also white and male, students disadvantaged by race and gender outside often feel more vulnerable inside the classroom as well.

What has this meant for classrooms that are composed of all women, or all women of color? Chinosole, in a cogent defense of Spelman as an all-Black institution, remarked that "I think it depends, if the [classroom] group that is homogeneous has been traditionally forced to internalize the value system, the education, the facts about a dominant group, then it's not the same kind of homogeneity that you would find in an all-white setting." Indeed, the all-women's classrooms like those at Spelman, Wheaton, San Francisco State, and Margaret Blanchard's class seemed like "safe" spaces. While unable there to directly confront the "Other" in the form of males, or whites, these members of marginalized groups, both white women and women of color, could begin to construct knowledge from newly articulated viewpoints on the world, in a process that might not have been possible in more heterogeneous settings.

The majority-female classrooms at Lewis and Clark, and Angela Davis's and Chinosole's majority women-of-color course at San Francisco State were the settings in which we saw the most powerful emergence of positional knowing. In a striking number of instances, discussions were led by young people of color. These classrooms also comprised members of dominant groups—white women and men at Lewis and Clark and white women at San Francisco State. But there were enough women of color present, in the context of strong support by the teacher, for them to make their voices heard (in contrast, say, to the situation of Michelle Barnett at Wheaton, who was alone, even though she felt very supported by Bev Clark). In those two settings in particular, those privileged by being white or male, like Daniel Ritter or Ted Michelini at Lewis and Clark or Ginnie Richards at San Francisco State, could begin to see their maleness or their whiteness, in the context of confronting other lives and experiences, as relational *positions*.

It is thus perhaps paradoxical, but necessary to point out, that while more privileged, middle-class white students and males need to learn from females, from African-American students, and from people of color, the latter, at least in part, need to be strong enough in number to explore their own lives on their own terms. The former benefit from being in classes where they are in the minority to offset their own positions of relative power, whereas the reverse is true for marginalized groups. And examination of these classrooms will attest that the teacher's support is crucial in any case, since the vocal women of color in Dorothy Berkson's and Grey Osterud's classes were still in the minority.

These instances particularly demonstrate the importance of seeing student and teacher "positionality" as relational. Context-specific variations govern the ways in which different gender, class, race, and other positions emerge through individual perspectives, confront each other, and combine to produce classroom knowledge. The "mix" of people in any classroom, in terms of overt and hidden aspects of their identities and group memberships, profoundly shapes the possibilities for creating consciously positional pedagogies. The particular situation and status of an institution within the class and racial hierarchy of American higher education helps determine the composition of its student body. The institutional context also helps determine the degree of intimacy and trust afforded in the classroom context for discussion of these issues. The classrooms in the liberal arts colleges, like the community of graduate students in Chinosole's and Angela Davis's class, were places where students knew and trusted each other and formed relationships outside the classroom as well.

To focus on frameworks of positionality is not to deny the importance of individuals. While we have marked the uniqueness of the professors with whom we worked, the students also showed us that individuals construct, move within, and move beyond their societal and classroom positions in very different and creative ways. The power of Nancy Ichimura's and Elisabeth Stitt's journal entries, the forcefulness of a Ned Sharp or a Ron Underwood, or the candor of a Wendy Johnson, can neither be reduced to nor explained by their social positions, yet were major factors in the evolution of the discourse and production of positional knowledge in their classrooms.

The last barrier to positional pedagogies is an ideological one. Institutional and disciplinary frameworks both reflect, as in a fractured mirror revealing many facets of the same thing, the power of the dominant ideologies of our culture to shape individual consciousness. The capacity of many people to tolerate the severe inequities of capitalism depends on their acceptance of the fundamental idea of the marketplace, where everyone competes on equal terms for places on a fixed ladder. Undergirding this principle of the equality of opportunity is the equally powerful ideology of individualism. People are set up to compete as atomized individuals in the marketplace, have political rights as individuals, and are assumed to occupy different positions in society primarily on the basis of individual merit. Yet these conceptualizations of basic individual *equalities* of opportunity and rights mask deep structural *inequalities* of power, position, and possibility in the lives of many people. The cumulative effects of these inequalities over many generations have tended to imprison some groups indefinitely at the lower rungs of the ladder.

These tensions between ideology and reality are, of course, deeply embedded in our educational system. *Individual* upward mobility, defined as moving up within or even leaving the working class, has been available through education, a carrot for the ambitious or fortunate few that would show everyone else that failure was their fault. But, as we have observed about institutions of higher education, the educational system reflects the power and status hierarchies of the broader society and is therefore itself highly stratified: it prepares people for their places on different steps of the economic ladder.

Educational hierarchies have also been reinforced by the ideologies of racism and sexism, which have held that certain *inherent group* characteristics of people of color, some immigrants, and women constitute appropriate barriers to their attainments of success. Our society's ideology of classlessness assumes that working-class white males fail only because of their alleged drawbacks as *individuals*. In this ideological context, our groping to understand the ways we are all situated historically and contextually—as members of different groups with differing relationships to the structures of power, has to be profoundly limited.

On the other hand, there has been an equally long educational tradition of both accommodation and resistance, one in which immigrants, workers, people of color, and women of all classes have taken on the promise of the American dream, gained educations that moved them beyond the lives of their parents, and sometimes even challenged the antidemocratic ideologies and practices of the system itself. Most recently, the demands of the Civil Rights movement, the women's movement, and the other "liberation movements" the 1960s combined with other educational reforms, such as the GI Bill to produce the first sizeable cohort of working-class and "minority" students to attend college.[11]

The professors with whom we worked fall into a long tradition of teachers committed to using education to promote the advancement of such students. One of the themes in this book has turned out to be the conflict, for both teachers and students, between enacting the dominant ideologies of individualism and exploring the structural inequalities that have oppressed people as members of groups so that they can resist these inequalities. But to explore these social structures positionally, teachers require not only theoretical frameworks to explain them, but also alternative pedagogical approaches.

Ideologies, which are integrated conceptual frameworks for understanding a society and culture, profoundly influence epistemologies, or ways of knowing, as well as pedagogies, or methods for constructing classroom knowledge. In the classroom, as many have noted and Carmen Luke has cogently analyzed, many so-called "democratic" pedagogical approaches entail giving female students and other "minorities" equal rights or "access" to classroom discourses *as individuals,* ignoring the power relations within and outside that continue to disadvantage them as members of oppressed groups and leave the language and terms of the discourse unchanged.[12]

Progressive educators like Paulo Freire and others have long engaged in alternative approaches, which reflect their rejection of competitive and individualistic models of academic success and their wish to challenge the social inequalities played out in the classroom.[13] However, during the past two decades in the academy, feminist thinkers and writers, both white and women of color, theorists of race, culture, and ethnicity, as well as gay and lesbian theorists have begun to offer analyses of kinds of historical exploitation different from those noted by Marxists like Freire, who have emphasized class. Feminist educational thinkers like Jennifer Gore, Elizabeth Ellsworth, Carmen Luke, Patti Lather, and Kathleen Weiler, among others, have pointed out that no single concept of oppressed or dominant groups, and therefore no one "liberatory pedagogy," even feminist pedagogy, can suffice.[14] Ellsworth writes:

> [Henry Giroux says]: "All voices and their differences become unified (against human) suffering." [This] formula assumes a classroom of participants unified on the side of the subordinated against the subordinators. . . . It fails to confront dynamics of subordination present among classroom participants and within classroom participants, in the form of multiple and contradictory subject positions.[15]

She goes on to say that unity—"interpersonal, personal, and political"— among students is always fragmentary and unstable, not a given, which needs to be "chosen and struggled for."

In attempts to wrestle with the *intersection* of these "dynamics of subordination," some feminists, African-American theorists, and multicultural theorists have begun to use concepts of positionality to examine issues of exploitation and unequal power among various groups. Some thinkers have emphasized gender, race, and other markers of identity as *relational* variables always in the process of mutually defining each other.[16] Others have examined the connections among language, meaning, and political power in constructing those relationships, and explored the postmodern concern with "representation of the other" as a way of illuminating various kinds of "difference."[17]

However, in spite of the classroom as an obvious site in which to explore the production of knowledge through relational and positional lenses, it has proved exceptionally difficult—at least judged by the classrooms we visited—to confront and work through these issues there. The dominant view that casts each person as an equally placed individual in this society also constructs that individual, normatively, as white, heterosexual, male, and middle class. For every difference from this norm, whether by gender, race, class, sexual orientation, or age, we have observed different struggles for positional understandings and different ideological, epistemological, and pedagogical barriers to their realization.

Social-Class Differences

There is, first, little available language to talk about class differences among students, or between students as a group and others outside the academy who are not so privileged. We saw this problem perhaps most strongly at

Towson, whose students cast themselves as upwardly mobile individuals, without acknowledging the deep anxiety and worry in that quest. Grey Osterud pointed out to us that we could not simply recommend that students face their own positions in the social class structure. First, she said, they had to learn to *distance themselves* from the clichés of the "American Dream":

> Their actual experience is one in which they don't understand their class location. They don't even understand that they have one. . . . So it's really important to keep separating their statements from the people who articulate them. I would first say to students, "What I'm hearing is all the dominant ideology about class mobility in American society. Let's start writing it all down." And then we sit back and look at our list. And say, OK, this is an ideology, this is a belief system. What are the assumptions of this belief system? . . . What does it mean that this ideology assumes that there are class divisions . . . that remain constant, that there is a fixed class system within which each individual can change location, without it making a damn bit of difference to how the whole system works?

She suggested that only after this distancing could the students really examine what their class position is, and "the immense amount of pain there is around these issues in their lives."[18]

The failure to acknowledge social class *privilege* also deeply plagued the discussions in the predominantly white-middle-class settings we studied. Many female students found the perspectives of Women's Studies personally liberating, as in the words of a Lewis and Clark student who said, "I have the freedom and the confidence to look at things in a new way." But many European Americans tended to perceive themselves only as individuals, missing their own connection to the economic and political structures that privilege them in relation to other women and men. As Grey Osterud put it, "People feel empowered to speak of their own experiences and construct theory on that basis, and that is good. But they do not feel impelled to include other people's experiences in their explanatory frameworks." While some white female students clearly saw that, in the words of Elisabeth Stitt from Wheaton, "the women's perspective has been ignored and overlooked," they viewed the impact of feminism solely in individual terms. As Susan Cotter from Wheaton put it, "Going out into the world and working is what I want to do someday, and if feminism and working and living can't coexist, then you have a problem."

The absence of a discourse of social class also may be a reason for the relative silence in Phillips's class, and the hesitancy in Wade-Gayles's class, about social-class divisions within the Black community—in Atlanta and elsewhere. Both Emory and Spelman, although Emory much more so as a predominantly white institution, occupy relatively elite positions within the academic power structure, so that their students are relatively privileged members of their communities. And these social-class relationships were very difficult to discuss.

Privilege, Whiteness, and Racism

Going beyond, but directly related to, the absence of a theory of relative class privilege is the inability of white students to take a relational view of racism. Unable to understand their own positions in society vis-à-vis more privileged and powerful whites, the Towson students tended also to blame Black people for their oppression, and to see themselves as threatened by civil rights, particularly Affirmative Action programs. The white students had trouble seeing themselves as white, in seeing racism as part of a social structure in which their own lives were embedded, and, therefore, had trouble coping with their own racism except, sometimes, in terms of individual guilt. In a recent essay, Beverly Daniel Tatum spoke of the necessity (and difficulty) of achieving an antiracist stance as part of the development of a healthy "white identity," echoing Elizabeth Spelman's book-length dismantling of feminism's equation of "woman" with white women.[19] Bev Clark, Dorothy Berkson, Grey Osterud, K Edgington, Carla Trujillo, and Gloria Wade-Gayles, as well as others in our study, struggled with this issue constantly, while Mona Phillips, as seen in chapter 3, struggled with the reverse problem, that of claiming a cohesive identity for Black women that white feminists' appropriation of the term "woman" had denied them.

Sexual Orientation

The assumptions that govern the silences about class and race, namely that being middle class and white are "normal" conditions of life rather than privileged positions within networks of power, have also governed silences about sexual orientation, an aspect of positionality that, like social class, can remain invisible in the classroom. For example, the power of heterosexual privilege to organize students' assumptions about what constitutes valid knowledge and authority became very clear to us as we compared the struggles by Kersti Yllo and Bianca Murphy to define the sources, in their personal lives, of their authority as teachers.

It has been fascinating for us to notice that with more material available on gay and lesbian lives and issues, it has become easier for lesbian students and faculty to acknowledge their own positions as members of a particular group, with histories and ideological stances of their own. For example, Bev Clark told us in a recent interview that she had gained new insights from lesbian colleagues that led to more openness in the classroom on the part of her lesbian students. Bianca Cody Murphy's candor in class certainly helped gay and lesbian students feel more comfortable outside the classroom, as it helped all students to view heterosexuality as a culturally conditioned orientation rather than a universally valid assumption.

Gender and Race: The Challenges of Identity Politics

The barriers to positional thinking in analyses of gender and race are qualitatively different from those produced by social-class and heterosexual privileges. For one thing, differences of social class and sexual orientation are often hidden, at least in the classroom, making for easy assumptions about sameness on the surface. And since people come to the academy to enter the middle class, class divisions are especially difficult to address. But women and, to a large extent, people of color, not being male and white, are visible in important contexts as "different," as the clearly marked "Other." They have had to develop oppositional approaches to the privileged positions of the dominant group.

The "consciousness-raising" practices of the women's movement of the 1960s and 1970s, upon which the earliest versions of feminist pedagogy were based, reflected an epistemology based on personal experience to forge an emerging common culture of feminism. However, various strands diverged in the late 1970s and early 1980s, reflecting a persistent and age-old dualism in feminist thought. Although one major theoretical approach of feminism has been to assert the essential sameness of women and men, and thus women's claim to equal treatment, another prominent strain has formulated a psychological structure, a politics, and a pedagogy that celebrates women's particular attributes—a set of theories based on "difference."[20] Early versions of feminist pedagogy, as described in chapter 1 exemplified this division in feminist ideology, reflecting transformation of the early traditions of consciousness raising into ideas about the sisterhood of all women, as well as biologically grounded notions of women's nature and identity as dichotomously different from men's.

But such ideas about the essential commonality of all women, represented by a phase of feminist theory known as "cultural feminism," demonstrate a failure to take into account those differences *among* women, such as social class, heterosexual privilege, and whiteness, that the dominant culture would have us ignore. As a result, women of color and lesbians began to adopt a conscious stance from which to categorize, resist, and transform their own oppression—against the hegemony of privileged white women within feminism. This movement for the articulation of group membership (that also included groups other than women) became known as "identity politics." As Linda Alcoff defines it:

> [The] suggestion [in identity politics] is to recognize one's identity as always a construction yet also a necessary point of departure. . . . I think that just as Jewish people can choose [to emphasize] their Jewishness, so black men, women of all races, and other members of more immediately recognizable oppressed groups can practice identity politics as a political point of departure.[21]

However, our impressions of the ways in which ideas about "identity" were expressed in these classrooms suggest that this kind of theorizing often falls into fixed and absolute categories, which are at least as resistant to positional understandings as the silences about social class and homosexuality. The process of claiming group identities becomes rigid and confining, as noted by the students in Osterud's class. It tends to proceed in terms of a series of oppositions against a succession of essentialized "Others"—woman against man, Black against white, Chicana/o against Black *and* white, and so on. The invisibility and silence about differences other than the one determining each category of "identity" aggravates these tendencies to fix each group into a unidimensional and unbreakable mold without even considering the social contexts that give rise to such categories in the first place. Faced with multiple and contradictory aspects of identity, as in the case of Black women (who are erased by racism from the category "woman" and by sexism from the category "Black"), "identity politics" creates endless add-on categories and subgroups, all of which multiply the ways that people are irreducibly separate from each other.

Thus, in the discussion of *Sula* in Bev Clark's class, students were operating within a construct of women's essential nature that viewed men as the absent "Other." They made connections to *Sula* on the basis of gender alone, with lesbianism and blackness functioning as "add-on" categories of identity. By considering characters in the novel in terms of their "lesbian" or "straight" aspects and ignoring their race, students could continue to see themselves as exemplars of an abstract essence called "women," apart from the social relationships of race and heterosexuality that gave themselves privilege.

Another example of the reductiveness of interpretations based on any single category of identity is reflected in the confusion of Laurie Finke's students about gender and class analyses, from which she tried to rescue them with her point about positionality. Or we can turn to Mona Phillips's class, where the idea of restructuring the whole society for Black people, no longer "wearing those clothes [because whites' clothes] aren't our clothes," perhaps reflected a racial and cultural identification that obscured social-class differences among the students, and between students and members of the Black community outside.

Indeed, as we have been reviewing our work with barriers to positional epistemologies in mind, we were struck by a commonality we saw between some ideologies of "cultural" feminism, the epistemological stage of "subjective knowing," defined by the authors of *Women's Ways of Knowing* (discussed in chapter 4), and the individualism of the dominant culture. As an epistemological stance, subjective knowing represents an ultimate reliance on the authority of personal intuition and each person's individual experience, as the grounds for assessing the validity of knowledge or truth claims. The idea that "woman's nature" is profoundly different from that of men, so that only a woman could understand another woman, could thus be read in some ways as a "subjective" phase of feminism, extending the notion of an individual's uniqueness into that of a group's uniqueness. Perhaps the concern of students at Wheaton and Lewis and Clark about women's stories of oppression ("they are all hanging themselves") came partially from their subjective identification with these stories because they, too, were women and saw themselves as facing similar experiences.

The feminist historian Joan Scott points out that this focus on subjective "experience" as a source of valid knowledge indicates a failure to understand that experiences, as well as identities, have no real meaning prior to their interpretations, and are therefore constructed in the light of the theoretical frameworks available to understand them.[22] In the same light, comments by Mona Phillips's students that "subjective" readings of Black peoples' lives could only come from Black authors is yet another reflection of this epistemology of identity politics. In an example of the pitfalls, noted by Scott, of relying on "experience" as a basis for knowledge, the students were implying that only women can understand women's "experiences," only Black people can understand the experiences of African-Americans, and white women can understand women of color only through the piece of their common identity that is sex-linked. As Louise Bobosink, Clark's student, described this process:

While white women can never expect to express a total understanding of the Black woman's experience they can express concern and understanding in those areas of Black women's lives and literature that parallel their own.

From the perspective of identity politics, "true" understanding of another becomes possible only in the increasingly limited ways that the "Other" is seen as "the same." In the extreme, such views of the sources of meaning and truth are strikingly solipsistic, as Belenky et al. point out in relation to "subjective knowing" as well.[23] Grey Osterud noted in her recent interview with us,

Late adolescents especially are concerned about negotiating their identity, and that makes some of them more individualized, and if identity politics is seen as the basis for knowledge, then no one's getting beyond that. But I do think that in the period of time when you observed these people's practice, that was a real phenomenon in the state of feminist politics. You draw a distinction between identity projects, on the one hand, and positionality, on the other, but the fact is that it keeps collapsing in the actual transcripts, as those things are not clearly separated.

Mainstream scholars, particularly critics of "multiculturalism," express distress at what they see as the increasing fragmentation of such approaches, and often reassert the need for maintaining the universalism of traditional views in the face of such self-centered relativism. However, in contrast to the idea that ultimate truth must reside either (or both) "nowhere" or "everywhere," positional epistemologies assert the contextual groundedness of valid knowledge. In contrast to the isolation of fixed "identities," positional approaches bring different forms of "identity" into relation to each other, showing, for example, how gendered experiences, far from being "natural," are constructed by class and race, and vice versa, each factor contextualizing and specifying the circumstances under which the others are experienced.

Our classroom observations have shown us, moreover, that the process of constructing essentialized "identities" is self-reinforcing and cumulative. Because white men do not mark or position themselves in terms of gender or race, but simply as "people," women are forced to become "women," not just "people," themselves. They must then use gender as a category to describe themselves rather than as a marker for an unequal power relationship. In other words, only women are seen to have gender. Similarly, because white women do not mark themselves in terms of race, but simply as "women," women of color—look at the terminology here!—must carry race as their category alone. In this context, white women have no color. By contrast, positional approaches view race as a marker of relationship, of inequality, in which all are implicated. When such relations of privilege are acknowledged and explored, identity politics can become, as Linda Alcoff suggests, a point of departure rather than a dead end.

According to the feminist philosopher of science Sandra Harding, it is not their "experience" or "identity" per se that prevents members of dominant groups from fully understanding the experiences of others, but rather their naïveté about what she calls their "social locations" of dominance:

> All of us live in social locations that make social arrangements appear intuitive, that have been created and made to appear natural by the power of the dominant groups. It is not necessary to have any particular form of experience in order to learn how to generate less partial and distorted belief from the perspective of women's lives. It is only necessary to learn how to overcome the "spontaneous consciousness" of thought that begins in one's dominant social location. . . . [Since, for example] African Americans exist only in historically specific configurations of class, gender, sexuality and culture, then the subject or agent of African American (knowledge) must be multiple. The lives that provide the starting points for African American thought will then also provide the starting points for feminist, socialist, gay and lesbian, and other emancipatory thought. Thus it is not only African Americans who have the obligation to generate knowledge from the perspective of African American lives.[24]

In spite of a long positional and constructivist tradition in the sociology of knowledge, going back to Marx and Gramsci and embracing contemporary feminist thinkers such as Sandra Harding, Dorothy Smith, or Donna Haraway,[25] these classrooms reveal the difficulties many students face in looking at their own lives as embedded in social structures of class and race as well as gender and heterosexuality. Positional pedagogies could help them to explore those categories not as natural states, or as normal or abnormal conditions, but as different positions within a structural power dynamics, which these students could imagine challenging. As Harding puts it:

> Teachers daily face the challenge to articulate a relationship between experience and knowledge seeking which has not been preconceptualized. . . . [to energize] our students and colleagues to seek objective perspectives on their own lives as a way to produce liberatory knowledge out of their own [transformed] social situations.[26]

Authentic knowledge about each other, we suggest, is available through a comparative critique of the structural, historical, and personal aspects of one's own and others' situations and lives, an epistemology captured by the final stage of "constructed knowing" proposed by Belenky et al. in *Women's Ways of Knowing*.[27] Partly, however, such forms of consciousness depend on events outside the academy. Because there has been a conscious women's movement and a conscious movement against racism, there have also been moments of community between white women and women of color that we have observed in our classrooms. But the absence of cross-racial projects in the society at large, and the increase of racial and class differences, is mirrored in the silences about white racism and class privilege that we noticed everywhere. Grey Osterud told us that it was only after the civil unrest in Los Angeles that her class at San Jose State really started to talk about the material conditions of their lives. Even then the only way they could talk about change, she said, was in terms of communities of the past; as she noted:

> The task of building a movement must start with building community, and you have nothing to work with if you don't have that. The ones who do that work best at least belong to a community with some sense of culture and tradition.

This lack of viable political communities, with a strong sense of historical consciousness and social agendas, underlies the lack of positional theories of social change in our classrooms. Although it is not surprising that the academy alone cannot change this situation, it *is* remarkable, and energizing, to see how far and in what ways our informants have struggled with these issues, and how empowered, at times, students have felt as a result.

CHAPTER EIGHT

Looking Back, Looking Forward

*There is this element of both being somebody who does research on pedagogy
and somebody who is the subject of research on pedagogy. It's quite
bizarre. What I think is so peculiar about feminist research is the interaction which really does question the traditional set-up of research.*

—Laurie Finke, personal conversation

*I'm in the middle of my life—and I'm not talking about midlife—I'm in
the middle of it, just like you're in the middle of yours. So I'm constantly
shifting and learning.* —Mona Phillips, personal conversation

A COMMON COMPLAINT among field workers is the refusal of their
research subjects, or participants, to remain motionless before and after their
portraits are sketched.[1] However, after a talk with Laurie Finke, at the
National Women's Studies Conference in June 1990, about her work in feminist teaching and the pedagogical unconscious, it struck us that our informants' evolution as teachers was worth watching if we wanted to deepen our
understanding of the dynamics of feminist classrooms. We decided to interview all seventeen professors at the end of our study to capture their "shifting and learning" since we first observed them.

At various times during the writing of this book we felt like writers of
fiction, who often comment on the difficulty of controlling their fictional
characters as they take on a life of their own and refuse to behave in expected
ways. Ironically, it was only when we gave up "control" over these teacher
participants and invited their reactions to our written work that we were
able to expand our understanding of the construction of meaning that took
place in their classrooms. Each conversation among us built upon earlier levels of understanding, bringing to the surface deeper layers of meaning.

In our concluding interviews, we asked each of these participants to react
to what we had written about her, and to reflect on major issues in her teaching. Throughout we had the sense of looking both backward and forward:
backward as they provided yet another level of interpretation of the teaching

we observed, and forward into emerging versions of feminist pedagogy. Like us, these teacher/scholars were concerned with issues of positionality, with their personal situations within increasingly complex relational networks. They explored how to widen the grounds for sharing their authority with students, and how to encompass increasingly multiple cultural identities in the classroom. They were also thoughtful about the limitations, and possibilities, for creating classroom communities, particularly feminist communities. Indeed, after these interviews, we remain convinced of both the importance of people's positions for creating knowledge and their limitations. Barrie Thorne, the Director of Women's Studies at the University of Southern California, captured these limitations when she wrote us:

> I find poignancy and limitations in what has become a litany of social-self-categories when the categories are NOT understood as fluid, as relational, and shifting, as full of multiple meanings, as far from unitary, as only a starting point for further understanding and inquiry.[2]

LOOKING BACKWARD: A METHODOLOGY OF POSITIONALITY

In chapter 1, we expressed how we saw positionality as a central lens for exploring both feminist classrooms and our emerging methodology. As we conclude this book, we see more clearly the parallels between a *pedagogy* of positionality and a *methodology* of positionality. Interaction and exchanges with our informants have enhanced our understanding of their contexts as well as our ability to depict their construction of meaning in their classes and beyond. During this process we recognized the strength of our yearning for a master narrative, the narrative that will "get it right" once and for all. But when research becomes a collaborative relationship between "subjects" and researchers, this yearning is continually checked. These interactive processes have made us more deconstructive, more aware of our own positions, and more tolerant of our ambiguities and disagreements.

A web of relationships is the metaphor that best captures the parallels between research and pedagogy. As we look back on this work, we see this web connecting all of the professors who read and commented on various drafts of the chapters—not only with us but with each other. This interconnectedness between researchers and informants puts in question traditional research epistemologies, in which subjects basically provide data for detached investigators to manipulate. In contrast, our participants are active agents whose "shifting and learning," and their engaging narratives, have shaped the study. Several, including Laurie Finke and Bev Clarke, have engaged in their own research on pedagogy at the same time they were "subjects" of our research. Borrowing from Margaret Collins, a student at Lewis and Clark whom we quoted in chapter 3, our web of relationships has shown why the "straight line" of traditional scientific research, with its binary opposition of subject and object, does not "have a chance to survive" in a feminist methodology.

Chantal Tetreault's ethnography of a feminist classroom helped sharpen our awareness of the importance of differing social positions. Just as students became authorities to one another when they were, as she put it, "explicit about themselves as social and political actors with respect to a text or issue," defining "themselves contextually (in relation to the specific class material)," so our professor participants became authorities to us and to one another, as we all explicitly defined ourselves as engaged social and political actors in relation to a shared text.[3] This reciprocal, grounded understanding has shaped our revisions of the chapters on mastery, voice, authority, and positionality.

One of the most important things we have learned is the power of social structures of privilege to shape not only the production of classroom knowledge, as discussed in chapter 7, but also the analytical frameworks we have used. The dynamics of gender, race, class, and sexual orientation have informed all our constructions. Our awareness of "difference" with regard to ourselves and our informants has been particularly marked in our interactions with women of color.

Beginning with our first observations at Spelman, we have continuously been reminded, by explicit conversations and implicit understanding, of the complex positions of women of color observed by white women, of women of color once again the "objects" of research. Sometimes we relied too heavily on spoken, rational discourse, ignoring subtle undercurrents of meaning. In several instances, the reactions of one of our participants of color to our analysis of another woman of color helped us to perceive a situation in a clarifying new light.

For example, Chinosole cautioned us against engaging in analyses that divorce individual classrooms from the political and social context of the university. This is particularly relevant in critiquing classrooms from the perspective of positional dynamics, which at first may appear as a great improvement over the traditional approach, where one position (that of dominant males) prevails. Observing that it is not enough to mix students up and get them to talk to one another, Chinosole proposed some useful questions to guide classroom analyses: What has been the pattern of race (or gender or class) relations within the institution in a particular academic year? Have things happened in the environment that place students of color in much greater need of support than they might be in less tumultuous times? If students lay bare their experiences, especially in the charged context of racist incidents, will it be at the expense of the least privileged group? She brought the last point home by relating this experience:

> I was at UC Santa Barbara talking about women's studies and the need to put in material about women of color and issues of the disadvantaged, and a young white woman, very wealthy, came up to me and said: "Well, this means that you don't support the advantages that people like myself and my mother presently have in the system." I said, "That's right." "You want to kind of equalize things more," she said. I said, "That's right." She said, "Well, why should I support that?" I said, "Well, you know, you have a point."

As in the case of this student, or that of Mark Adams in Gloria Wade-Gayles's class at Emory, the exposure of privileged students to a critique of existing social arrangements does not necessarily make them more willing to give up some of their advantages for a more equal and just society. One way we had unconsciously enacted our own privilege as white female academics was to overstate the beneficial effects of the oasis of an "integrated" classroom on the unequal society outside.

Our dominant position as white researchers was made clear to us also through our work with Carla Trujillo, who told us recently:

> At first I felt very strongly that your interpretation and mine were different. I felt like I was being used. But after reading the second draft, I felt a lot better because you had really listened to me.

Helen Valance, one of Trujillo's students, had gained a heightened awareness of her prejudices toward women of color by taking Trujillo's course, Women in Groups. She also told us that she had wanted more discussion about voices that were "not congruent with the majority opinion or the fears that women of one racial or ethnic group have about each other." We interpreted this comment as reflecting Trujillo's "failure" to raise such issues or to connect personal disclosures to theories that might make sense of them. However, when we spoke to Trujillo about her perceptions of what happened in class, we learned that the classroom dynamics were far more complex than we had discerned. From Trujillo's perspective, even though Helen wanted to understand her racism at a deeper level, she also resisted at every turn, saying that she was on the spot when questioned. Because Trujillo worried that Helen was "so unstable and so unsure," she held back from pushing her as far as she might have.

It was not that Trujillo lacked the tools for helping Helen, or any other student, for that matter, to work on her racism; she had selected various readings, discussions, and exercises just for that purpose. Rather, she worried about protecting the other students, particularly those who were in the process of disclosing incidents of sexual abuse. If we had not received feedback from Trujillo, we might have "blamed" her for Helen's unwillingness to deal with her racism, and failed to address the complexities of Trujillo's attempts to confront messy and hidden issues.

Trujillo also reminded us of the burden faced by women of color in having their classroom authority frequently challenged by their students, most often white females and men of color. Reflecting on the class we observed, she said, "I used to ride home with Erica Huggins after that class, and I used to tell her how mad I would get sometimes at the racism that was being played out."[4] It was not until this year at Berkeley that Trujillo began to feel that her authority as a professor, who is a woman of color, a Chicana, was not being challenged.[5]

Trujillo obviously saw us as white researchers challenging her authority and competence. Such encounters expose relations of power and domination, not only because we are European American women and she is Latina, but because as researchers we were enacting some of the positions of racial and ethnic inequality that are present in academic life. If we had not shown her what we had written, these relations would have remained obscured.

While we have found that cross-cultural and cross-ethnic research is often messy and painful, we believe that our struggles to be articulate about the positions held by both teachers and researchers is a precondition for criticizing existing social arrangements. When Chinosole appeared on a panel with us at a recent national conference, she elaborated on the intersection of women's studies and cultural studies. She put what we said about her in the context of the need for "an expansive understanding of people and places with an acute awareness of positionality."[6]

Another powerful insight into the effects of privilege on methodology, as well as our tendency to view our suggestions for classroom discourse as a "cure-all," came to us from Grey Osterud, this time in relation to the issue of social class. One unanticipated result of our methodology was the burgeoning interest of some of our informants in each other. Sometimes, like Laurie Finke, they remarked on how they saw themselves in others. At other times, they criticized our analysis of other teachers as too simplistic or flawed. What commonly gave one informant the authority to discuss another were commonalities of experience, as in the comments of women of color about each other.

As someone who had worked with working-class and poorer students, Osterud was disturbed by our analysis of the discussion of social class in K Edgington's classroom:

> I had to stop reading and quit this project. For twenty-four hours, I had to walk around and think about it—it was just obsessive. You haven't analyzed what's going on there. . . . I tried to think about why this is so disconcerting.

We had criticized these students for not critically analyzing their own class positions. Osterud learned from her students at San Jose State University, who are "a lot like those at Towson, . . . that such an analysis wouldn't work because of their lack of identification with a social-class location if they're white and if they're not new immigrants." What she found useful was to help students understand which of their statements represent the dominant ideology about class mobility in American society. This enables them to "free up their [and their family's] relationship to social class, to see the contradictions in the belief that there is a class system within which individuals can change class location without it making a bit of difference to how the system works." She continued:

> Once you've developed some understanding of what an ideology is, then you can ask: What does it mean that this ideology assumes that there are class divisions and structures and inequalities that remain constant? What does it mean for people to believe that they themselves can move around in this system? Only after you've done that can you possibly go back and, with students, examine their often contradictory class locations. Only after they think about this in ideological terms can they deal with the immense amount of pain that there is around these issues in their lives.

As we discussed in chapter 7, Osterud helped us elaborate how social-class identities, as well as sexual orientations, remained unmarked categories in the classroom, and why such disclosures could be so painful for students. More generally, our participants' processes of teaching us about themselves, and therefore about ourselves, seemed to parallel the ways we saw students become authorities to one another as they sharpened their positional understandings.

LOOKING FORWARD: BROADENING INTERPRETATIVE AUTHORITY

As we spoke to our participants about their current concerns as teachers in the spring of 1993, we were struck by how many of them were increasingly conscious of issues involving "pedagogies of positionality." For example, Laurie Finke, Dorothy Berkson, and Mona Phillips were all struggling to more explicitly "position" their authority in relation to that of students, so as to increase the students' share.

While she was still teaching at Lewis and Clark, Laurie Finke started having students in her class on feminist theory keep a diary on their term projects as they researched and wrote them. Her purpose was "to focus their attention as much on the process of theorizing as on its products—the theories themselves—and to create spaces in which they might glimpse some of the unconscious processes that accompany learning."[7] In her article, "Knowledge as Bait," Finke presents the interesting case study of a self-confident senior student, who nonetheless had significant difficulties with the nonauthoritarian context of Finke's classroom, with her relinquishing of "certain forms of authority and mastery."

Much of the student's distress was centered around Finke's reluctance to reveal the kind of term paper she wanted. It reached a "peak with the evaluation of her rough draft," the time, as Finke observed, when students recognize that the teacher will judge their work. As the student's diary progressed, it become apparent that she was as resistant to being freed *from* Finke's authority as some students are in their resistance *to* authority. Finke concluded that this process-oriented mode of teaching proceeds "much like the analytic situation, . . . not progressively through time, but through resistance and 'breakthroughs, leaps, discontinuities, regressions and deferred action.'"[8]

Finke's next project is to incorporate each student's position into the classroom discourse in order to foster collaboration rather than individualism. As she told us:

I'm becoming increasingly conscious of our model of teaching where students relate individually to the teacher, but there's not any real sense of how they relate to and learn from each other.[9]

Finke continues to experiment with pedagogies that reframe relationships among students as well as between student and teacher. Her practice, which we initially observed in 1986, of beginning with students' questions has been pushed one step further at Kenyon College, where she now charges students with designing her senior seminar course in Women's Studies a semester in advance.

Another person who has given considerable thought to redefining the nature of her authority is Dorothy Berkson. Although "the journal revolt" was only a single incident in the classroom of one of the most highly regarded professors at Lewis and Clark, that experience, as well as our interpretation of it as an example of the contradictions inherent in feminist authority, spurred her to rethink these issues and see that the journals themselves were problematic.

Paradoxically, her response to this challenge has been to reshape her writing assignments to become more structured.[10] She began to use "teaching" logs, an idea that was circulating at Lewis and Clark at the time, to demystify the process of interpretation by linking the students' emotional connections to texts with their intellectual analyses.

She now instructs her students to select a passage that puzzles or engages them or triggers a strong emotional reaction. Believing that some of the best criticism starts with such reactions, she asks the students next to paraphrase the passage they've chosen, understand what it means, or, in a sense, master it. They are then asked to look at it again, to become conscious of what cannot be captured by paraphrase as well as any concerns or questions that escaped them before. They finally place the passage in the context of the entire text, using the following questions: "Where does it happen? Are there other passages that relate to it, that contradict it? that confirm it? that raise more questions about it?" Concluding with a summary of where this procedure has taken them, they turn in these "logs" at the end of each class. Returned to the students with Berkson's comments, the logs then become the basis for the students' formal paper.

Berkson believes that this process forces students to reengage with the text over and over again, to engage in continuous reinterpretation of the text rather than to think they have arrived at some final mastery. She went on to say:

I have been struggling with how to give them the methodology so that they have power over the text. I used to do that just as a demonstration in class and then expect them to be able to do it on paper; the process gives them a methodology for writing a paper. They are discovering the meaning of the text as they write. They don't need to ask, "Well, what exactly is it that you want?" I've tried to demystify the process.

Berkson has observed that discussions are now more focused and students' responses much deeper. Feeling in charge of the tools of literary interpretation, they more readily offer to read their logs, either to initiate or facilitate the course of discussion. Through this process they learn not only that there is no single interpretation of a literary work, but also that there are constraints on the meaning of a text: you cannot just impose any interpretation upon it.

Berkson has noticed other effects as well. Dyslexic students gain a way to control their writing, a formula to follow so that they don't feel at sea about what to do. Successful English majors become more aware of the process of interpretation. She also has seen an enormous effect on gay and lesbian students, who are noticeably freer to speak about their positions as members of sexual minorities. Berkson has also observed that this process breaks down the differences between the ways male and female students write; as she remarked:

> The male students no longer get to create closed systems of interpretation that say this is THE interpretation of the text. This particular format doesn't allow them to do that. It keeps the process open-ended, and I think that is what particularly empowers the female students.

This new method has freed Berkson to voice her own opinions more vigorously, by saying, for example, "I read this differently. And this is how I got there. Did anyone else read it differently?" She said: "I think that as I figure out better ways to help them get their authority clearer, I have been more comfortable with my own." That comfort is tied to making the distinction clearer between her authority as a reader in the class and her authority as a teacher. Although she is a more experienced reader who models various interpretations, as a reader she is equal to her students in authority. Her authority as a teacher is exercised in her requirement that students follow the format she has devised, which is graded in their formal papers.

Thus the paradox in Berkson's pedagogy: by becoming more prescriptive, she has given the students more freedom—a better grounding in the text that enables them to "take the authority they need." Their greater confidence, in turn, allows her to express her own views with more conviction. As with Finke, explicit recognition of the different positions of teacher and students allowed for a conscious renegotiation of their relationship in the classroom in order to broaden the range and depth of literary interpretations.

Mona Phillips at Spelman has also sought recently to make her position as an authority explicit to her students, so that they can take more responsibility for their learning. She assigns her classes books by Paulo Freire (such as *The Pedagogy of the Oppressed*) and by bell hooks on critical and feminist pedagogies. She told us in an interview in April 1993:

> And what we do then is talk about the student-teacher relationship. . . . We look at those pieces side by side and we say what kind of relationship we are going to have in this class. . . . They then feel freer to make changes. They said [about one book] why don't we move this around and do this and that, and I said, fine. It also gave me room enough to be honest about my own inconsistencies. While I changed my reading list I am still firm on deadlines.

By "always talking about teaching and learning as you're teaching and learning," she makes students conscious about their roles in creating knowledge. This cultivation of their "third eye" is necessary since their "folk have . . . historically constructed knowledge in a different way." She especially wants those students aspiring to graduate school to enter that phase of their education conscious that what they will be hearing is only "one possibility out of an array of possibilities."

LOOKING FORWARD: CONFRONTING MULTIPLE IDENTITIES

Another important issue for some of our informants stems from their increasing awareness of the multiple identities present in their classrooms. Patricia MacCorquodale, Mona Phillips, Beverly Clark, and Bianca Cody Murphy told us of recent resistances and breakthroughs related to the power relations implicit in these identities. The hidden and shifting dynamics of power in each context reminds us of Laurie Finke's point that "what is significant about teaching (may not always be) available for conscious and rational analysis."

At the time we observed Pat MacCorquodale's class in 1987, "feminism" was a word that was avoided by the women's community at the University of Arizona. Since then, she has become much more explicit about her identity and perspectives as a feminist. In a recent interview she told us: "I decided I might as well label myself that way because students are going to figure it out in the end, anyway. But what I've found in teaching regular sociology courses is that when you identify yourself as a feminist in a class like that, then you become a lightning rod."

MacCorquodale reflected on the consequences of this openness in an essay, "Political Correctness as a Resistance to Diversity," in which she analyzed the course evaluations in her Introduction to Sociology courses, which typically enroll five hundred students.[11] Several factors pushed her to do this analysis. One was an incident following a short video presentation on the relationship between population growth, land distribution, and hunger, using the conflict in El Salvador as an example. MacCorquodale found a note on the projector saying, "Why should we care if people are hungry in Central America? Just tell me what will be on the exam." Another was her general sense that the level of student resistance to discussions of sexism, racism, and First World hegemony has escalated, and that this resistance has become increasingly emotional since conservatives promulgated the idea of "political correctness." As she observed, "The ultimate irony is that those who bring charges of political correctness act as if the systematic exclusion of women and minorities from the academy is not political."

From the course evaluations MacCorquodale found that even though only 12 percent of the students complained about bias in the course, their written comments expressed deeply held beliefs in the objectivity of mainstream knowledge, and a presumption that paying attention to gender, race, and ethnicity deviated from the fundamental purpose of this course in sociology. Such resistance took the form of seeing MacCorquodale as a "griping," "offensive," and man-hating feminist.

She decided that before students could understand issues of difference, teachers must pay attention to the unconscious and emotional factors in learning, such as students' projections of their own values, positions, and rights upon the world. MacCorquodale believes that students have to see their opinions and positions as partial perspectives, develop a wariness of simple categories, and become aware that knowledge is socially constructed and contextual. However, an environment in which there are five hundred students in a class is the antithesis of one that nurtures student critiques of sociological knowledge or of their developing perspectives as learners. To

MacCorquodale, what was needed is "a small-group setting characterized by intense discussion and introspective analysis." In concluding her essay, she remarked on the irony "that this small-group context is urgently needed at the same time that budget pressures and enrollment patterns are creating demands for larger and larger classes."

The smaller group context at liberal arts colleges such as Wheaton is indeed a more conducive climate for dealing with such issues. Beverly Clark has been preoccupied in the years since we observed her with the problem of how a white professor and a group of white students can tackle the topic of race in America. The issue of confronting multiple group identities means a struggle to help her students "appreciate people who are non-white, and/or non-male and/or non–upper class, or move them in a new place from where they are." She went on:

> I want them to think of other possibilities in life than what they start with. . . . There are some things I think they kind of get, but they don't live their whiteness; I don't live my whiteness. I'm working hard to see how to do that.

She has noticed that while students are not reluctant to raise questions about race in a small-group setting, they often remain silent in the larger group. Clark spoke about these patterns of resistance and breakthrough in ways reminiscent of Toni Morrison's description of a society engaged in all kinds of intellectual feats to erase race from a world seething with its presence.[12] As "whiteness" is a basic and unconscious component of American ideology, according to Morrison, Clark's students have difficulty conceptualizing whiteness, seeing their own identities in positional terms in reaction to people of color, and learning to distinguish, in Beverly Tatum's terminology, between being white and being racist.[13]

Clark has found that it helps European American students to talk explicitly about their own racial position if she gives them a great deal of exposure to African-American perspectives. Another approach is to make them conscious of how one group's experiences—that of Black women, for instance—has been represented by authors ignorant about the feelings and experiences of Black women, as in the case of Harriet Beecher Stowe:

> [She] completely ignores the position of Black women, implies that the best place to be is in the home, the house, the kitchen . . . and assumes that slaves want to be house slaves. . . . yet one of the reasons

a woman slave might want to be a field slave is that the opportunities for rape were simply less available. You wouldn't necessarily have to worry about where certain white males were in the house all the time. Stowe was oblivious to this aspect of a slave woman's life.

Clark also tries to increase her students' consciousness of their own positions by helping them grasp the social positions of the authors they are reading, as well as their own:

I want to get to questions like considering Frederick Douglass or Stowe, Who has the most impact and who is the most credible? There was a fair amount of gendering in the responses to Stowe. I asked, Who got caught up in the story of *Uncle Tom's Cabin?* Now, not all the women raised their hands, but everyone who did was a woman. And so we talked a little bit about it, you know, What does it mean if it has no impact on the males? The men were the ones who had been raising questions about it: "Is she overdoing it sometimes?"

Marking readings in this way as "gendered" and "raced" is a way of broadening interpretive authority. Clark's questions show how a teacher may reveal, or conceal, aspects of student identities by the teacher's approach to the text. It is not so much a question of denying or affirming identities, but of understanding how they are constructed in different settings.

As another illustration of how context shapes the exploration of multiple identities, Mona Phillips has been expanding the arena of discourse by putting Black women's experiences at the center and in a global context. Her aim is to help students "see similarities in oppressive structures across class and race and ethnicity . . . [and see] racial dominance [and] the way that capitalism functions in terms of the eternal search for markets." She went on:

Other people have said this . . . as Black women get older, we become much more clear about the different levels of oppression. And everything conspires against us really thinking in a systematic way about gender until we get older. . . . It's [also] the first time I've felt comfortable doing a little bit of cross-cultural stuff.

Phillips has worked to make her students more aware of their multiple identities by explicitly placing them in relation to others—white women, as seen through Naomi Wolf's *The Beauty Myth* ("in very clear ways it's really written about white women, but to see how some of her larger issues affect us all"), and other Black women in America and Africa. To discuss a novel from Senegal, she brought in a colleague from Gambia, who could talk "about Islam and women and Africa in a way that I wouldn't have access to." She took her students on a field trip to New Orleans and the Mississippi Delta to observe the legacies of African culture that still thrive in the area. While students came away depressed by the stark poverty of the inhabitants, "when you see a lot of the African that's still there," she noted, "it's also invigorating."

Bianca Cody Murphy's struggle has been with the fashioning of identities as tied to issues of public avowal and expression. Themes of silence and voice wound their way through much of her interview, conducted in March 1993, about facing issues of lesbianism and sexuality in the classroom. The public debate about gays in the military, the evasiveness of the policy of "don't ask, don't tell," seemed to mirror the critical issues in Murphy's class, namely, the costs and benefits of self-disclosure, on the one hand, and silence, on the other.

Murphy was firmer than ever on the need, albeit the pain, of publicly affirming her lesbianism:

> I can't just say, oh, my lover and I, we, because people could say, Oh, she told us but did she really want us to know? So now I say quite clearly I'm a lesbian. I'm not saying my partner, meaning my work partner, I want to make sure you got it, I'm a lesbian.

Why? Partly she put it in terms of the proposed military policy. "I was aghast. You're in the military and they don't want you to talk about it, how can you not talk about it?!" Finally she asserted, "I wish it wasn't important to society but as long as lesbians and gay men are oppressed, I have to say that I'm a lesbian."

As we have seen, Murphy's (and Carla Trujillo's) honesty about her own sexuality partly gives her the authority to speak for others. Paradoxically, as she explains, her disclosures create a climate that can embrace a range of differences, so that student experiences can be validated or remain concealed; in a sense, she articulates the unspoken identities of the diverse, sometimes oppressed, groups in her classroom:

> I have to voice a lot of difference for them. It's not appropriate for them to say "I'm an incest victim." I have to assume the diversity of

my audience . . . that their experiences are validated without them having to be spoken. I assume that they are people who have been victims of incest, who have been raped, that they are people who have a lot of sexual activity and no sexual activity, that they are gay men and lesbian women and people who are bisexual and that all of that is okay. I'm not asking them to talk about it, but I have to say it all out loud, which is also why I had to come out.

Murphy's candid approach, which affirms and protects her students, showed us the mistake of assuming automatic "healing" effects from students' personal disclosures. Our innocence about the role of the unconscious and our belief that everything, even the pain of oppression, is available for "airing" through conscious and rational analysis was once again challenged. Murphy pointed out that enabling students to fashion a voice does not necessarily mean that they will or should talk at that particular moment in the class, but that they may be able to identify themselves in a more appropriate context. That her disclosures validated both student experiences and their concealments reminded us again of the powerful effect of the teacher's authority in relation to the multiple identities in her classroom.

As it turned out, the class we observed in the spring of 1991 was Angela Davis's last one at San Francisco State, because that fall she took a position at the University of California, Santa Cruz. As she looks back, she sees how the Wild Women in Music and Literature course informed her teaching at Santa Cruz: she continues the practice of using nontheoretical texts by women of color to discover theoretical points of departure for the construction of feminist theory. She told us in a recent interview:

The basic question that my students and I confront is how to bring together issues of race, class, gender, and sexuality without necessarily privileging one over the other. The issues are how you handle these tensions, and how you develop a language and a vocabulary that allow you to address them.

The diversity of Davis's students—they are primarily graduate students and women of color—leads her to look at interrelationships among various groups of people of color, going beyond the traditional construction of race relations as Black and white. She and her students are working to talk about the experiences, theories, and cultural productions of women of color in relation to one another rather than always in relation to the dominant white cul-

242

ture. "I'm quite interested in how this identity has come into being in a relatively short period of time," Davis said, "and in ways that Black women are often perceived as the exemplary women of color." For instance, Davis noted that women-of-color feminists are frequently expected to know the literature that Black feminists have produced while there is no similar mandate for African-American feminists to familiarize themselves with the "really exciting work that's being done by Asian-American or Latina feminists."

Her more recent teaching leads Davis to remark that she would conceptualize "Wild Women" differently today. Rather than placing the history and cultural productions of African-American women at the center, she would develop a more complex model, "one which thinks about Black women in relation to the political constructions of women of color."

LOOKING FORWARD:
FEMINIST COMMUNITIES AND
THE PROCESSION OF EDUCATED MEN

Beverly Guy-Sheftall of Spelman College was one of the plenary-session speakers at a national conference in April 1993 on curriculum integration, at which we met informants from four of the six institutions we visited. She spoke of the hurdles to achieving a feminist transformation of the academy:

> The ability to understand—and celebrate—the differences between us will be among our greatest challenges in the twenty-first century. But can overwhelmingly white universities truly embrace multiculturalism so that it exists someplace other than in mission statements and college catalogs? We're talking about transforming the entire university and a stubborn, ingrained power structure.[14]

Alongside our seventeen professors' feminist work in their classrooms is the "stubborn and ingrained power structure" of the university system. As we have looked back through our informants' eyes at developments within their universities, we found that institutional issues were also bound up with questions of positionality. What will be the next direction of these colleges (or, in the larger universities, the women's studies programs), given steadily diminishing resources? What are the prospects for the growth and enhancement of feminist communities within the academy?

As with individual professors' awareness of positional issues, we have found a relationship between the extent to which an institution has specified its identity and mission and the continuing success of feminist projects there. The institution we see most strongly using its societal niche to guide its curriculum is Spelman, which, because of its status as an historically African-American college, is never allowed to forget its position within "the dark enclosure" of race and gender in the United States. When we spoke to Beverly Guy-Sheftall at the April 1993 conference, she emphasized how every community of learning can provide only a partial perspective on the world. She and other Spelman colleagues have therefore begun to argue the need for oppressed racial groups to take up their own histories both nationally and worldwide in order to develop the knowledge they need.

The project that has been particularly "compelling to the faculty" in this context is the development of a required sophomore General Studies course based on the African Diaspora, which Mona Phillips planned to teach in the fall of 1993. Beginning with the diaspora, they "fan out into the global" to consider relationships among structures of capitalism, international ties of religion and culture, and the intersection of race and gender issues, while also focusing on the positions of their own students within these frameworks. This interdisciplinary course has also moved beyond traditional classroom learning to include the trip to New Orleans and the Delta that Phillips and her students joined. The culminating event for the 1993 course was a jazz concert in the Sisters' Chapel that included lectures and discussions of the movement of African music through the Caribbean and Latin American countries.

Because Wheaton College became coeducational in 1988, nearly twenty years later than some of its "sister" campuses, it benefited from the knowledge that at other colleges this change had led to the repression of women students in the classroom and in the community culture. At Wheaton, the administration and much of the faculty forged a new commitment to make the college "differently coeducational," seeking to encourage both "female" and "male" strengths and interests and to create a truly egalitarian community both inside and outside the classroom. This challenge has led to a diminished interest in the content issues of "balancing the curriculum," and more institutional and individual attention to pedagogical issues, specifically concern that male students not dominate class discussions.

Feminist goals continue to enjoy a supportive atmosphere. The Women's Studies program thrives amid enthusiastic student interest, with growing numbers of majors and over ninety students enrolled in the most recent introductory course. However, the college has not achieved genuine racial and ethnic diversity, a structural flaw making the efforts of teachers like Beverly Clark to confront issues of "whiteness" doubly difficult.

Clark's frustrations in this regard reminded us of the only real effort at structural change made by any of our informants, namely, Grey Osterud at Lewis and Clark. Osterud's experiences showed her that gender integration had to move beyond the terms of the white culture. Although her students might begin to grasp these issues, they would then move on to other courses and nothing would change. She told us a story of a mixed racial/ethnic group of students returning from Kenya (all were enrolled in Osterud's Colonial American History course) who wondered why they had to go to Africa to experience a world where Blacks were in charge of themselves. The group wanted to deal with racial inequality in a college where African-Americans would be the cultural majority. Osterud worked with these students to develop an exchange with Spelman and Morehouse colleges, in which students from Lewis and Clark would spend a quarter in Atlanta, and Spelman and Morehouse students would spend the next in Portland. The proposal was never administratively reviewed because of an institutional crisis of authority at Lewis and Clark at the time, even though Osterud and the students presented it at an "Ideas Exchange." Resistance by some students to this proposed change was described in an interview with Ned Sharp as "a mean-spirited attack on some cultural exchange that Grey was fronting for the minority students."[15]

The failure of Lewis and Clark as an institution to give a more multicultural and internationalist context to issues of gender may also have had something to do with the increasing marginalization of the Gender Studies program. Dorothy Berkson, the only one of our three informants who remains there today, increasingly finds contradictions between the feminist pedagogy of her classroom and the drift of the larger institution's culture and values. As she sees it, there has been a muting of enthusiasm for the feminist ways of teaching and learning that predominated in the years following the Women's Studies seminar in the summer of 1983. As she told Tetreault, the loss of feminist professors like "you and Grey and Laurie," as well as the conservative backlash of the eighties, had allowed "certain individuals to become more vocal, and to feel it's OK to oppose feminism and gender studies. Some of them have a lot of power right now":

I feel as if every time I turn a corner, there's a barrier—an institutional barrier. There are no incentives, there are no rewards. There is no excitement coming from the people in power about gender issues and feminist pedagogy any more. [On the other hand,] there is, from the students, an enormous enthusiasm and excitement.

Furthermore, the women's community at Lewis and Clark has persisted, in the form of a continuing faculty study group that meets regularly and "has co-opted the technology the institution gives us" by communicating through E-mail. "So between E-mail and the research group, we do have a feminist community. But it doesn't have the kind of institutional support it did have. We are not in the center as we were for a while." Berkson went on:

> I don't think there has been a backlash against us individually, no. But it's disturbing because we could be doing much more. We were in a position five or six years ago to do something dramatically wonderful. And, basically, the position we're in now is trying to maintain what we have and not lose it.

The issues involving participants at the larger universities had not changed since we visited. For example, Sara Coulter and Elaine Hedges, the directors of the Towson project, initiated an outreach project to ten local community colleges and have recently obtained funding from the Ford Foundation to establish a national dissemination center on curriculum integration. At the University of Arizona, feminist faculty members associated with SIROW have continued to gain funding for feminist projects that further their land-grant populist philosophy by collaborating with other faculty members from institutions of higher education in the West. Their emphasis continues to be on course content—internationalizing the Women's Studies curriculum and infusing international perspectives into the curriculum—due in part to the interests of funding agencies.[16] However, informal seminars on pedagogy continue to reflect the persistent concern of feminists that "women faculty have less legitimate authority . . . especially with male students and male colleagues." They have sponsored discussions between themselves and personnel from Student Affairs and the Counseling Center about female students' problems with low self-esteem and sexual violence. In addition, the group discussed teaching politically controversial topics to recalcitrant students, a need that echoes MacCorquodale's experiences. For Karen Anderson, the current director of Women's Studies, the most important effect of these seminars was to let faculty know that they were not alone in confronting these issues in their classrooms. Although Women's Studies faculty at Arizona assume that knowledge of content is separate from and more important than process issues, they increasingly see the importance of pedagogy.

Recent cutbacks in higher education in California are endangering the special contribution that Women Studies at San Francisco State has the potential to make, as women of color are in a position to build a department that nourishes the personal, political, and academic potential of working-class students, many of whom are women of color. However, despite a recent highly positive accreditation report on the program, every faculty member's involvement in women's community issues, and innovative courses like the one taught recently by Chinosole, Women in Cross-Cultural Organizing, the department, like others at San Francisco State, has endured cutbacks that seriously erode all of its gains.* "Such a place," said Chinosole, "is situated to be the most negatively impacted by budget cuts because of the nature of the student body. California is increasingly reluctant to fund state education, which is the only place people of color, the newly arrived, and the poor can expect to get educated. Pedagogy, economics, and politics all go together."

We have also noticed another troubling trend: Angela Davis left San Francisco State for a position at the University of California at Santa Cruz; Carla Trujillo now teaches part-time at Berkeley; and during the past two years, Chinosole has divided her time between teaching at San Francisco State University and Dartmouth, where she is a visiting professor in African and African-American Studies. Commenting on the demands of the administrative side of academic feminist work, she said in a recent published interview "that one thing you have to do in academia is always be ready to become destitute again."[17] When the interviewer exclaimed, "I don't want to hear that," she went on:

> Even though I received tenure, I know that I have to be ready to walk away from it if it's necessary, if it means being involved in a racist project. And walk to where . . . I would be in a position to do a lot more research, because I think that's my natural inclination anyway, and not so much administrative work, which can just be a form of being Aunt Jemima.

We detect a pattern in the more elite universities, who now seek to diversify their faculties, raiding the less elite institutions who pioneered these multicultural fields.

Perhaps it is Chinosole's cross-institutional perspective, or perhaps it is just her approach to the world, but once again she has exemplified to us the

---

*The Ethnic Studies Department at San Francisco State challenged the location of Wild Women in Music and Literature in the Women Studies Department, claiming that it was their curricular purview. The Curriculum Committee decided in favor of Ethnic Studies, and so the course is no longer taught.

need for freedom to resist institutional ties. Indeed, another angle with which to examine the importance of institutional cultures is to look at the experiences of those of our professor informants who have left the institutions in which we first met them. These moves have allowed them to look forward and back from the perspectives they gained in new contexts for teaching and learning. For example, Leslie Flemming's interest in teaching has grown since she became Dean of Arts and Humanities at the University of Maine, where more attention is paid to teaching than at Arizona. She told us that "since becoming Dean in an institution where teaching has always been more important than research, I have a much greater respect for the work that the faculty is putting into teaching than when I was doing it myself." Conversely, Laurie Finke found she missed Lewis and Clark for its emphasis on student-generated learning.

The influence of institutional epistemologies, or views of what constitutes good teaching and successful learning, was driven home clearly in our interview with Margaret Blanchard, who left Towson partly because of her frustration at her marginalization there. She took a position in the master's degree program at Vermont College, a nonresidential external-degree program that serves returning adult students. Students' programs of study develop from their own experiences and are determined by their own questions. The pedagogy of her new institution—students work primarily on their own, meeting with their professors and each other at regular intervals—is in harmony with the trajectory of Blanchard's own development; and she no longer feels the need to "provide answers to questions the students never thought of asking." Commenting on her current role, which is to help students with their own thinking processes and to facilitate networking among them, she noted: "I need to enter into their world to see what their questions are. When I see that they are not going deep enough, then I need to help them go deeper. It is important to ask them why they care about something."

Although Blanchard has found the change from Towson's traditional atmosphere liberating, she acknowledges that one limitation of this student-centered epistemology has been its lack of ongoing communal discourse. Even though students come together for monthly seminars, there is less of a sense of community among the professors and students than Blanchard had found at Towson, which provided a community of discourse more accessible at traditional universities.

Like Margaret Blanchard, Grey Osterud left her institution in search of a community more congenial to her commitments as a feminist educator. Her

Lewis and Clark experience showed her that what she needed was a "much more racially and ethnically diverse student body and a different social-class composition, where I could take for granted some awareness that race and ethnicity were problematic." After leaving Lewis and Clark, she took a position at San Jose State in the California State University system. Osterud found the diverse student body she was looking for; there is no one ethnic or racial majority at San Jose.[18]

San Jose State is like many other institutions in California, whose richly diverse multiethnic population feeds the illusion of a multicultural paradise in which groups can overcome their own ethnocentrism and achieve a level of harmonious pluralism. In spite of its pluralism, students and faculty members at San Jose State pay little attention to the power relations of gender, ethnicity, and sexuality. In Osterud's classroom, she found that students subscribed to the notion that everyone is an individual, and consistently avoided talking about the social contexts in which they lived their lives. The students of color were socialized to believe that class mobility can solve the problems of racial inequality.

The costs of suppressing the circumstances of their lives and masking racial and ethnic tensions were dramatically exposed in the civil unrest that followed the initial verdict in the Rodney King trial. There was a race riot on campus and beyond, with the accompanying marks of civil turmoil—floodlights, sharpshooters on the dorm roofs, and helicopters overhead—and a considerable amount of property damage and student injuries as a result. When classes resumed, students' accounts of the riots triggered extended discussions about their experiences with race and inequality. Students realized how precarious the civility was among different groups and how easily it was disrupted.

For the first time, Osterud found students wanting to go beyond the confines of their own groups to think about interrelated racial and ethnic issues. She saw a dramatic example of this kind of recognition when a white female told how she had been forced to flee a dormitory. She said, "I never thought I'd be beaten up because of my race." A woman from East Palo Alto, a segregated Black community, walked across the room to hug her and said, "I understand exactly how you feel." Osterud concluded:

> Finally people saw [issues of] inequality. Before there had been a lot of talk about immigrant parents, and negotiating cultural differences and group identities. That stuff . . . basically disappeared and they wanted to know about inequality, about group organization to redress

it, about political movements and how anybody had dealt with these
issues.

It is only within communities that have some sense of their position in
history, as well as a common culture, Osterud concluded, that oppositional
ideologies and coalitions can be constructed. Ironically, the longer immi-
grant ethnic communities are in California and achieve a position in the stable working class, the more these communities are eroded. People lose their
sense of group identification and common interests, prerequisites to constructing a political movement. She observed a strong sense of individualism, of isolation, of anomie. Osterud has not figured out a pedagogy that can
overcome these deep personal and structural problems; her only hope is to
teach students about positional politics that could bring different groups of
the dispossessed together.[19]

As Osterud, Blanchard, and other participants continue to search for
institutional contexts congenial to the feminist educational communities
they envision, their recent experiences have much to say about the larger
political and social contexts of the academy. The continuation of feminist
gains in institutions of higher education is not by any means guaranteed.
Feminist projects require a mix of intellectual ferment, administrative support, and a critical mass of faculty members working together for a long
period of time.

Looking back on these classrooms and institutions, moreover, it is apparent to us that even further reconceptualizations of the educational needs of
our student bodies are needed. Understanding pedagogy as the comprehensive process of constructing classroom knowledge, we envision less individualistic and more communal models of learning, bringing together different
groups of people within classrooms and beyond. Such models need to be
built on the exploration and acceptance of people's commonalities and differences within an increasingly complex and fragmented social order.

These professor participants have bravely "fanned out" in different direc-
tions to explore a wide range of social issues previously repressed in academic
discourse, including racism, class inequality, homophobia, and sexual abuse.
While their efforts have shown the centrality of the teacher's role in uncovering these "voices from the bywaters," these "unspeakable things unspoken,"
they have also revealed the limitations of single classroom settings in tran-
scending the dominant epistemologies of the larger institutions.

The absence of community noted by Grey Osterud is endemic to American culture. Thus the difficulty, and the necessity, of consciously building

discourse communities like the one envisioned by Guy-Sheftall at Spelman, or the "different form of coeducation" at Wheaton. Proponents of such projects understand that an awareness of positionality, difference, and the possibility of making connections across forms of difference once they are acknowledged is central to the construction of knowledge. Such settings, and beyond, are places to look for a resurgence of feminist activism.

Our most recent conversations with our participants had a finality to them, a sense of saying good-bye. Yet, as we look backward and forward, we see that we have created a collectivity of feminist teachers. We understand now, more than ever, the need for collective work on pedagogy because we are all facing similar challenges. We have no choice but to continue this collective work since, as Dorothy Berkson told us more than six years ago, "unless this generation or the next has some sense of being empowered, of asking different kinds of questions and thinking in different ways, there will be no future."

NOTES

Chapter 1. Breaking Through Illusion

1. We first encountered the quotation from Adrienne Rich in a paper by Renato Rosaldo entitled "Symbolic Violence: A Battle Raging in Academe," American Anthropological Association Annual Meeting, Phoenix, Arizona, 1988. The journal entry by Nancy Ichimura, quoting Emily Dickinson's poetry, was read in a class at Lewis and Clark College, October 1986.

2. Oscar F. Porter, *Undergraduate Completion and Persistence at Four-year Colleges and Universities* (Washington, D.C.: National Institute of Independent Colleges and Universities, 1989).

3. Yolanda T. Moses, "The Challenge of Diversity, Anthropological Perspectives on University Culture," *Education and Urban Society* 22 (4 [1990]): 403.

4. Ibid., pp. 403–4. See also Vincent Tinto, *Leaving College: Rethinking the Causes and Curses of Student Attrition* (Chicago: University of Chicago Press, 1987).

5. Roberta Hall, and Bernice Sandler, *The Classroom Climate: A Chilly One for Women?* Project on the Status and Education of Women (Washington, D.C.: Association of American Colleges, 1982).

6. See, among other works: Catherine Krupnick, "Women and Men in the Classroom, Inequality and Its Remedies," *On Teaching and Learning,* Journal of the Derek Bok Center for Teaching and Learning, Harvard University (May 1985): 18–25; and Cheris Kramarae and Paula Treichler, "Power Relationships in the Classroom," in *Gender in the Classroom: Power and Pedagogy,* ed. Susan Gabriel and Isaiah Smithson (Urbana and Chicago: University of Illinois Press, 1990), pp. 41–59.

7. Carol Gilligan, *In a Different Voice: Psychological Theory and Women's Development* (Cambridge, Mass.: Harvard University Press, 1982); Jean Baker Miller, *Towards a New Psychology of Women* (Boston: Beacon Press, 1976).

8. Mary Belenky, Blythe Clinchy, Nancy Goldberger, and Jill Mattuck Tarule, *Women's Ways of Knowing: The Development of Self, Voice, and Mind* (New York: Basic Books, 1986). See also William Perry, *Forms of Intellectual and Ethical Development in the College Years* (New York: Holt, Rinehart and Winston, 1970).

9. Deborah Tannen, "Teachers' Classroom Strategies Should Recognize That Men and Women Use Language Differently," *Chronicle of Higher Education,* June 19,

1991, p. B2. Tannen is the author of the widely known *You Just Don't Under-stand: Women and Men in Conversation* (New York: Morrow, 1990).

10. Jane Roland Martin, "Becoming Educated: A Journey of Alienation or Integra-tion?" *Journal of Education* 167 (3 [1985]): 871–84; Richard Rodriguez, *Hunger of Memory* (Boston: Godine, 1982).

11. See, among many other examples: Gilligan, *In a Different Voice;* Sandra Gilbert and Susan Gubar, *The Madwoman in the Attic* (New Haven, Conn.: Yale Univer-sity Press, 1979); Gerda Lerner, "Placing Women in History: A 1975 Perspec-tive," in *Liberating Women's History: Theoretical and Critical Essays,* ed. Bernice Carroll (Urbana and Chicago: University of Illinois Press, 1976), pp. 357–67; Jane Roland Martin, *Reclaiming a Conversation: The Ideal of the Educated Woman* (New Haven, Conn.: Yale University Press, 1985); Elizabeth Kamarck Min-nich, Jean O'Barr, and Rachel Rosenfeld, eds., *Reconstructing the Academy, Women's Education and Women's Studies* (Chicago: University of Chicago Press, 1988); Marilyn Schuster and Susan Van Dyne, "Placing Women in the Liberal Arts: Stages of Curriculum Transformation," *Harvard Educational Review* 54 (4 [1984]): 413–28; Mary Kay Tetreault, "Feminist Phase Theory: An Experience-Derived Evaluation Model," *Journal of Higher Education* 56 (4 [1985]): 363–84; and Marcia Westkott, "Feminist Criticism of the Social Sciences," *Harvard Edu-cational Review* 49 (4 [1979]): 422–30.

12. Allan Bloom, *The Closing of the American Mind* (New York: Touchstone Books, 1988); E. D. Hirsch, Jr., *Cultural Literacy: What Every American Needs to Know* (Boston: Houghton Mifflin, 1987); Dinesh D'Souza, *Illiberal Education: The Pol-itics of Race and Sex on Campus* (New York: Free Press, 1991).

13. John Searles, "The Storm over the University," *New York Review of Books,* December 6, 1990, pp. 36–42.

14. Renato Rosaldo, "Others of Invention: Ethnicity and Its Discontents," [Village] *Voice Literary Supplement* (82 [February 1990]): 29.

15. Gary Wills, "Man of the Year," *New York Review of Books,* November 21, 1991, p. 18.

16. Yolanda Moses, *Black Women in Academe: Issues and Strategies* (Washington, D.C.: Association of American Colleges, 1989), p. 14.

17. Although there has been much discussion of the state of the American universi-ty in recent years, there is relatively little research on the college classroom itself. See Ernest L. Boyer, *College: The Undergraduate Experience in America* (New York: Harper & Row, 1988); K. Patricia Cross, *Accent on Teaching* (San Francis-co: Jossey-Bass, 1976); Kenneth E. Ebel, *The Aims of College Teaching* (San Fran-cisco: Jossey-Bass, 1984); Carolyn L. Ellner and Carol P. Barnes, *Studies of Col-lege Teaching* (Lexington, Mass.: Lexington Books, 1983); Joseph Katz and Mildred Henry, *Turning Professors into Teachers* (New York: American Council on Education and Macmillan, 1988). Even academic novels devote little atten-tion to teaching. With the exception of May Sarton's *A Small Room* (New York: Norton, 1976), there are no extended portraits of classroom life in the work of authors who humorously and poignantly present academics' doubts about the meaning of the scholarly life; spout passion for departmental politics, faculty

governance, academic freedom, and conflicts with administrators; and describe struggles with sexual desire. See, for example, Kingsley Amis, *Lucky Jim* (New York: Viking Penguin, 1976); Gerald Warner Brace, *The Department* (Chicago: University of Chicago Press, 1968); Amanda Cross, *Death in a Tenured Position* (New York: Ballantine, 1986); John Galbraith, *A Tenured Professor* (Boston: Houghton Mifflin, 1990); David Lodge, *Changing Places* (New York: Viking Penguin 1979), Nice Work (New York: Viking Penguin, 1990), *Small World* (New York: Warner 1989); Mary McCarthy, *The Groves of Academe* (New York: Harcourt Brace 1952).

18. For accounts and analyses of the gendered nature of teaching, both historically and in the present, see: Sara Freedman, Jane Jackson, and Katherine Bowles, "The Other End of the Corridor: The Effects of Teaching on Teachers," *Radical Teacher* 23 (1984): 2–23; Madeline Grumet, "Pedagogy for Patriarchy: The Feminization of Teaching, *Interchange on Educational Policy* 12 (2–3 [1981]): 165–84; Nancy Hoffman, *Women's "True" Profession: Voices from the History of Teaching* (New York: Feminist Press and McGraw-Hill, 1981); Susan Laird, "Reforming 'Women's True Profession': A Case for 'Feminist Pedagogy' in Teacher Education?" *Harvard Educational Review* 58 (4 [1988]): 449–63; and Kathleen Weiler, *Women Teaching for Change: Gender, Class and Power* (South Hadley, Mass.: Bergin and Garvey, 1988).

19. Belenky et al., *Women's Ways of Knowing,* p. 198.

20. See Mary Kay Tetreault, *Women in America: Half of History* (Boston: Houghton Mifflin, 1979). See also Miller, *Towards a New Psychology of Women;* Gerda Lerner, *The Majority Finds Its Past: Placing Women in History* (New York: Oxford University Press, 1979); Nancy Cott, *The Bonds of Womanhood: "Women's Sphere" in New England, 1780–1835* (New Haven, Conn.: Yale University Press, 1977).

21. We both received doctorates in Education at Boston University, Tetreault in 1979 and Maher in 1980. Tetreault began teaching in 1980 at Lewis and Clark College in Portland, Oregon, and Maher started work at Wheaton College in Norton, Massachusetts, in 1981. For our work see Frances Maher and Kathleen Dunn, "The Practice of Feminist Teaching: A Case Study of the Interaction Among Curriculum, Pedagogy, and Female Cognitive Development," working paper, Wellesley College Center for Research on Women, 1984; Frances Maher, "Pedagogies for the Gender-Balanced Classroom," *Journal of Thought* 20 (3 [1985]): 48–64; Frances Maher, "Toward a Richer Theory of Feminist Pedagogy," *Journal of Education* 169 (3 [1987]): 91–99; Mary Kay Tetreault, "Phases of Thinking About Women in History: A Report Card on the Textbooks," *Women's Studies Quarterly* 13 (3 and 4 [1985]): 35–47; Mary Kay Tetreault, "Integrating Women's History: The Case of United States History Textbooks," *The History Teacher* 19 (2 [1986]): 211–62; and Mary Kay Tetreault, "It's So Opinioney," *Journal of Education* 168 (2 [1986]): 78–95.

22. By the year 1982 there were about 30,000 women's studies courses in the United States. See Marilyn Boxer, "For and About Women: The Theory and Practice of Women's Studies in the United States," *Signs* 7 (2 [1982]): 661–95.

23. For feminist approaches to epistemology, see Linda Alcoff, "Cultural Feminism versus Post-Structuralism: The Identity Crisis in Feminist Theory," *Signs* 13 (3 [1988]): 405–36; Donna Haraway, "Situated Knowledges: The Science Question in Feminism and the Privilege of Partial Perspective," *Feminist Studies* 14 (3 [1988]): 575–99; Sandra Harding, *The Science Question in Feminism* (Ithaca, N.Y.: Cornell University Press, 1987); Frances Mascia-Lees, Patricia Sharpe, and Colleen Cohen, "The Postmodernist Turn in Anthropology: Cautions from a Feminist Perspective," *Signs* 15 (1 [1989]): 7–33.

24. For early explorations of feminist research methodologies, see Helen Longino, "Scientific Objectivity and Feminist Theorizing," *Liberal Education* (Fall 1981): 187–95; Patti Lather, "Feminist Perspectives on Empowering Research Methodologies," *Women's Studies International Forum* 11 (6 [1988]): 569–81; Liz Stanley and Sue Wise, *Breaking Out: Feminist Consciousness and Feminist Research* (London: Routledge & Kegan Paul, 1983); and Westkott, "Feminist Criticism of the Social Sciences."

25. Paulo Freire, *Pedagogy of the Oppressed* (New York: Continuum, 1970). For comparisons of feminist pedagogies and other democratic and progressive pedagogical approaches, see Maher, "Toward a Richer Theory of Feminist Pedagogy"; Jennifer Gore, "What Can We Do for You! What *Can* "We" Do For "You?": Struggling over Empowerment in Critical and Feminist Pedagogy," *Educational Foundations* (Summer 1990): 5–26; Berenice Fisher, "What Is Feminist Pedagogy?" *Radical Teacher* 18 (1978): 20–25; Kathleen Weiler, "Freire and a Feminist Pedagogy of Difference," *Harvard Educational Review* 61 (4 [1991]): 449–74.

26. Maher, "Pedagogies for the Gender-Balanced Classroom," p. 49.

27. Although we also had planned to work with three men, none of the classes they taught in the semester we observed turned out to be appropriate.

28. We chose students who represented the range of students in each classroom. We looked for females and males, students of color and European Americans, older and younger students, more and less verbal students, and so on. Some students struck us by their classroom performances as being particularly insightful or unusual, and we always followed up on them. We interviewed approximately five to six students per professor.

29. See, besides the articles on feminist pedagogy already cited: Charlotte Bunch and Sandra Pollack, eds., *Learning Our Way: Essays in Feminist Education* (Trumansberg, N.Y.: Crossing Press, 1983); Margo Culley and Catherine Portuges, eds., *Gendered Subjects: The Dynamics of Feminist Teaching* (London: Routledge & Kegan Paul, 1985); Barbara Hillyer Davis, ed. "Feminist Education," special issue of *The Journal of Thought, an Interdisciplinary Quarterly* 20 (2 [Fall 1985]); and Nancy Schniedewind and Frances Maher, eds., "Feminist Pedagogy," special issue of *Women's Studies Quarterly* (Fall & Winter 1987). See also the journal *Feminist Teacher,* Wheaton College, Norton, MA 02766.

30. Gilligan, *In a Different Voice;* Belenky et al., *Women's Ways of Knowing;* and Jane Roland Martin, *Reclaiming a Conversation* (New Haven, Conn.: Yale University Press, 1985).

31. James Clifford, "Introduction: Partial Truths," in *Writing Culture: The Poetics and Politics of Ethnography,* ed. James Clifford and George Marcus (Berkeley: University of California Press, 1986), p. 22. See also George Marcus and Michael Fischer, *Anthropology as Cultural Critique: An Experimental Moment in the Human Sciences* (Chicago: University of Chicago Press, 1986), and Marjorie Shostak, *Nisa: The Life and Words of a !kung Woman* (New York: Vintage, 1983).

32. Dorothy Berkson, personal communication, Tenth Annual Gender Studies Symposium, Lewis and Clark College, April 1991.

33. Sara Coulter, personal communication, 1992.

34. Elizabeth Ellsworth, "Why Doesn't This Feel Empowering? Working Through the Repressive Myths of Critical Pedagogy," *Harvard Educational Review* 59 (4 [1989]):297–324; bell hooks, "From Skepticism to Feminism," *Women's Review of Books* 7 (5 [1990]):29. For earlier explorations of conflict in the feminist classroom, see, for example, Barbara Hillyer Davis, "Teaching the Feminist Minority," *Women's Studies Quarterly* 9 (4 [1981]):7–9; Susan Geiger and Jacqueline N. Zita, "White Traders: The Caveat Emptor of Women's Studies," *Journal of Thought* 20 (3 [1985]):106–21; John Schilb, "Pedagogy of the Oppressors?" in Culley and Portuges, *Gendered Subjects,* pp. 253–64.

35. hooks, "From Skepticism to Feminism."

36. For an interesting discussion of how race shapes white women's lives, see Ruth Frankenberg, *White Women, Race Matters: The Social Construction of Whiteness* (Minneapolis: University of Minnesota Press, 1993).

37. Elizabeth Spelman, *Inessential Woman: Problems of Exclusion in Feminist Thought* (Boston: Beacon Press, 1988), esp. pp. 178–87.

38. Recent literature on feminist pedagogy includes Susan Gabriel and Isaiah Smithson, eds., *Gender in the Classroom: Power and Pedagogy* (Urbana and Chicago: University of Illinois Press, 1990); Jennifer Gore, *The Struggle for Pedagogies: Critical and Feminist Discourses as Regimes of Truth* (New York and London: Routledge, 1993); Carmen Luke, and Jennifer Gore, eds., *Feminisms and Critical Pedagogy* (New York and London: Routledge, 1992); and Anne Statham, Laurel Richardson, and Judith A. Cook, *Gender and University Teaching* (Albany: State University of New York Press, 1991).

39. Laurie Finke, personal communication, 1991.

40. Renato Rosaldo and other postmodern anthropologists have written about the validity of a range of emotions for coming to an understanding of one's subjects. See Renato Rosaldo, *Culture and Truth: The Remaking of Social Analysis* (Boston: Beacon Press, 1989), esp. pp. 172, 173.

41. Jill Tarule, personal communication, 1990.

42. Alcoff, "Cultural Feminism versus Post-Structuralism."

43. Judith Stacey, "Can There Be a Feminist Ethnography?" *Women's Studies International Forum* 11 (1 [1988]): 21–27.

Chapter 2. Creating a Kaleidoscope: Portraits of Six Institutions

1. Virginia Woolf, *Three Guineas* (New York: Harcourt, Brace, 1938), p. 94; Susan Hardy Aiken, Karen Anderson, Myra Dinnerstein, Judy Nolte Lensink, and

Patricia MacCorquodale, *Changing Our Minds* (Albany: State University of New York Press, 1988), p. xviii.

2. The profiles of each campus represent our point of view at the time we observed in classrooms and interviewed professors and students. We provide an updated view of each professor and her institution in chapter 8 as a way of capturing their changes.

3. Nadya Aisenberg and Mona Harrington, *Women of Academe: Outsiders in the Sacred Grove* (Amherst: University of Massachusetts Press, 1988).

4. Correspondence with Chinosole, June 1992.

5. Of the 34,725 students enrolled in the fall of 1988, 1 percent were American Indian, 2.6 percent were Asian, 1.6 percent were Black, 7.5 percent were Hispanic, and 80.5 percent were white. Foreign students accounted for 6.7 percent.

6. See "Changing Our Minds: The Problematics of Curriculum Integration," in Aiken et al. *Changing Our Minds,* pp. 154, 144.

7. MacCorquodale, who completed her undergraduate degree at Carleton College in 1972 and her Ph.D. at the University of Wisconsin in 1978, began teaching at the university at the age of twenty-eight, and was the lone tenure-track woman in the Sociology Department for six years. Her research, which emphasizes sex equity, comprised a number of projects that have gender as their unifying theme: gender and justice, a study of inequities in legal outcomes and in the experiences of attorneys and judges; gender and ethnic identities, a comparison of the socialization and family relations in Mexican-American and Anglo families; the effect of sex roles on the expression of sexuality; and the integration of women's studies into the curriculum. For example, see Patricia MacCorquodale, Martha W. Gilliland, Jeffrey P. Kash, and Andrew Jameton, *Engineers and Economic Conversion: from the Military to the Marketplace* (New York: Springer Verlag, 1993); Patricia MacCorquodale, "Stability and Change in Gender Relations," *Sociological Theory* 8 [1990]: 136–52; "Identity: Gender and Ethnic Dimensions," in *Mexican American Identity,* ed. Martha Bernal and Phyllis Martinelli (Encino, CA: Floricanto Press, 1993): 115–38; and Patricia MacCorquodale and Gary F. Jensen, "Women in Law: Partners or Tokens?" *Gender and Society* 7, no. 4 (1993).

   Educational equity was also the focus for a research project supported by a Kellogg National Fellowship Award. By visiting occupational, educational, and health care institutions throughout the world, she sought to examine her hypothesis that people have a basic understanding of gender stemming from the family, which they transport into organizations. This three-year award was an opportunity for her to travel. During 1987, she went to both Nicaragua and China.

8. *Lo Que Pasa* (Tucson), 10 (March 30, 1987): 3. Recent data in the *Chronicle of Higher Education* (December 1990) ranked the University of Arizona twentieth in expenditures on research and development activities.

9. The 1986 *Directory of Faculty Research in Women's Studies* contains the names of forty-eight women and men who are actively engaged in writing books and articles and hosting major conferences on feminist scholarship. For example,

research sponsored by SIROW included a history of women in the Southwest, work on Chicana literature, and research on low-income widows and health and on sex differences in language. Dinnerstein and the women's studies scholars in the SIROW region brought in more than $787,000 in 1986–87. At this writing SIROW has brought in $6 million. With funding from the National Endowment for the Humanities, the Ford Foundation, and the Department of Education, SIROW had projects at the University of Arizona and at community colleges in eighteen western states and thirty-four four-year colleges in the West, including a two-state project to integrate scholarship on women into international studies in seven universities. Even though a research university, UA's projects reflect its nonelitist land-grant orientation.

10. Interview with Patricia MacCorquodale, April 1987. The 1985–86 Annual Report of the Women's Studies Program describes a major and over thirty courses in history, literature, sociology, anthropology, humanities, and other disciplines. By 1986, these courses had enrolled over 11,000 women.

11. This preoccupation with winning a place for women in the curriculum was reflected in the university's mainstreaming project. Even though it was virtually the first on campus to focus on teaching improvement, the emphasis was on curriculum integration rather than pedagogy. During each year of the project, a steering committee of Women's Studies faculty (the authors of *Changing Our Minds*) conducted interdisciplinary seminars in feminist theory and pedagogy for approximately ten participants. In addition to the seminars, participants read the work of feminist scholars, prepared bibliographies, and held consultations with feminist specialists in their individual disciplines about the relationship of the new scholarship on women to their pedagogy and research.

12. Seminar leaders decided to focus on tenured faculty members, reasoning that they would be more likely than untenured faculty to remain at the university. Because of this, forty-two of the forty-five project participants were white, middle-class males.

13. In addition to Aiken et al., *Changing Our Minds,* see "Trying Transformations: Curriculum Integration and the Problem of Resistance," *Signs* 12 (1987): 255–75.

14. Aiken et al., *Changing Our Minds,* p. 162.

15. Flemming first came to the university in 1972 as an instructor in Hindi and Urdu. She received her Ph.D. from the University of Wisconsin in 1973 and graduated from Carleton College in 1965. Although she was aware of the women's movement before she agreed to participate in the curriculum integration seminars, she had not been seriously involved in women's studies in either her research or her teaching.

Her scholarly interest in Urdu fiction took her to India in 1982. When we met her in 1987, she was working on a book about American women missionaries in North India from 1870 to 1930 and their interactions with Indian women, particularly in educational and medical institutions. She attributed this shift to her desire to do a project reflecting her newfound interest in women and religion. See, for example, *Women's Work for Women: Missionaries and Social*

Change in Asia, (Boulder, Colo.: Westview Press, 1989), and "A New Humanity: American Women Missionaries' Ideals for Indian Women, 1870–1930," in *Western Women and Imperialism: Complicity and Resistance,* ed. Nupur Chaudhuri and Margaret Strobel (Bloomington: Indiana University Press, 1992), pp. 191–206. Flemming left the University of Arizona in 1990 to become Dean of the College of Arts and Humanities at the University of Maine, Orono.

She had become interested in India only after she felt she had to forsake her aspirations to be an English professor. She had been advised against pursuing a doctorate in English by professors at Carleton, where she received her B.A., and encouraged instead to seek a graduate degree in teaching because "English departments aren't very hospitable to women." She was awarded a Fulbright Teaching Assistantship in English, which took her to India.

16. See Flemming's chapter, "New Visions, New Methods: The Mainstreaming Experience in Retrospect," in Aiken et al., *Changing Our Minds,* pp. 54–56.

17. The size and complexity of the university are reflected in its organization, student body, and faculty. The 1,200 faculty members are organized into twelve colleges, many of which are professional: agriculture, architecture, business, education, engineering, law, medicine, mines, nursing, and pharmacy. The largest college, and the one in which all our informants were tenured, is the College of Arts and Sciences. In 1987, 89.8 percent of the tenure-track faculty were men.

18. See "Transforming the Curriculum," pamphlet available from Integrating the Scholarship on Women, Transforming the Curriculum Project, Towson State University, p. 1.

19. The faculty teaching load is twelve hours per week, with little assigned time given for research.

20. In 1988, the student body of 16,000 students comprised 15,000 undergraduates, 66 percent of whom were full-time and 59 percent of whom were women. While most students were of traditional age, eighteen to twenty-two, about 2,000 were between twenty-five and thirty-five. Only 1,244, or 8 percent of the students, were African-Americans, while 1.7 percent were Asian, 0.09 percent Hispanic, 0.02 percent Native American, and 216 foreign-born that year. (*TSU Factbook,* Fall 1988, Office of Institutional Research, Towson State University.) African-American students are concentrated in several other campuses in the Baltimore area, among them Morgan State University and Coppin University.

21. The majority of students are from the top two-thirds of their high school class. The university's student retention rate is high: 84 percent of first-time, full-time freshmen enrolled in the fall of 1988 returned for a second year (*TSU Factbook*). All quotations in this section are taken from interviews conducted while we were on campus in October and November 1989. This quote is from an interview with K Edgington, one of our professor informants.

22. Florence Howe, Susan Howard, and Mary Jo Boehm Strauss, eds. *Everywoman's Guide to Colleges and Universities* (Old Westbury, N.Y.: Feminist Press, 1982), p. 162. See also Sara Coulter, "Career Politics and the Practice of Women's Studies," in *Rocking the Boat: Academic Women and Academic Processes,* edited by Gloria

De Sole and Lenore Hoffman (New York: Modern Language Association, 1981), pp. 77–81; and Elaine Hedges and Ingrid Wendt, *In Her Own Image: Women Working in the Arts* (New York: Feminist Press and McGraw Hill, 1980).

23. Support for the project came from a $250,000 grant from the Fund for the Improvement of Postsecondary Education (FIPSE). In eleven workshops, participants read and discussed the new scholarship on women, created new syllabi, and worked with twenty-five consultants who participated at different times. The project also sponsored four short conferences on various aspects of curriculum integration and published a newsletter three times a year. See Sara Coulter, K Edgington, and Elaine Hedges, eds., "Resources for Curriculum Change," unpublished paper, Towson State University, 1986, p. 3. Under the aggressive and far-reaching leadership of Coulter and Hedges, the success of the Towson Project was bound up with creating a regional and national reputation for the institution and the work they were doing, perhaps not unrelated to their concern for the growing status of their institution. Thus they initiated a second FIPSE grant with five community colleges in the Baltimore area from 1988 to 1990. In the fall of 1990, the Institute for Teaching and Research on Women (ITROW) was established to foster research on women, with an emphasis on applied research, and to continue the work of curriculum transformation.

24. Of the 540 faculty members at Towson State in 1989, 79 percent were male and 21 percent were female. Of the 467 tenure-track faculty members, 66 percent were men and 33 percent were women (*TSU Factbook*).

25. For example, we had expected to observe the teaching of Daniel Jones, Chair of the English Department, but health problems during the semester we were on campus prevented his participation.

26. Virginia "Ginny" Anderson began her teaching career as a seventh-grade general science and biology teacher, later gaining a master's degree in Science Education from the University of Georgia. As she put it, "I came off the street in 1968 to teach here." She taught only General Biology, had no departmental or committee duties, and easily got tenure. She wanted to get promoted, so she got a doctorate in Science Education at the University of Maryland, College Park, in 1984. In 1982, she had begun to publish in the field of science teaching. Her recent book, co-authored with Barbara Walvoord, Lucille McCarthy, John Dreihan, Susan Robinson, and A. Kimbrough Sherman, is entitled *Writing and Thinking in College* (Urbana, Ill.: National Council of Teachers of English, 1991). In addition, she won the Ohio Science Teaching Award for innovations in the field of science teaching, and in 1993 received a grant to develop an urban education science curriculum.

27. K Edgington received her B.A. in English in 1973, and her doctorate in Literary Studies in 1976, both from the American University in Washington. She began to think about her teaching when she participated in a seminar with other graduate students exploring different methods of teaching and literary criticism. It was there also that she began to explore feminism: "We had our own girls' network and we had ladies' luncheons several times during the semester in which we plotted, and eventually we began including women

authors in our courses." Her research interests are in Canadian women's literature, Margaret Atwood in particular. At this writing, in 1994, she is finally
being considered for tenure.

28. Blanchard attested to the value of the mainstreaming seminar in relation to her
feeling connected to the women in the group. She received her BA at Incarnate
Word College, San Antonio, Texas, in 1960. When she began teaching at Towson State, the rest of her time had been taken up with activism within the
women's movement, particularly the collective of the national feminist magazine *Women: A Journal of Liberation.* She was also pursuing her own creative writing and a doctorate at the Union Graduate School, a respected external-degree
doctoral program. In 1990, she completed her doctoral work on women and
intuition, which involved writing a novel, *Queen Bea* (so far unpublished), and a
book on intuition, *The Rest of the Deer: An Intuitive Study of Intuition* (Portland,
Maine: Astarte Press, 1993). In 1990 she accepted a position teaching at the
Vermont College Graduate Program in Montpelier.

   She wrote us: "I hope somewhere you emphasize the point that my being so
marginal for so long to the academic establishment, was less a personal choice,
or accident, than the result of how the system does not reward good teaching or
even take it into consideration, and how it exploits so many excellent women
teachers" (personal correspondence, December 1991). In fact, she once led a
movement of adjunct professors that succeeded in doubling their pay.

29. The anthropologist Shirley Brice Heath has observed how heavily professors
have been socialized into thinking they teach by asking questions. See Shirley
Brice Heath, *Ways with Words: Language, Life, and Work in Communities and
Classrooms* (New York: Cambridge University Press, 1983), p. 283.

30. Osterud has written extensive reflections on her teaching. See, for example,
three unpublished papers, "Teaching and Learning About Race at Lewis and
Clark College," 1987; "The Revolution in History 357: Feminism in Historical
Perspective," 1987; and "Gender Studies 200: Women and Men in American
Society" 1985, from which this excerpt is taken. Her research focuses on the
interplay of structural constraints on nineteenth-century farm women's lives
and their efforts both to change their situation and to strengthen mutuality in
their communities. Her most recent publication is *Bonds of Community: The Lives
of Farm Women in Nineteenth Century New York* (Ithaca, N.Y.: Cornell University
Press, 1991). She is currently working on a second volume. Osterud completed
her undergraduate degree at Radcliffe College in 1971 and her Ph.D. in American Civilization at Brown in 1984.

31. Finke's book is entitled *Feminist Theory, Women's Writing* (Ithaca, N.Y.: Cornell
University Press, 1992). For an example of using teaching as a point of departure for scholarly writing, see her article "Knowledge as Bait: Feminism, Voice
and the Pedagogical Unconscious," *College English* 55 (1993):7–27, in which she
argues that voices are not found but fashioned from relevant experiences that
surface in the discursive environment of the feminist classroom. Laurie Finke
graduated from Lake Forest College in 1974 and completed her Ph.D. at the
University of Pennsylvania in 1980.

32. In one course, for example, Berkson paired Mark Twain's *Huckleberry Finn* with Maya Angelou's *I Know Why the Caged Bird Sings* to illustrate the socialization of children into gender roles; in a course on the American Renaissance, she paired Harriet Beecher Stowe and Herman Melville. Her forthcoming book illustrates the way culture constructs gender systems and the way literature uses gender in the symbolic construction of differences. Berkson is the editor of the American Women Writers' Series Edition of Harriet Beecher Stowe's *Oldtown Folks* (New Brunswick, N.J.: Rutgers University Press, 1988). In 1989 she was the recipient of the Jane Bakerman Award for the best essay in feminist criticism, which is awarded by the American Culture, Popular Culture Association. See "Born and Bred in Different Nations: Margaret Fuller and Ralph Waldo Emerson," in *Patrons and Protégés,* ed. Shirley Marchalonis (New Brunswick, N.J.: Rutgers University Press, 1988), pp. 3–30. Berkson received her B.A. in 1961 from the University of Washington and her Ph.D. from the University of Illinois in 1978.

33. The present-day college is composed of an undergraduate college of approximately 1,800 students, which is the heart of the institution that also includes a Graduate School of Professional Studies and a law school. The college draws primarily traditional-age students from around the country. The student body, like the faculty, is predominantely white (85.9 percent). The ethnic minority enrollment in 1987 was 4.5 percent Asian-American, 1.2 percent African-American, and 1.3 percent Hispanic. Foreign students account for 6.3 percent.

34. Martha Frances Montague, *Lewis and Clark College 1867–1967* (Portland, Oreg.: Bindford and Mort, 1968), pp. 11–12, a reference we found in Susan Kirschner, Jane Monnig Atkinson, and Elizabeth Arch, "Reassessing Coeducation," in *Women's Place in the Academy,* ed. Marilyn Schuster and Susan Van Dyne (Totowa, N.J.: Rowman and Allanheld, 1985), pp. 30–31.

35. Kirschner et al., "Reassessing Coeducation," pp. 31–33.

36. In all, seventeen faculty members (eleven women and six men) of diverse disciplines and varying ranks and familiarity with feminist scholarship spent four weeks investigating feminist scholarship in four disciplines: anthropology, history, literature, and psychology. Each week visiting scholars, supported by the National Endowment for the Humanities, lectured and led discussions on the new scholarship on women in their discipline. With the exception of one session led by Florence Howe, there was no attention given to pedagogy. As Finke suggested, it was the General Studies Program and, to some extent, the Writing Across the Curriculum Project that helped faculty members reconceptualize their teaching.

37. The college redefined its mission to include the balanced exploration of the perspectives, traditions, and contributions of women and men. Jean Ward, the current director of the Gender Studies Program, and Mary Kay Tetreault were two of the five faculty representatives elected to the Mission Planning Committee.

38. The college received a grant in 1987 from the Quill Foundation to incorporate American minority and Third World women into the core curriculum.

39. Nancy Grey Osterud, "Teaching and Learning About Race at Lewis and Clark College," unpublished paper, Lewis and Clark College, Fall 1987.

40. An uproar ensued from faculty, students, and particularly alumnae who had given to the 1984 fund-raising campaign.

41. Alice Emerson, "Preface" to Bonnie Spanier, Alexander Bloom, and Darlene Boroviak, eds., *Toward a Balanced Curriculum: A Sourcebook for Initiating Gender Integration Projects* (Cambridge, Mass.: Schenkman, 1984).

42. Operating through a series of speakers, workshops, and several visiting scholars over a three-year period, the project, which began in 1980, was supported by the Fund for the Improvement of Postsecondary Education. It also gave small stipends to faculty to transform, or "gender-balance," selected courses. Although participation was completely voluntary, over half the 100 faculty members became involved to some extent, and a core group of twenty or so met in study groups, led workshops for other faculty, and used the project to extend, transform, and/or create their own scholarship.

43. Beverly Clark arrived at Wheaton in 1977, and Yllo and Maher in 1981.

44. By the time Yllo's class was observed in the fall of 1989, when men comprised about 25 percent of the students, coeducation was not a particular issue in her Families in Transition class, still all women. Bianca Cody Murphy, on the other hand, had 20 males (out of 115) in her Human Sexuality class for the spring of 1992.

45. "Learning Environments Task Force Report," Wheaton College, March 22, 1988.

46. Maher was informally in charge of the "pedagogy piece" of the Balanced Curriculum Project, and established the teaching workshops with several other colleagues.

47. Clark graduated from Swarthmore College in 1970 and got her Ph.D. from Brown University in 1979. Reflecting on her own graduate school experience in class one day, she said she had been drawn away from American Literature and into English Literature because the latter had more novels about women, the family, and society, and fewer isolated and male "quest stories." Besides her literature courses, her work at Wheaton has been largely in the area of writing; she developed a peer tutoring program from which she has written a textbook entitled *Talking About Writing: A Guide for Tutor and Teacher Conferences* (Ann Arbor: University of Michigan Press, 1985). Her research interests have been many and broad: she has studied "school stories" and other aspects of children's literature, and has written several articles with students, two which are forthcoming on the Feminist Criticism course. One, co-authored with Heather Braun, Susan Dearing, et al., is entitled "Giving Voice to Feminist Criticism: A Conversation," in *Teaching Theory to Undergraduates,* ed. William Cain and Dianne Sadoff (New York: Modern Language Association, 1993).

48. Murphy combines teaching at Wheaton with a clinical practice and an active research life in Boston, where she studies issues of families in the nuclear age and gay and lesbian lifestyles. She graduated from Marymount Manhattan College in 1971 and received her Ed.D. in Counseling Psychology from Boston University in 1982. Her many publications include "Lesbian Couples and Their Parents," *Journal of Counseling and Development* 68 (1989): 46–51, and "Educat-

ing Mental Health Professionals About Gay and Lesbian Issues," in *Coming Out of the Classroom Closet,* ed. Karen M. Harbeck (New York: Harrington Park Press, 1992), pp. 229–46.

49. The *1993–1994 Student Handbook* says:

> The issue for the College is not that gays and lesbians are part of the community, but rather that they may choose to become a visible and vocal part of the community. . . . [We] must not confuse the demands of lesbian, gay and bisexual people for their human rights with proselytizing and sexual aggression. The College has a responsibility to protect students from all forms of sexual aggression, both heterosexual and homosexual; it also has a responsibility to respond positively when members of the community request to participate fully and openly in the life of the community (p. 7).

50. Yllo got her B.A. at Dennison in 1974. Receiving her Ph.D. in sociology at the University of New Hampshire in 1981, she wrote her dissertation on marital rape, which she turned into a book, *License to Rape,* co-authored with David Finkelhor, one of the scholars at UNH's Center for the Study of Family Violence. Since then, she has edited a book of essays, *Feminist Perspectives on Wife Abuse* (Newbury Park, Calif.: Sage, 1988). More recently, she has been doing work at Children's Hospital in Boston, as part of a team of clinicians and researchers investigating family violence.

51. In the fall of 1991, 12 percent of the entering freshmen were students of color, which included Asians and Hispanics but which were mostly African-American. This percentage had held steady for the previous five years. The gender ratio of this class was 66 percent female to 34 percent male, from 70 percent to 30 percent the previous year. The majority of students come from New England, with a group from the middle Atlantic states and a smattering from the West Coast, the Southwest, and the Southeast.

52. The students included nine black women, one white woman, an exchange student, and two men from Morehouse College. Maher was in the class as part of our exploratory visit before making a decision to include Spelman among the institutions we observed.

53. Beverly Guy-Sheftall, Anna Julia Cooper Professor of English and Women's Studies, graduated from Spelman and returned to her alma mater to teach English. She was centrally involved with Spelman's new mission, having been primarily responsible for attaining a grant from the Charles Stewart Mott Foundation, which established the Women's Research and Resource Center and provided for the establishment of a minor in Women's Studies. Later, two grants from the Ford Foundation, from 1983 to 1985 and from 1987 to 1989, provided for the integration of scholarship on women, particularly Black Women's Studies, into the curriculum. Guy-Sheftall is founding co-editor of *SAGE: A Scholarly Journal on Black Women,* which was started in 1984 and is housed at the Center.

Guy-Sheftall told us that although, for the time being, there was no conflict between the ideology of the school and the ideology of Black Women's

Studies, nevertheless the majority of the faculty were still white and conservative. Johnnetta Cole became president of Spelman in 1987.

54. Gloria Wade-Gayles first came to Spelman in 1983, and by the time of our visit was a full-time member of the English Department. Wade-Gayles received her B.A. in 1959 from Le Moyne College and her doctorate in American Studies in 1981 from Emory University, and is the author of a critical study of Black Women writers, *No Crystal Stair: Visions of Race and Sex in Black Women's Fiction* (New York: Pilgrim Press, 1984). She received tenure at Spelman in 1991. During the fall of 1991 she was a fellow at the W. E. B. Du Bois Institute at Harvard, where she was doing work on Alice Walker's novels. Most recently she published a memoir, *Pushed Back to Strength: A Black Woman's Journey Home* (Boston: Beacon Press, 1993).

55. From Mona Phillips's Sociology of Women class, March 12, 1990.

56. Morehouse, the prominent all-male college that is Spelman's counterpart, lies across the street, unfenced.

57. According to a handout from the Public Relations Office, "Spelman is the nation's oldest and largest private, undergraduate liberal arts college for Black women. Enrollment is approximately 1700. . . . Spelman was the only historically Black college to be included in the *U.S. News and World Report*'s 1988 listing of the nation's top colleges and universities." After a substantial gift from John D. Rockefeller in 1884, which included naming a dormitory after his mother-in-law, Lucy Henry Spelman, the school was renamed Spelman; it gained college status in 1887 and graduated its first students in 1901. The faculty numbers about 114 full-time members; 65 percent are female and 35 percent male. The students, all undergraduates and primarily traditional college age, come from forty-six states and four countries, with 26 percent from Georgia.

58. From National Public Radio transcript, "All Things Considered," 1989. As Mona Phillips put it, "Now we are also getting more students who are like Johnnetta—internationalists and socially conscious. . . . there's something about having a woman at the head of the school that transforms the place." Ethel Githii died of cancer in 1992.

59. Since 1987, entering freshman at Spelman have had the highest SAT scores of all students at historically African-American colleges and universities. *Speaking of Spelman* (a collection of excerpts from selected newspaper and magazine articles about the college), ed. TaRessa Stone, n.d. In her study of Black college students, Jacqueline Fleming found that they do better at Black colleges, and that Spelman students showed the best academic development of all the Black schools. See Jacqueline Fleming, *Blacks in College: A Comparative Study of Students' Success in Black and White Institutions* (San Francisco: Jossey-Bass, 1984).

60. Interview with Johnnetta Cole, *Washington Post*, "Style" section, November 11, 1988, p. B3.

61. Phillips graduated from Spelman in 1976 and did graduate work at the University of Michigan, where she got her doctorate in Sociology in 1982. After teaching at the University of Tennessee for three years, she returned to Spelman in 1986. Her research and writing on Black women's lives draw largely upon fic-

tion to elucidate the place of Black women within the Black community and the larger society. One forthcoming article is titled "Telling the Stories of the Internal Colony: Gendered Analyses of Space, History and Conduits," *SAGE.* Another is "Racism, Sexism and Social Class: Implications for Studying Health, Disease and Well-Being," *American Journal of Preventive Medicine.*

62. Eric Alterman, "Black Universities, in Demand and in Trouble," *New York Times Magazine,* November 5, 1989, p. 63. As Alterman put it, "In 1979, Spelman received fewer than 1000 requests for a place in its freshman class; [in 1989] that number nearly doubled" (p. 62). Because of what Cole called "the push of racism," increasing numbers of more privileged Black students are choosing historically Black institutions like Spelman, Howard, and Morehouse over places like Harvard, Yale, and Michigan.

63. We had planned to observe Merle Woo's class, but her illness made it impossible.

64. Trujillo completed her undergraduate degree in 1979 at the University of California, Davis, and received her Ph.D. from the University of Wisconsin in 1984. Her scholarly work is an analysis of sexuality derived from lesbianism, and she edited *Chicana Lesbians: The Girls Our Mothers Warned Us About* (Berkeley: Third Woman Press, 1991). In the introduction she explores the dual worlds of this group:

> In regard to the Chicana lesbian, who then is she? As one would surmise, the Chicana lesbian is similar to any other Chicana, or any other lesbian, yet her own experience is usually that of attempting to fit into two worlds, neither of which is readily accepting. . . . Chicana lesbians pose a threat to the Chicano community for a variety of reasons, primarily because they threaten the established social hierarchy of patriarchal control.

Trujillo is also the Director of Women and Graduate Students of Color in Engineering, at UC Berkeley.

65. Both Chinosole and Davis see themselves doing socially relevant scholarship that is tied to their activism and believe that the current energy in Black feminist theory is related to the upsurge in activism. Davis has a forthcoming book on the role played by early blues women and their music in the shaping of social consciousness during the first part of the twentieth century. She will soon begin work focusing on the differential criminalization—and the problematics associated with the incarceration—of women. See also Angela Davis, *Women, Race and Class* (New York: Random House, 1982); "Billie Holiday: Music and Social Consciousness," in *Speech and Power,* ed. Gerald Early (New York: Ecco Press, 1991), pp. 33–43; "Black Nationalism: The Sixties and the Nineties," in *Black Popular Culture,* ed. Gina Dent (Seattle: Bay Press, 1993), pp. 317–24.

Chinosole, who describes her research focus as Black feminist/Black lesbian literary theory and colonial discourse, particularly in relation to the work of Audre Lorde, is currently writing a book, *The Skeins of Self and Skin in the Autobiographical Writing of the African Diaspora.* She viewed the class that she and Davis taught, Wild Women in Music and Literature, as a strategic move to forge a correspondence among their scholarship, activism, and teaching commitments. For other publications, see "Audre Lorde and Matrilineal Diaspora," in *Wild Women in the Whirlwind,* ed. Joanne M. Braxton and Andree Nicola McLaughlin (New Brunswick, N.J.: Rutgers University Press, 1991), pp. 379–94; "Tryin' to Get Over: Narrative Posture in Equiano's Autobiography," in *The Art of Slave Narrative: Original Essays in Criticism and Theory,* ed. John Sekora and Darwin T. Turner (Macomb, Ill.: Western Illinois Press, 1982): pp. 45–54; "Conde as Contemporary Griot in *Segu,*" forthcoming in *Callaloo.*

66. Davis formulated this observation specifically so as to reflect the struggles that have taken place to change the Women Studies Department at San Francisco State.

67. Chinosole's and Davis's activism led to similar experiences. Both began their careers by being fired—Davis, before delivering her first lecture at UCLA, by Ronald Reagan and the Regents of the University of California for her membership in the Communist party, and Chinosole from Xavier University for her antiwar activities during the 1960s. Chinosole was fired a second time from San Francisco State by Ronald Reagan for, among other reasons, as she put it to us, "the institution's refusal to sanction Black Studies as an autonomous unit."

Both women have gripping stories of working to resist racism and sexism. A large "Free Angela Davis" poster in the Women Studies office is a reminder of the harrowing ordeal of her imprisonment in 1970 at the age of twenty-six. Angela Davis graduated magna cum laude from Brandeis University in 1965 and received her masters from UC San Diego in 1969. She advanced to doctoral candidacy at UCSD that same year, but the FBI absconded with her dissertation before she actually received her Ph.D. See *Angela Davis: An Autobiography* (New York: Random House, 1974; International Publishers, 1988).

Chinosole graduated from Edgewood College in 1964 and went to Africa for a second time in the 1970s to teach English. She stayed in Angola after independence, worked for the coalition government, and taught in one of the movement's schools until her capture and imprisonment in August 1975. An article that appeared in the *Washington Post* ("Surviving Angola's War," March 7, 1976) chronicles Chinosole's survival during Angola's war and the brutality and turmoil she witnessed. She received her Ph.D. from the University of Oregon in 1986.

68. The ethnic composition of San Francisco State in 1988 was 0.07 percent Native American, 26.9 percent Asian, 7.4 percent African-American, 7.5 percent Latino, and 51.8 percent white. Foreign students account for 5.7 percent. Even though the campus has student dormitories, the majority of the 24,200 students live off campus.

69. Trujillo took a straw poll in her Women in Groups class, which revealed that a number of students had full-time jobs and others worked at least twenty hours a week. Only three of the thirty-five students did not work for pay, and one of those was the mother of a small infant.

70. San Francisco State is one of twenty campuses in the California State University system.

71. See William Barlow and Peter Shapiro, *An End to Silence: The San Francisco State College Student Movement in the 60s* (New York: Pegasus, 1971). Doell, who received her undergraduate degree in Biochemistry from the University of California, Berkeley, in 1952 and her Ph.D. in 1956, assumed a tenure-track position in 1970. She attributed her interdisciplinary interests to this change in course assignments. This fascination with interdisciplinary work created tensions with the norms of her department—the pressure to do experimental biological research—particularly in the tenure and promotion process. Her interdisciplinary interests led her first to environmental studies and later to the interrelations between feminist philosophy and biology. See her articles, written with Helen Longino, "Body, Bias and Behavior: A Comparative Analysis of Reasoning in Two Areas of Biological Science," *Signs* 9 (1983): 206–27, and "Sex Hormones and Human Behavior: A Critique of the Linear Model," *Journal of Homosexuality* 15 (1988): 55–78. Her current research interest is the relationship between biology and gender, which was fed in part by the teaching of a general studies course called Biological Sex and Cultural Gender. See, for example, "Whose Research Is This? Values and Biology," in *Engendering Knowledge: Feminists in Academe,* ed. Joan E. Hartman and Ellen Messer-Davidow (Knoxville: University of Tennessee Press, 1991), pp. 121–39.

72. Chinosole is committed to serving a broad range of students, not just radical students or students of color, even though such students tended to gravitate to Women Studies.

Chapter 3. Mastery

1. The first question was asked of psychologist Carol Gilligan after she introduced her study exploring girls' development and education to a group of adolescent girls at Emma Willard School. The second is Gilligan's reading of the possible question behind the question. See Carol Gilligan, Nona Lyons, and Trudy Hanmer, *Making Connections: The Relational Worlds of Adolescent Girls at Emma Willard School* (Cambridge, Mass.: Harvard University Press, 1990), pp. 2, 4.

2. See, for example Richard Rodriguez, *Hunger of Memory* (Boston: Godine, 1982), and Mike Rose, *Lives on the Boundary* (New York: Penguin, 1989).

3. Laurie Finke, "Knowledge as Bait: Feminism, Voice, and the Pedagogical Unconscious," *College English* 55 (1 [1993]): 7–27. See also Constance Penley, "Teaching in Your Sleep: Feminism and Psychoanalysis" in *Theory in the Classroom,* ed. Carey Nelson (Urbana and Chicago: University of Illinois Press, 1986), pp. 129–48.

4. Paulo Freire, *The Pedagogy of the Oppressed* (New York: Continuum, 1970); Renato Rosaldo, *Culture and Truth* (Boston: Beacon Press, 1989).

5. Of the fifty-eight students present on the day we assessed gender and race, seventeen were white males and forty-one were females, of whom eight were African-Americans, two were Asian, and the rest white.

6. Deborah Tannen, *You Just Don't Understand: Women and Men in Conversation* (New York: Morrow, 1990).

7. Patricia Hill Collins, *Black Feminist Thought: Knowledge, Consciousness and the Pol-*

itics of Empowerment (Boston: Unwin Hyman, 1990). See also bell hooks, *Talking Back: Thinking Feminist, Thinking Black* (Boston: South End Press, 1989).

8. TaRessa Stone, director of Public Relations and Special Events, Spelman College, *Speaking of Spelman,* n. d., p. 3. These academically able students do indeed flourish at Spelman.

9. Among the books Phillips used were Paula Giddings, *When and Where I Enter: The Impact of Black Women on Race and Sex in America* (New York: Morrow, 1984); and Jacqueline Jones, *Labor of Love, Labor of Sorrow: Black Women, Work, and the Family from Slavery to the Present* (New York: Basic Books, 1985).

10. By American feminism, Clark meant theoretical frameworks that emphasize women as an oppressed group in society and are concerned with issues of power and inequality, and also approaches that seek commonalities among women, such as their nurturing qualities, relational experiences and qualities, and so on. By French approaches, she meant an emphasis on deconstruction (undoing and multiplying the differences *among* and *within* women, and between women and men) and on psychoanalytic issues such as the role of sexuality, violence, and the unconscious for both women and men.

11. This view of knowledge was greatly influenced by her interest in deconstructionism, which she defined in class one day: "Deconstruction is a process of finding self-contradictions, a process of undermining oppositions . . . the idea is not to destroy the oppositions but to undo them, with an effort to show the underlying values implied. . . . What we end up valuing in a text is not unity but contradiction, disunity."

12. The students in the class were mostly white, traditional-age juniors and seniors; one was an African-American woman. There were also several older students, one in her early forties and two in their mid-twenties. See Judith Fetterley, *The Resisting Reader: A Feminist Approach to American Fiction* (Bloomington: Indiana University Press, 1976).

13. Angela Carter, "The Company of Wolves," in *The Norton Anthology of Literature by Women,* ed. Sandra Gilbert and Susan Gubar (New York: Norton, 1985), pp. 2326–34.

14. Collins, *Black Feminist Thought,* p. 189.

15. Toril Moi, *Sexual/Textual Politics: Feminist Literary Theory* (London and New York: Methuen, 1985).

16. Interview with Angela Davis and Chinosole, March 19, 1991. See also Angela Y. Davis, "The Black Woman's Role in the Community of Slaves," *Black Scholar* 3 (4 [1971]) pp. 2–15.

17. In addition to two course readers that included relevant articles, students read Joanne M. Braxton and Andree Nicola McLaughlin eds., *Wild Women in the Whirlwind* (New Brunswick, N.J.: Rutgers University Press, 1990) and saw a video of Zora Neale Hurston's fables.

18. Collins, *Black Feminist Thought,* p. 185.

19. When Lori was asked why they are called the Forty-Nine Songs she said: "I think it has to do with a Western cultural tradition that comes out of 'Forty-niners,' like forging something new. Almost like the Americans who came [West]."

20. These ideas were presented by Chinosole at the meetings of the American Educational Research Association, San Francisco, April 1992.

21. For an interesting analysis of these two poles of feminism and the necessary oscillation between them, see Ann Snitow, "A Gender Diary," in *Conflicts in Feminism,* ed. Marianne Hirsch and Evelyn Fox Keller (New York and London: Routledge & Kegan Paul, 1990), pp. 9–43.

22. Kimberle Crenshaw, "Whose Story Is It Anyway? Feminist and Antiracist Appropriations of Anita Hill," in *Race-ing Justice, Engendering Power,* ed. Toni Morrison (Pantheon: New York, 1992), pp. 403–36. In her book *Inessential Woman: Problems of Exclusion in Feminist Thought* (Boston: Beacon Press, 1988), the feminist political scientist Elizabeth Spelman says, "Black women's being Black somehow calls into question their counting as straightforward examples of 'women,' but white women's being white does not. As long as 'women' are compared to 'Blacks' a decision will have to be made about whether to classify Black women as 'Black' or as 'women,' but not about whether to classify white women as 'white' or as 'women'" (p. 169).

23. See Mary Belenky, Blythe Clinchy, Nancy Goldberger, and Jill Tarule, *Women's Ways of Knowing: The Development of Self, Voice, and Mind* (New York: Basic Books, 1986), and Tannen, *You Just Don't Understand.*

Chapter 4. Voice

1. *Sula* (New York: Knopf, 1974) p. 52. Carol Gilligan, *In a Different Voice: Psychological Theory and Women's Development* (Cambridge, Mass.: Harvard University Press, 1982).

2. Carol Gilligan, Nona Lyons, and Trudy Hanmer, *Making Connections: The Relational Worlds of Adolescent Girls at Emma Willard School* (Cambridge, Mass.: Harvard University Press, 1990), pp. 1–5.

3. Gilligan et al., *Making Connections,* p. 4.

4. Diane Fuss, *Essentially Speaking: Feminism, Nature and Difference* (New York: Routledge, 1989).

5. Personal correspondence, November 11, 1993. See Sherri Tucker, "'Where the Blues and the Truth Lay Hiding': Rememory of Jazz in Black Women's Fiction," *Frontiers* 13 (2 [1992]):26–44.

6. Male students were in the minority in all of the coeducational classes we observed.

7. Personal correspondence with Nancy Grey Osterud, June 13, 1992.

8. Ibid.

9. Theoretical works included Sandra Gilbert and Susan Gubar, *The Madwoman in the Attic* (New Haven, Conn.: Yale University Press, 1979); Gilligan, *In a Different Voice;* Elaine Showalter, "Feminist Criticism in the Wilderness," in *Writing and Sexual Difference,* ed. Elizabeth Abel (Chicago: University of Chicago Press, 1982).

10. Thomas H. Johnson, ed., *Complete Poems of Emily Dickinson* (New York: Macmillan, 1967), poem 288:

I'm Nobody! Who are you?
Are you—Nobody—Too?
Then there's a pair of us?
Don't tell! They'd advertise—
you know!

How dreary—to be—Somebody!
How public—like a frog—
To tell one's name—the live-
long June
to an admiring Bog!

11. Ibid., poem 327:

Before I got my eye put out
I liked as well to see—
As other Creatures, that have
Eyes
And know no other way—

But were it told to me—Today—
That I might have the sky
For mine—I tell you that my
heart
Would split, for size of me—
The Meadows—mine—
The Mountains—mine—
All Forests—Stintless Stars—
As much of Noon as I could
take
Between my finite eyes—

The Motions of the Dipping
Birds
The Morning's Amber Road—
for mine—to look at when I
liked—
The News would strike me dead—

So safer—guess—with must my
soul
Upon the Window pane—
Where other Creatures put their eyes—
Incautious—of the Sun—

12. Nancy was drawing upon what the anthropologists Shirley and Edwin Ardener call "the Wild Zone." In the Ardeners' conceptualization of culture, women are "a muted group, the boundaries of whose culture and reality overlap but are not wholly contained by the dominant (male) group. . . . Both muted and dominant

groups generate beliefs or order ideas of social reality at the unconscious level but dominant groups control the forms or structures in which consciousness can be articulated" (Elaine Showalter, "Feminist Criticism in the Wilderness," in Abel, *Writing and Sexual Differences,* pp. 129–48). Nancy Ichimura, "Taking a 'Walk on the Wild Side' Through the Poems of Emily Dickinson," paper presented at the Lewis and Clark Gender Studies Symposium, April 6, 1987.

13. The course examined the historical development of modern feminism in England and America. Students read both major statements of feminist theory and historical works. See, for example, Mary Wollstonecraft, *A Vindication of the Rights of Woman* (Troy, N.Y.: Whitston, 1982 [1790]); Margaret Fuller, *Woman in the Nineteenth Century* (Columbia: University of South Carolina Press, 1980); bell hooks, *Ain't I a Woman? Black Women and Feminism* (Boston: South End Press, 1982); Barbara Taylor, *Eve and the New Jerusalem: Socialism and Feminism in the Nineteenth Century* (New York: Pantheon, 1983); Ellen Carol DuBois, *Feminism and Suffrage: The Emergence of an Independent Women's Movement* (Ithaca, N.Y.: Cornell University Press, 1978).

14. Personal correspondence with Nancy Grey Osterud, June 13, 1992.

15. The findings from Trujillo's dissertation, which she described as an extremely political act because of its topic, were published as "A Comparative Examination of Classroom Interactions Between Professors and Minority and Non-Minority College Students," *American Educational Research Journal* 23 (4 [Winter 1986]): 629–42. Trujillo found that professors interacted differently at a significant level with minority students and had significantly lower academic expectations of them.

16. In Adrienne Rich, *On Lies, Secrets, and Silence: Selected Prose 1966–1978* (New York: Norton, 1979), pp. 185–94.

17. Grey Osterud has also observed that one of the challenges of women's studies classrooms is how to get a group working together collaboratively without encouraging a false unity that assumes all women share a common identity.

18. Rich, *On Lies, Secrets, and Silence,* p. 187.

Chapter 5. Authority

1. Susan Hardy Aiken, Karen Anderson, Myra Dinnerstein, Judy Nolte Lensink, and Patricia MacCorquodale, *Changing Our Minds* (Albany: State University of New York Press, 1988), p. xviii.

2. Upon retiring from Columbia University, the feminist literary scholar Carolyn Heilbrun likened the male-run world of American colleges and universities—where 88 percent of presidents, provosts, and chancellors and 87 percent of full professors are men—to a secret treehouse club where girls are not allowed. See Anne Matthews, "Rage in a Tenured Position," *New York Times Magazine,* November 8, 1992, p. 47. See also Anthony de Palma, "Rare in Ivy League, Women Who Work as Full Professors," *New York Times,* January 24, 1993, p. 1, which points out that the higher the prestige of any academic job, the fewer occupants of that job are women; even though women now comprise 52 percent of students, they make up only 13 percent of full professors and 27.6 percent of

all professors, but 38 percent of community college teachers (as well as about half of all high school teachers and over two-thirds of elementary school teachers).

3. Aiken et al., *Changing Our Minds,* p. 145.

4. Laurie Finke, "Knowledge as Bait: Feminism, Voice, and the Pedagogical Unconscious," *College English* 55 (1 [1993]): 1.

5. See, for example, Sandra Harding, *The Science Question in Feminism* (Ithaca, N.Y.: Cornell University Press, 1986); and Evelyn Fox Keller, *Reflections on Gender and Science* (New Haven, Conn.: Yale University Press, 1984).

6. Doell's interdisciplinary work was also accompanied by exhilarating connections with colleagues across departmental boundaries. One of the by-products of those connections was the funding of a seminar to bring together faculty members from the sciences, social sciences, and humanities to develop an interdisciplinary general education program. Seventeen years later the seminar is still functioning and the program, called NEXA, (Greek for convergence) offers a wide range of courses that pair, for instance, philosophy professors with physicists and English professors with biologists. We observed NEXA seminar in which eighteen faculty members from the sciences, humanities, and social sciences engaged in a year-long seminar whose topic was the social construction of knowledge. The theme for the evening we were present was Feminism and Science, a topic central to Doell's NEXA course, Biological Sex and Cultural Gender. Doell was very much the authority during the discussion, not only because the group had read one of her articles but because of the thoughtful way she presented her ideas about the relationship between the social construction of gender and the social construction of science.

7. Among the products that the students produce in the Biological Literature class are a library research paper, a review of the literature on a particular topic, an actual grant proposal for the funding of research, and an original research paper.

8. Interestingly enough, the course, which met for an hour and a half twice a week, did not count for Biology credit because it was a class in writing skills.

9. Flemming also told us that she was much more concerned about authority in her large lecture classes than in small seminar settings. For a discussion of the reasons women professors are evaluated as less effective than their male colleagues despite equivalent levels of professional performance see Anne Statham, Laurel Richardson, and Judith A. Cook, *Gender and University Teaching: A Negotiated Difference* (Albany: State University of New York Press, 1991).

10. Aiken et al., *Changing Our Minds,* p. 53.

11. Ibid., p. 45.

12. Flemming developed and taught a course entitled Women and Religion, but it was not offered the semester we observed.

13. Virginia Woolf, *Three Guineas* (New York: Harcourt, Brace, 1938), p. 50. Leslie Flemming first came to our attention during a conversation with a white female student in Oriental Studies, who was married to a graduate student from the Middle East. She praised Flemming's teaching, particularly the sensitive position she brought to the study of non-Western cultures.

14. David Finkelhor and Kersti Yllo, *License to Rape* (New York: Holt, Rinehart and Winston, 1985).

15. Adrienne Rich, "Compulsory Heterosexuality and Lesbian Existence," *Signs* 5 (4 [1980]): 631–60.

16. Virginia Woolf, *A Room of One's Own* (New York: Harcourt, Brace, 1929), pp. 72–73.

17. Susan Gabriel and Isaiah Smithson, eds., *Gender in the Classroom: Power and Pedagogy* (Urbana and Chicago: University of Illinois Press, 1990).

18. See Finke, "Knowledge as Bait," p. 3.

Chapter 6. Positionality

1. Linda Alcoff, "Cultural Feminism versus Post-Structuralism: The Identity Crisis in Feminist Theory," *Signs* 13 (3 [1988]): 433–34.

2. Personal conversation with Jill Tarule, November 1990.

3. Donna Haraway, "Situated Knowledges: The Science Question in Feminism and the Privilege of Partial Perspective," *Feminist Studies* 14 (March 1988): 575–99.

4. Toni Morrison, *Sula* (New York: Knopf, 1974). *Sula,* a novel set in rural Ohio in the early 1900s, is about two Black women, Sula and Nel, close friends since girlhood. The narrator says about Sula and Nel, "Being neither white nor male, they had to figure out something else to be." In a recent article Morrison wrote, "I knew . . . this novel would be about people in a Black community not just foregrounded but totally dominant, and that it would be about Black women, also foregrounded and dominant." Toni Morrison, "Unspeakable Things Unspoken; The Afro-American Presence in American Literature," *Michigan Quarterly Review* 28 (1 [1989]): 23.

5. Morrison, *Sula,* p. 52.

6. Morrison, "Unspeakable Things Unspoken," p. 12.

7. Gloria Naylor, *The Women of Brewster Place* (New York: Penguin, 1980), italics added. This novel portrays the difficult lives of a community of women in an isolated and poverty-stricken cul-de-sac in a large city. The wall in the book separates Brewster Place, this street of Black families, from the world outside.

8. Gloria Wade-Gayles, *No Crystal Stair: Visions of Race and Sex in Black Women's Fiction* (New York: Pilgrim Press, 1984).

9. We did not research Emory the way we did the other institutions, nor spend time there except to observe in Wade-Gayles's class and to interview her and her students. The school is a prestigious Southern university where students of color account for approximately 17 percent of the student body.

10. Of the twenty-six students enrolled, thirteen were African-American women, seven were African-American men, four were white women, and two were white men.

11. William Faulkner, *The Sound and the Fury* (New York: Random House, 1984). This novel of a white Southern family, the Compsons, whose decay and agony is portrayed through the eyes of several characters—most notably Benjie, a thirty-three-year-old mentally retarded man, and Quentin, a tortured young man who

goes north to Harvard and ultimately commits suicide—is all about issues of class and downward mobility; race and the racism that constructs the Black person as other; and gender, in terms, among other issues, of the promiscuous sexuality of Caddie, Quentin's beloved sister.

12. William Wells Brown, *Clotel* (New York: Arno Press, 1969).

13. There are several published accounts of experiences like this. Bell hooks says that at Stanford, "I was in an environment where Black peoples' class backgrounds and values were radically different than my own. To overcome my feelings of isolation I bonded with workers, with Black women who labored as maids, as secretaries" (*Talking Back: Thinking Feminist, Thinking Black* [Boston: South End Press, 1989], p. 100). See also Laurie Nisonoff, Susan Tracy, and Stanley Warner, "Stories Out of School, Poor and Working-Class Students at a Small Liberal Arts College," *Radical Teacher* 11, no. 41: 15–19, an article about working-class students at Hampshire College. For an account of working-class professors in academia, see Jake Ryan and Charles Sackrey, *Strangers in Paradise* (Boston: South End Press, 1984).

14. Personal conversation with Jane Roland Martin, November 1990. In his teaching in a working-class community college, Ira Shor found that women students talked more than the men for complex class and gender reasons. See Ira Shor, *Critical Teaching for Everyday Life* (Boston: South End Press, 1980).

15. One of the surprises of this research has been the difference in classroom discourse between freshman and upper-division students. We observed a freshman general studies course taught by David Savage at Lewis and Clark and decided not to include it because the data were so much richer in classes with a majority of juniors and seniors.

16. At Lewis and Clark, the graduate programs are in education and other professional areas; those programs enroll students of more modest social-class backgrounds than does the college. Maggie Gilbert's religious beliefs may also have marginalized her; she had a fundamentalist background, albeit a socially liberal one. The Lewis and Clark faculty tended perhaps to be from less advantaged backgrounds than the students. At the Women's Studies seminar in 1981, Florence Howe asked faculty participants to talk about their mothers' lives. Upon the conclusion of the seventeen or so stories among the participants, she remarked that she was surprised how few mothers had been educated, suggesting that, at least among the faculty in the seminar, most came from lower social-class origins.

17. Noticing over the years at Lewis and Clark and later in other settings that women students tend to be more reluctant to read from their journals than are male students, Grey Osterud eventually realized that most women students were reluctant to hold the floor for extended periods without getting feedback from others, making eye contact with others, or being certain that they were understood. In short, most have a more interactive conversational style.

18. Personal correspondence with Nancy Grey Osterud, June 13, 1992.

19. Zora Neale Hurston, *Of Mules and Men* (New York: Negro University Press, 1935).

20. Bettye Saar is a well-known African-American artist who often juxtaposes contradictory ideas.

21. Johnnetta B. Cole, *Conversations: Straight Talk with America's Sister President* (New York: Doubleday, 1993), p. 58.

22. Eighty percent of the students at Spelman get financial aid, most of it "need-based." About 60 percent of Wheaton students get financial aid.

Chapter 7. Toward Positional Pedagogies

1. Noami Wolf, *The Beauty Myth: How Images of Beauty Are Used Against Women* (New York: Doubleday, 1992). Phillips explained, "This is what happens to the analysis when you bring in race in a very specific way. Naomi Wolf does not. But race is there, and it's whites. And she just assumes it's women."

2. Carmen Luke, "Feminist Politics in Radical Pedagogy," in *Feminisms and Critical Pedagogy,* ed. Carmen Luke and Jennifer Gore (New York and London: Routledge, 1992), p. 47.

3. See Donna Haraway, "Situated Knowledges: The Science Question in Feminism and the Privilege of Partial Perspective," *Feminist Studies* 14 (3 [1988]): 575–99.

4. Much of the discussion in this chapter about the relationships among positionality, community, and social and political change was explored in an interview between Maher and Grey Osterud on March 31, 1993. To her we owe much of the sharpening of our thoughts on these issues.

5. See Sandra Harding, *The Science Question in Feminism* (Ithaca, N.Y.: Cornell University Press, 1987), for a particularly useful summary of the different approaches of feminism to the scientific disciplines, some approaches aiming to improve them by widening their scope, others seeking as well to challenge their assumptions.

6. Kersti Yllo, ed., *Feminist Perspectives on Wife Abuse* (Newbury Park, Calif.: Sage, 1988).

7. Judith Stacey and Barrie Thorne, "The Missing Feminist Revolution in Sociology," *Social Problems* 32 (4 [1985]): 301–16.

8. Chantal Tetreault, "Metacommunication in a Women's Studies Classroom," unpublished senior honors thesis, Vassar College, 1991.

9. Frances Maher faced 90 students in an Introduction to Women's Studies class in the spring of 1993 at Wheaton College. While the students were divided into discussion groups led by upper-class students once a week, the gulf between course topics and materials, on the one hand, and students' questions and experiences, on the other, was never really bridged. At the University of California at Santa Cruz, her son, Matthew, took Bettina Aptheker's Introduction to Feminism with 500 other students.

10. See Tony Kushner's editorial, "University or Trade School," *New York Times,* June 28, 1993, p. A17. He says about the proposed cuts in liberal arts at CUNY: "A more disturbing assumption is that the people most affected by downsizing and consolidation—our growing minority population—need to be trained not as thinkers, writers and artists but as service sector employees. This is racist and classist." (As well as economically unwise, since the pace of social

change will require people who are broadly educated rather than narrowly "trained.")

11. There is an extensive literature in American educational history exploring these struggles and ideological contradictions. For an excellent summary analysis, see David Nasaw, *Schooled to Order: A Social History of Public Schooling in the United States* (New York: Oxford University Press, 1979).

12. Luke, "Feminist Politics in Radical Pedagogy," p. 32.

13. Paulo Freire, *The Pedagogy of the Oppressed* (New York: Continuum, 1970).

14. See, for example, Elizabeth Ellsworth, "Why Doesn't This Feel Empowering? Working Through the Repressive Myths of Critical Pedagogy," *Harvard Educational Review* 59 (4 [1989]): 297–324; and Jennifer Gore, "What Can We Do for You! What *Can* 'We' Do for 'You'?: Stuggling over Empowerment in Critical and Feminist Pedagogy," *Educational Foundations* (Summer 1990): 5–26. See also Jennifer Gore, *The Struggle for Pedagogies: Critical and Feminist Discourses as Regimes of Truth* (New York and London: Routledge, 1993); Patti Lather, *Getting Smart: Feminist Research and Pedagogy with/in the Postmodern* (New York and London: Routledge, 1991); Luke and Gore, *Feminisms and Critical Pedagogy;* and Kathleen Weiler, "Freire and a Feminist Pedagogy of Difference," *Harvard Educational Review* 61 (4 [1991]): 449–74.

15. Ellsworth, "Why Doesn't This Feel Empowering?" pp. 314–15.

16. See, for example, Jane Flax, "Postmodernism and Gender Relations in Feminist Theory," *Signs* 12 (4 [1987]): 621–43. She says:

> Until we see gender as a social relation, rather than an opposition of inherently different beings, we will not be able to identify the variations and limitations of different women's (or men's) powers and oppressions within particular societies. . . . We need to know how women's activities are affected by, but also how they affect, or enable, or compensate for . . . men's activities, as well as their implications in class or race relations. (p. 641)

17. See, for example, Frances Mascia-Lees, Patricia Sharpe, and Colleen Cohen, "The Postmodernist Turn in Anthropology: Cautions from a Feminist Perspective," *Signs* 15 (1 [1989]): 7–33. These authors note that the evolution of feminist theory, in coming to terms with diversity, "bears relation to the postmodern deconstruction of the subject, but it stems from a very different source: the political confrontation between white feminists and women of color" (p. 23). See also Marianne Hirsch and Evelyn Fox Keller, eds., *Conflicts in Feminism* (New York and London: Routledge, 1990); Toni Morrison, ed., *Race-ing Justice, Engendering Power* (New York: Pantheon, 1992). For issues of representation, see, for example, James Clifford and George Marcus, eds., *Writing Culture: The Poetics and Politics of Ethnography* (Berkeley: University of California Press, 1986); and Renato Rosaldo, *Culture and Truth: The Remaking of Social Analysis* (Boston: Beacon Press, 1989).

18. As mentioned earlier, Paulo Freire's work articulates a pedagogy for oppressed peoples. Based on a Marxist model of class oppression, his philosophy is a sophisticated model for "renaming the world" from their position. However, in

universities it has been influential mainly within schools of education, where it has typically been either reduced to a list of teaching methods or elaborated by educational theorists who speak little of specific classroom applications. An exception is the work of Ira Shor, whose *Critical Teaching in Everyday Life* (Boston: South End Press, 1980) is about exercises and approaches for working with working-class students on the issues in their lives. Articles in *Radical Teacher* also address specific teaching situations such as those encountered by K Edgington here.

19. Beverly Daniel Tatum, "Talking About Race, Learning About Racism: The Application of Racial Identity Development Theory in the Classroom," *Harvard Educational Review* 62 (1 [1992]): 1–24. See also Elizabeth Spelman, *Inessential Women* (Boston: Beacon Press, 1988), p. 169, quoted on page 271.

20. For a description of the development of different strands of feminist thought and politics throughout the 1960s and early 1970s, see Alice Echols, *Daring to Be Bad: Radical Feminism in America, 1967–75* (Minneapolis: University of Minnesota Press, 1989). See also Ann Snitow, "A Gender Diary," in *Conflicts in Feminism,* ed. Marianne Hirsch and Evelyn Fox Keller (New York and London: Routledge, 1990), pp. 9–43.

21. Linda Alcoff, "Cultural Feminism versus Post-Structuralism: The Identity Crisis in Feminist Theory," *Signs* 13 (3 [1988]): 432.

22. Joan Scott, "Experience," in *Feminists Theorize the Political,* ed. Judith Butler and Joan Scott (New York and London: Routledge, 1992), pp. 22–40.

23. See Mary Belenky, Blythe Clinchy, Nancy Goldberger, and Jill Tarule, *Women's Ways of Knowing: The Development of Self, Voice, and Mind* (New York: Basic Books, 1986), chap. 4, esp. pp. 83, 84. Different from "subjective knowing" is these authors' conceptualization of "connected knowing," which is learning about another through an engaged and empathetic, rather than distanced and "separate," attitude toward the other's point of view.

24. Sandra Harding, *Whose Science? Whose Knowledge? Thinking from Women's Lives* (Ithaca, N.Y.: Cornell University Press, 1992), p. 287.

25. See ibid. and Haraway, "Situated Knowledges." See also Dorothy Smith, *The Everyday World as Problematic: A Feminist Sociology* (Boston: Northeastern University Press, 1987).

26. Harding, *Whose Science?* pp. 271, 295.

27. See Belenky et al., *Women's Ways of Knowing,* chap. 7.

Chapter 8. Looking Back, Looking Forward

1. John Van Maanen, *Tales of the Field: On Writing Ethnography* (Chicago: University of Chicago Press, 1988), p. 39*n* 8. See also Laurie Finke, "Knowledge as Bait: Feminism, Voice, and the Pedagogical Unconscious," *College English* 55 (1 [1993]): 7–27.

2. Personal correspondence, September 6, 1993.

3. Chantal Tetreault, "Metacommunication in a Women's Studies Classroom," unpublished senior honors thesis, Vassar College, 1991.

4. Erica Huggins is a former professor at San Francisco State who was prominent

in the Black Panther party in the 1960s. She is presently working in the AIDS Shanti Project.

5. When we interviewed Trujillo in April 1993, she was teaching a course called Women of Color in the United States and continuing as Director of Women and Graduate Students of Color in Engineering, University of California, Berkeley.

6. Annual Meeting of the American Educational Research Association, San Francisco, April 1992.

7. Finke, "Knowledge as Bait," p. 20.

8. Ibid., p. 16.

9. Interview with Laurie Finke, June 1991.

10. Interview with Dorothy Berkson, April 1993.

11. Patricia MacCorquodale, "Political Correctness as a Resistance to Diversity," unpublished paper, University of Arizona, n. d. The courses MacCorquodale analyzed were taught in the fall of 1989 and 1990.

12. Toni Morrison, "Unspeakable Things Unspoken: The Afro-American Presence in American Literature," *Michigan Quarterly Review* 28 (1 [1989]): 1–34.

13. Beverly Daniel Tatum, "Talking About Race, Learning About Racism: The Application of Racial Identity Development Theory in the Classroom," *Harvard Educational Review* 62 (1 [1992]): 1–24.

14. Gretchen Schmidhausler, "After Twenty Years, Scholarly Emphasis on Diversity Reinvigorated," *Black Issues in Higher Education* 10 (5 [May 6, 1993]): 30–33.

15. Interview with Ned Sharp, Lewis and Clark College, Spring 1987.

16. A number of projects have focused on the Middle East in part because the university is the national headquarters for the Middle Eastern Studies Association.

17. Sharon Elise, "Chinosole: That Precious Quality to Which We All Aspire But Is Difficult to Achieve: Freedom." *Wazo Weusi* (Spring/Summer 1993): 59–98.

18. The largest group is European Americans, followed by Asian and Asian-American students, Latinos, and African-Americans.

19. Grey Osterud left San Jose in 1992 to serve as the American editor of *Gender and History,* a journal devoted to historical questions about gender relations. She also works in a field-based history education program for elementary school students in the Boston public schools.

BIBLIOGRAPHY

Aiken, Susan Hardy, Karen Anderson, Myra Dinnerstein, Judy Nolte Lensink, and Patricia MacCorquodale. *Changing Our Minds*. Albany: State University of New York Press, 1988.

————. "Trying Transformations: Curriculum Integration and the Problem of Resistance." *Signs: Journal of Women in Culture and Society* 12 (1987): 255–75.

Aisenberg, Nadya, and Mona Harrington. *Women of Academe: Outsiders in the Sacred Grove*. Amherst: University of Massachusetts Press, 1988.

Alcoff, Linda. "Cultural Feminism versus Post-Structuralism: The Identity Crisis in Feminist Theory." *Signs: Journal of Women in Culture and Society* 13, no. 3 (March 1988): 405–36.

Alterman, Eric. "Black Universities, in Demand and in Trouble." *New York Times Magazine,* November 5, 1989, p. 61–3, 81–6.

Amis, Kingsley. *Lucky Jim*. New York: Penguin, 1976.

Anderson, Virginia, Barbara Walvoord, Lucille McCarthy, John Dreihan, Susan Robinson, and A. Kimbrough Sherman. *Writing and Thinking in College*. Urbana, Ill.: National Council of Teachers of English, 1991.

Barlow, William, and Peter Shapiro. *An End to Silence: The San Francisco State College Student Movement in the 60s*. New York: Pegasus, 1971.

Becker, Howard. *Making the Grade*. New York: Wiley, 1968.

Belenky, Mary, Blythe Clinchy, Nancy Goldberger, and Jill Mattuck Tarule. *Women's Ways of Knowing: The Development of Self, Voice, and Mind*. New York: Basic Books, 1986.

Bennett, William J. *American Education: Making It Work*. Washington D.C.: U.S. Government Printing Office, 1988.

Berkson, Dorothy, "Born and Bred in Different Nations: Margaret Fuller and Ralph Waldo Emerson." In *Patrons and Proteges,* edited by Shirley Marchalonis, 3–30. New Brunswick, N.J.: Rutgers University Press, 1988.

Berkson, Dorothy, ed. *Oldtown Folks,* by Harriet Beecher Stowe. American Women Writers Series. New Brunswick, N.J.: Rutgers University Press, 1988.

Blanchard, Margaret. *The Rest of the Deer: An Intuitive Study of Intuition*. Portland, Maine: Astarte Press, 1993.

Bloom, Allan. *The Closing of the American Mind.* New York: Touchstone Books, 1988.

Boxer, Marilyn. "For and About Women: The Theory and Practice of Women's Studies in the United States." *Signs: Journal of Women in Culture and Society* 7, no. 2 (Spring 1982): 661–95.

Boyer, Ernest L. *College: The Undergraduate Experience in America.* New York: Harper & Row, 1988.

Brace, Gerald Warner. *The Department.* Chicago: University of Chicago Press, 1968.

Braxton, Joanne, and Andree Nicola McLaughlin. *Wild Women in the Whirlwind.* New Brunswick, N.J.: Rutgers University Press, 1990.

Brown, William Wells. *Clotel.* New York: Arno Press, 1969.

Bunch, Charlotte, and Sandra Pollack. *Learning Our Way: Essays in Feminist Education.* Trumansburg, N.Y.: The Crossing Press, 1983.

Butler, Judith, and Joan Scott, eds. *Feminists Theorize the Political.* New York: Routledge, 1992.

Carey, Nelson. *Theory in the Classroom.* Urbana and Chicago: University of Illinois Press, 1986.

Carroll, Bernice, ed. *Liberating Women's History: Theoretical and Critical Essays.* Urbana and Chicago: University of Illinois Press, 1976.

Carter, Angela. "The Company of Wolves." In *The Norton Anthology of Literature by Women,* edited by Sandra Gilbert and Susan Gubar, pp. 2326–34. New York: Norton, 1985.

Chinosole. "Andre Lorde and Matrilineal Diaspora." In *Wild Women in the Whirlwind,* edited by Joanne M. Braxton and Andree Nicole McLaughlin, pp. 379–94. New Brunswick, N.J.: Rutgers University Press, 1991.

———. "Condé as Contemporary Griot in *Segu.*" In *Calloloo: A Journal of African Americans and African Arts and Letters* (1994).

———. "Surviving Angola's War," *Washington Post,* March 6, 1976.

———. "Trying to Get Over: Narrative Posture in Equiano's Autobiography." In *The Art of Slave Narrative: Original Essays in Criticism and Theory,* edited by John Sekora and Darwin Turner, pp. 45–54. Macomb, Ill.: Western Illinois Press, 1991.

Chodorow, Nancy. *The Reproduction of Mothering: Psychoanalysis and the Sociology of Gender.* Berkeley: University of California Press, 1978.

Clark, Beverly Lyon. "Introduction." In *The Making of a Schoolgirl,* by Evelyn Sharp New York: Oxford, 1989.

———. *Talking About Writing: A Guide for Tutor and Teacher Conference.* Ann Arbor: University of Michigan Press, 1985.

Clark, Beverly Lyon, Heather Braun, Susan Dearing, Kerry-Beth Garvey, Karen Gennari, Becky Hemperly, and Michelle Henneberry, "Giving Voice to Feminist Criticism, a Conversation." In *Teaching Theory to Undergraduates,* edited by William Cain and Dianne Sadoff. New York: Modern Language Association, 1993.

Clifford, James. "Introduction: Partial Truths." In *Writing Culture: The Poetics and Politics of Ethnography,* edited by James Clifford and George Marcus. Berkeley: University of California Press, 1986.

Clifford, James, and George Marcus, eds. *Writing Culture: The Poetics and Politics of Ethnography.* Berkeley: University of California Press, 1986.

Cole, Johnnetta B. *Conversations: Straight Talk with America's Sister President.* New York: Doubleday, 1993.

Collins, Patricia Hill. *Black Feminist Thought: Knowledge, Consciousness and the Politics of Empowerment.* Boston: Unwin Hyman, 1990.

Cott, Nancy. *The Bonds of Womanhood: "Women's Sphere" in New England, 1780–1835.* New Haven, Conn.: Yale University Press, 1977.

Coulter, Sara. "Career Politics and the Practice of Women's Studies." In *Rocking the Boat: Academic Women and Academic Processes,* edited by Gloria De Sole and Leonore Hoffman, pp. 77–81. New York: Modern Language Association, 1981.

Coulter, Sara, K Edgington, and Elaine Hedges, eds. "Resources for Curriculum Change." Unpublished paper, Towson State University, 1986.

Crenshaw, Kimberle. "Whose Story Is It Anyway? Feminist and Antiracist Appropriations of Anita Hill." In *Race-ing Justice, Engendering Power,* edited by Toni Morrison, pp. 403–36. New York: Pantheon, 1992.

Cross, Amanda. *Death in a Tenured Position.* New York: Ballantine, 1986.

Cross, K. Patricia. *Accent on Teaching.* San Francisco: Jossey-Bass, 1976.

Culley, Margo, and Catherine Portuges, eds. *Gendered Subjects: The Dynamics of Feminist Teaching.* London: Routledge & Kegan Paul, 1985.

Davis, Angela. *Angela Davis: An Autobiography.* New York: Random House, 1974.

———. "Billie Holiday: Music and Social Consciousness." In *Speech and Power,* edited by Gerald Early, pp. 33–43. New York: Ecco Press, 1991.

———. "Black Nationalism: The Sixties and The Nineties." In *Black Popular Culture,* edited by Gina Dent, pp. 317–24. Seattle: Bay Press, 1993.

———. "The Black Woman's Role in the Community of Slaves." *Black Scholar* 3, no. 4 (April 1971): 2–15.

———. *Women, Race and Class.* New York: Random House, 1982.

Davis, Barbara Hillyer. "Teaching the Feminist Minority." *Women's Studies Quarterly* 9, no. 4 (Winter 1981): 7–9.

Davis, Barbara Hillyer, ed. *"Feminist Education." The Journal of Thought: An Interdisciplinary Quarterly* 20, no. 2 (Fall 1985), special issue.

de Palma, Anthony. "Rare in Ivy League: Women Who Work as Full Professors." *New York Times,* January 24, 1993, p. 1.

Dickinson, Emily. *Complete Poems of Emily Dickinson.* Edited by Thomas H. Johnson. New York: Macmillan, 1967.

Doell, Ruth. "Whose Research Is This? Values and Biology." In *Engendering Knowledge: Feminists in Academe,* edited by Joan E. Hartman and Ellen Messer-Davidow, pp. 121–39. Knoxville: University of Tennessee Press, 1991.

Doell, Ruth, and Helen Longino. "Body, Bias, and Behavior: A Comparative Analysis of Reasoning in Two Areas of Biological Science." *Signs: Journal of Women in Culture and Society* 9 (1983): 206–27.

———. "Sex Hormones and Human Behavior: A Critique of the Linear Model." *Journal of Homosexuality* 15 (1988): 55–78.

D'Souza, Dinesh. *Illiberal Education: The Politics of Race and Sex on Campus.* New York: Free Press, 1991.

DuBois, Ellen. *Feminism and Suffrage: The Emergence of an Independent Women's Movement.* Ithaca, N.Y.: Cornell University Press, 1978.

Ebel, Kenneth E. *The Aims of College Teaching.* San Francisco: Jossey-Bass, 1984.

Echols, Alice. *Daring to be Bad: Radical Feminism in America, 1967–75.* Minneapolis: University of Minnesota Press, 1989.

Elbow, Peter. *Writing Without Teachers.* London: Oxford University Press, 1973.

Elise, Sharon. "Chinosole: That Precious Quality to Which We All Aspire But Is Difficult to Achieve; Freedom." *Wazo Weusi* (Spring/Summer 1993): 59–98.

Ellner, Carolyn L., and Carol P. Barnes. *Studies of College Teaching.* Lexington, Mass: Lexington Books, 1983.

Ellsworth, Elizabeth. "Why Doesn't This Feel Empowering? Working Through the Repressive Myths of Critical Pedagogy." *Harvard Educational Review* 59, no. 4 (April 1989): 297–324.

Faulkner, William. *The Sound and the Fury.* (1929). New York: Random House, 1984.

Fetterley, Judith. *The Resisting Reader: A Feminist Approach to American Fiction.* Bloomington: Indiana University Press, 1976.

Finke, Laurie. *Feminist Theory, Women's Writing.* Ithaca, N.Y.: Cornell University Press, 1992.

———. "Knowledge as Bait: Feminism, Voice, and the Pedagogical Unconscious." *College English* 55, no. 1 (January 1993): 7–27.

Finkelhor, David, and Kersti Yllo. *License to Rape: Sexual Abuse of Wives.* New York: Holt, Rinehart and Winston, 1985.

Fisher, Berenice. "What Is Feminist Pedagogy?" *Radical Teacher* 6 (1978): 18, 20–25.

Flax, Jane. "Postmodernism and Gender Relations in Feminist Theory." *Signs: Journal of Women in Culture and Society* 12, no. 4 (April 1987): 621–43.

Fleming, Jacqueline. *Blacks in College: A Comparative Study of Students' Success in Black and White Institutions.* San Francisco: Jossey-Bass, 1984.

Flemming, Leslie, "A New Humanity: American Women Missionaries' Ideals for Indian Women, 1870–1930." In *Western Women and Imperialism: Complicity and Resistance,* edited by Nupar Chaudhuri and Margaret Strobel, pp. 191–206. Bloomington, IN: Indiana University Press, 1992.

———. "New Visions, New Methods: The Mainstreaming Experience in Retrospect." In *Changing Our Minds,* edited by Susan Hardy Aiken Karen Anderson, Myra Dinnerstein, Judy Nolte Lensink, and Patricia MacCorquodale, pp. 39–58. Albany: State University of New York Press, 1988.

Flemming, Leslie, ed. *Women's Work for Women: Missionaries and Social Change in Asia.* Boulder, Colo.: Westview, 1989.

Frankenberg, Ruth. *White Women, Race Matters: The Social Construction of Whiteness.* Minneapolis: University of Minnesota Press, 1993.

Freedman, Sara, Jane Jackson, and Katherine Bowles. "The Other End of the Corridor: The Effects of Teaching on Teachers." *Radical Teacher* 23 (1984): 2–23.

Freire, Paulo. *The Pedagogy of the Oppressed.* New York: Continuum, 1970.

Fuller, Margaret. *Woman in the Nineteenth Century.* (1844) Columbia: University of South Carolina Press, 1980.

Fuss, Diana. *Essentially Speaking: Feminism, Nature, and Difference.* New York: Routledge and Kegan Paul, 1989.

Gabriel, Susan, and Isaiah Smithson, eds. *Gender in the Classroom: Power and Pedagogy.* Urbana and Chicago: University of Illinois Press, 1990.

Galbraith, John. *A Tenured Professor.* Boston: Houghton Mifflin, 1990.

Geiger, Susan, and Jacqueline N. Zita. "White Traders: The Caveat Emptor of Women's Studies." In *Journal of Thought* 20, no. 3 (Fall 1985): 106–21.

Giddings, Paula. *When and Where I Enter: The Impact of Black Women on Race and Sex in America.* New York: Morrow, 1984.

Gilbert, Sandra, and Susan Gubar. *The Madwoman in the Attic.* New Haven, Conn.: Yale University Press, 1979.

———, eds. *The Norton Anthology of Literature by Women.* New York: Norton, 1985.

Gilligan, Carol. *In a Different Voice: Psychological Theory and Women's Development.* Cambridge, Mass.: Harvard University Press, 1982.

Gilligan, Carol, Nona Lyons, and Trudy Hanmer. *Making Connections: The Relational Worlds of Adolescent Girls at Emma Willard School.* Cambridge, Mass.: Harvard University Press, 1990.

Gore, Jennifer. *The Struggle for Pedagogies: Critical and Feminist Discourses as Regimes of Truth.* New York and London: Routledge, 1993.

———. "What Can We Do for You! What *Can* 'We' Do for 'You'?: Struggling over Empowerment in Critical and Feminist Pedagogy." *Educational Foundations* (Summer 1990): 5–26.

Grumet, Madeline. "Pedagogy for Patriarchy: The Feminization of Teaching." *Interchange on Educational Policy* 12, no. 2–3 (1981): 165–84.

Hall, Roberta, and Bernice Sandler. *The Classroom Climate: A Chilly One for Women.* Project on the Status and Education of Women. Washington, D.C.: Association of American Colleges, 1982.

Haraway, Donna. "Situated Knowledges: The Science Question in Feminism and the Privilege of Partial Perspective." *Feminist Studies* 14, no. 3 (March 1988): 575–99.

Harding, Sandra. *The Science Question in Feminism.* Ithaca, N.Y.: Cornell University Press, 1987.

———. *Whose Science? Whose Knowledge? Thinking from Women's Lives.* Ithaca, N.Y.: Cornell University Press, 1992.

Hartman, Joan E., and Ellen Messer-Davidow, eds. *Engendering Knowledge: Feminists in Academe.* Knoxville: University of Tennessee Press, 1991.

Heath, Shirley Brice. *Ways with Words: Language, Life, and Work in Communities and Classrooms.* New York: Cambridge University Press, 1983.

Hedges, Elaine, and Ingrid Wendt, eds., *In Her Own Image: Women Working in the Arts.* New York: Feminist Press and McGraw Hill, 1980.

Hirsch, E. D., Jr. *Cultural Literacy: What Every American Needs to Know.* Boston: Houghton Mifflin, 1987.

Hirsch, Marianne, and Evelyn Fox Keller, eds. *Conflicts in Feminism.* New York and London: Routledge, 1990.

Hoffman, Nancy. *Women's "True" Profession: Voices from the History of Teaching.* New York: Feminist Press and McGraw-Hill, 1981.

hooks, bell. *Ain't I a Woman: Black Women and Feminism.* Boston: South End Press, 1982.

————. "From Skepticism to Feminism." *Women's Review of Books* 7, no. 5 (February 1990): 29.

————. *Talking Back: Thinking Feminist, Thinking Black.* Boston: South End Press, 1989.

Howe, Florence, Suzanne Howard, and Mary Jo Boehm Strauss. *Everywoman's Guide to Colleges and Universities.* Old Westbury, N.Y.: Feminist Press, 1982.

Hurston, Zora Neale. *Of Mules and Men.* New York: Negro University Press, 1935.

Jones, Jacqueline. *Labor of Love, Labor of Sorrow: Black Women, Work, and the Family from Slavery to the Present.* New York: Basic Books, 1985.

Katz, Joseph, and Mildred Henry. *Turning Professors into Teachers.* New York: American Council on Education and Macmillan, 1988.

Keller, Evelyn Fox. *Reflections on Gender and Science.* New Haven, Conn.: Yale University Press, 1984.

Kirschner, Susan, Jane Monnig Atkinson, and Elizabeth Arch. "Reassessing Coeducation." In *Women's Place in the Academy: Transforming the Liberal Arts Curriculum,* edited by Marilyn Schuster and Susan Van Dyne, pp. 30–47. Totowa, N.J.: Rowman and Allanheld, 1985.

Kramarae, Cheris, and Paula Treichler. "Power Relationships in the Classroom." In *Gender in the Classroom: Power and Pedagogy,* edited by Susan Gabriel and Isaiah Smithson, pp. 41–59. Urbana and Chicago: University of Illinois Press, 1990.

Krieger, Nancy et al. "Racism, Sexism, and Social Class: Implications for Studying Health, Disease, and Well-Being." *American Journal of Preventive Medicine* 9, no. 6, supp. (November/December 1993): 82–122.

Krupnick, Catherine. "Women and Men in the Classroom: Inequality and Its Remedies." In *On Teaching and Learning.* Journal of the Derek Bok Center for Teaching and Learning. Harvard University (May 1985): 18–25.

Laird, Susan. "Reforming 'Women's True Profession': A Case for 'Feminist Pedagogy' in Teacher Education?" *Harvard Educational Review* 58, no. 4 (November 1988): 449–63.

Lather, Patti. "Feminist Perspectives on Empowering Research Methodologies." *Women's Studies International Forum* 11, no. 6 (1988): 569–81.

————. *Getting Smart: Feminist Research and Pedagogy Within the Postmodern.* New York and London: Routledge, 1991.

Lerner, Gerda. *The Majority Finds Its Past: Placing Women in History.* New York: Oxford University Press, 1979.

————. "Placing Women in History: A 1975 Perspective." In *Liberating Women's History: Theoretical and Critical Essays,* edited by Bernice Carroll, pp. 357–67. Urbana and Chicago: University of Illinois Press, 1976.

Lodge, David. *Changing Places.* New York: Viking Penguin, 1979.

————. *Nice Work.* New York: Viking Penguin, 1990.

————. *Small World: An Academic Romance.* New York: Warner, 1989.

Longino, Helen. "Scientific Objectivity and Feminist Theorizing." *Liberal Education* (Fall 1981): 187–95.

Lo Que Pasa 10 (March 30, 1987): 3.

Lorde, Audre. *Sister Outsider.* Freedom, Calif.: Crossing Press, 1984.

Luke, Carmen. "Feminist Politics in Radical Pedagogy." In *Feminisms and Critical Pedagogy,* edited by Carmen Luke, and Jennifer Gore, pp. 25–53. New York and London: Routledge & Kegan Paul, 1992.

Luke, Carmen, and Jennifer Gore, eds. *Feminisms and Critical Pedagogy.* New York and London: Routledge & Kegan Paul, 1992.

MacCorquodale, Patricia. "Indentity: Gender and Ethnic Dimensions." In *Mexican American Identity,* edited by Martha Bernal and Phyllis Martinelli, pp. 115–38. Encino, Calif.: Floricanto Press, 1993.

———. "Political Correctness as a Resistance to Diversity." Unpublished paper, University of Arizona, no date.

———. "Stability and Change in Gender Relations." *Sociological Theory* 8 (1990).

MacCorquodale, Patricia, Martha W. Gilliand, Jeffrey P. Kash, and Andrew Jameton. *Engineers and Economic Conversion: From the Military to the Marketplace.* New York: Springer Verlag, 1993, pp. 136–52

MacCorquodale, Patricia, and Gary F. Jensen. "Women in Law: Partners or Tokens?" *Gender and Society* 7, no. 4 (1993).

Maher, Frances. "Classroom Pedagogy and the New Scholarship on Women." In *Gendered Subjects: The Dynamics of Feminist Teaching,* edited by Margo Culley and Catherine Portuges, pp. 29–48. London: Routledge & Kegan Paul, 1985.

———. "Pedagogies for the Gender-Balanced Classroom." *Journal of Thought* 20, no. 3 (Fall 1985): 48–64.

———. "Toward a Richer Theory of Feminist Pedagogy." *Journal of Education* 169, no. 3 (1987): 91–99.

Maher, Frances, and Kathleen Dunn. "The Practice of Feminist Teaching: A Case Study of the Interaction Among Curriculum, Pedagogy, and Female Cognitive Development." Working paper, Wellesley College Center for Research on Women, 1984.

Marcus, George, and Michael Fischer. *Anthropology as Cultural Critique: An Experimental Moment in the Human Sciences.* Chicago: University of Chicago Press, 1986.

Martin, Jane Roland. "Becoming Educated: A Journey of Alienation or Integration." *Journal of Education* 167, no. 3 (1985): 871–84.

———. *Reclaiming a Conversation: The Ideal of the Educated Woman.* New Haven, Conn.: Yale University Press, 1985.

Mascia-Lees, Frances, Patricia Sharpe, and Colleen Cohen. "The Postmodernist Turn in Anthropology: Cautions from a Feminist Perspective." *Signs: Journal of Women in Culture and Society* 15, no. 1 (January 1989): 7–33.

———. "White Women and Black Men: Differential Responses to Reading Black Women's Texts." *College English* 52, no. 2 (February 1990): 142–53.

Matthews, Anne. "Rage in a Tenured Position." *New York Times Magazine,* November 8, 1992.

McCarthy, Mary. *The Groves of Academe.* New York: Harcourt Brace, 1952.

Miller, Jean Baker. *Toward a New Psychology of Women.* Boston: Beacon Press, 1976.

Minnich, Elizabeth Kamarck, Jean O'Barr, and Rachel Rosenfeld, eds. *Reconstructing the Academy: Women's Education and Women's Studies.* Chicago: University of Chicago Press, 1988.

Moi, Toril. *Sexual/Textual Politics: Feminist Literary Theory.* London and New York: Methuen, 1985.

Montague, Martha Frances. *Lewis and Clark College 1867–1967.* Portland, Oreg.: Bindford and Mort, 1968.

Morrison, Toni. *Sula.* New York: Alfred A. Knopf, 1974.

———. "Unspeakable Things Unspoken: The Afro-American Presence in American Literature." *Michigan Quarterly Review* 28, no. 1 (1989): 1–34.

———, ed. *Race-ing Justice, Engendering Power.* New York: Pantheon, 1992.

Moses, Yolanda. *Black Women in Academe: Issues and Strategies.* Washington, D.C.: Association of American Colleges, 1989.

———. "The Challenge of Diversity: Anthropological Perspectives on University Culture." *Education and Urban Society* 22, no. 4 (August 1990): 402–12.

Murphy, Bianca Cody. "Educating Mental-Health Professionals About Gay and Lesbian Issues." In *Coming Out of the Classroom Closet,* edited by Karen M. Harbeck, pp. 229–46. New York: Harrington Park Press, 1992.

———. "Lesbian Couples and Their Parents." *Journal of Counseling and Development* 68 (1989): 46–51.

Nasaw, David. *Schooled to Order: A Social History of Public Schooling in the United States.* New York: Oxford University Press, 1979.

Naylor, Gloria. *The Women of Brewster Place.* New York: Penguin, 1980.

Nisonoff, Laurie, Susan Tracy, and Stanley Warner. "Stories Out of School: Poor and Working-Class Students at a Small Liberal Arts College." *Radical Teacher* 11, no. 41 (1991): 15–19.

Osterud, Nancy Grey. *Bonds of Community: The Lives of Farm Women in Nineteenth Century New York.* Ithaca, N.Y.: Cornell University Press, 1991.

———. "Teaching and Learning About Race at Lewis and Clark." Unpublished manuscript, Lewis and Clark College, 1987.

Penley, Constance. "Teaching in Your Sleep: Feminism and Psychoanalysis." In *Theory in the Classroom,* edited by Carey Nelson, pp. 129–48. Urbana and Chicago: University of Illinois Press, 1986.

Perry, William. *Forms of Intellectual and Ethical Development in the College Years.* New York: Holt, Rinehart and Winston, 1970.

Phillips, Mona. "Gender, Race, and Ideology: Women Teaching and Learning about Women, Values, and Law." *Focus on Law Studies: Teaching about Law in the Liberal Arts* 5, no. 2 (Spring 1991).

———. "'I Bring the History of My Experience': Black Women Professors at Spelman College and Their Lives." In *Black Women in the Academy: Promise and Perils,* edited by Lois Benjamin. Gainesville: University of Florida Press, in press.

———. "Telling the Stories of the Internal Colony: Gendered Analyses of Space, History and Conduits." *SAGE: A Scholarly Journal on Black Women* (forthcoming).

———, co-investigator. "Survey Measures of Stress and Strain for African-American

Women" (three-year reseach project funded by the Centers for Disease Control, 1994–1997).

Phillips, Mona, Andrew Billingsley, and Eleda Jackson. "'Wind's Going to Blow, So Why Not Change?': Change, Transformations, and Tradition at Butler Street Baptist Church." In *Religion in the Contemporary South: Diversity, Community, and Identity,* edited by Daryl White, pp. 117–23. Athens: University of Georgia Press, 1994.

Porter, Oscar F. *Undergraduate Completion and Persistence at Four-Year Colleges and Universities.* Washington, D.C.: The National Institute of Independent Colleges and Universities, 1989.

Rich, Adrienne. "Compulsory Heterosexuality and Lesbian Existence." *Signs: Journal of Women in Culture and Society* 5, no. 4 (1980): 631–60.

————. *On Lies, Secrets, and Silence: Selected Prose, 1966–1978.* New York: Norton, 1979.

Rodriguez, Richard. *Hunger of Memory.* Boston: David R. Godine, 1982.

Rosaldo, Renato. *Culture and Truth: The Remaking of Social Analysis.* Boston: Beacon Press, 1989.

————. "Others of Invention: Ethnicity and Its Discontents." [Village] *Voice Literary Supplement* 82 (February 1990): 27–29.

————. "Symbolic Violence: A Battle Raging in Academe." Paper presented at the annual meeting of the American Anthropological Association, Phoenix, Arizona, November 1988.

Rose, Mike. *Lives on the Boundary: A Moving Account of the Struggles and Achievement of American's Educational Underclass.* New York: Penguin, 1990.

Rowbotham, Sheila. *Woman's Consciousness, Man's World.* New York: Penguin, 1974.

Ryan, Jake, and Charles Sackrey. *Strangers in Paradise.* Boston: South End Press, 1984.

Sarton, May. *The Small Room.* New York: Norton, 1976.

Schilb, John. "Pedagogy of the Oppressors?" In *Gendered Subjects: The Dynamics of Feminist Teaching,* edited by Margo Culley and Catherine Portuges, pp. 253–64. London: Routledge & Kegan Paul, 1985.

Schmidhausler, Gretchen. "After Twenty Years, Scholarly Emphasis on Diversity Reinvigorated." *Black Issues in Higher Education* 10, no. 5 (May 6, 1993): 30–33.

Schmitz, Betty. *Integrating Women's Studies into the Curriculum.* Old Westbury, N.Y.: Feminist Press, 1985.

Schniedewind, Nancy, and Frances Maher, eds. "Feminist Pedagogy." *Women's Studies Quarterly* (Fall & Winter 1987), special issue.

Schuster, Marilyn, and Susan Van Dyne. "Placing Women in the Liberal Arts: Stages of Curriculum Transformation." *Harvard Educational Review* 54, no. 4 (November 1984): 413–28.

————. *Women's Place in the Academy.* Totowa, N.J.: Rowman & Allenheld, 1985.

Scott, Joan. "Experience." In *Feminists Theorize the Political,* edited by Judith Butler and Joan Scott, pp. 22–40. New York and London: Routledge, 1992.

Searles, John. "The Storm over the University." *New York Review of Books,* December 6, 1990, pp. 36–42.

Shor, Ira. *Critical Teaching and Everyday Life.* Boston: South End Press, 1980.

Shostak, Marjorie. *Nisa: The Life and Words of a !kung Woman.* New York: Vintage, 1983.

Showalter, Elaine. "Feminist Criticism in the Wilderness." In *Writing and Sexual Difference,* edited by Elizabeth Abel, pp. 129–48. Chicago: University of Chicago Press, 1982.

Smith, Dorothy. *The Everyday World as Problematic: A Feminist Sociology.* Boston: Northeastern University Press, 1987.

Snitow, Ann. "A Gender Diary." In *Conflicts in Feminism,* edited by Marianne Hirsch and Evelyn Fox Keller, pp. 9–43. New York and London: Routledge, 1990.

Spanier, Bonnie, Alexander Bloom, and Darlene Boroviak. *Toward a Balanced Curriculum: A Sourcebook for Initiating Gender Integration Projects.* Cambridge, Mass.: Schenkman, 1984.

Spelman, Elizabeth V. *Inessential Woman: Problems of Exclusion in Feminist Thought.* Boston: Beacon Press, 1988.

Stacey, Judith. "Can There Be a Feminist Ethnography?" *Women's Studies International Forum* 11, no. 1 (1988): 21–27.

Stacey, Judith, and Barrie Thorne. "The Missing Feminist Revolution in Sociology." *Social Problems* 32, no. 4 (April 1985): 301–16.

Stanley, Liz, and Sue Wise. *Breaking Out: Feminist Consciousness and Feminist Research.* London: Routledge & Kegan Paul, 1983.

Statham, Anne, Laurel Richardson, and Judith A. Cook. *Gender and University Teaching: A Negotiated Difference.* Albany: State University of New York Press, 1991.

Stone, TaRessa. *Speaking of Spelman.* Office of Public Relations, Spelman College, n.d.

Tannen, Deborah. "Teachers' Classroom Strategies Should Recognize That Men and Women Use Language Differently." *Chronicle of Higher Education,* June 19, 1991, B1–B2.

———. *You Just Don't Understand: Women and Men in Conversation.* New York: Morrow, 1990.

Tatum, Beverly Daniel. "Talking About Race, Learning About Racism: The Application of Racial Identity Development Theory in the Classroom." *Harvard Educational Review* 62, no. 1 (January 1992): 1–24.

Taylor, Barbara. *Eve and the New Jerusalem: Socialism and Feminism in the Nineteenth Century.* New York: Pantheon, 1983.

Tetreault, Chantal. "Metacommunication in a Women's Studies Classroom." Unpublished senior honors thesis, Vassar College, 1991.

Tetreault, Mary Kay. "Classrooms for Diversity: Rethinking Curriculum and Pedagogy." In *Multicultural Education: Issues and Perspectives,* edited by J. Banks and C. Banks. Boston: Allyn & Bacon, 1992.

———. "Feminist Phase Theory: An Experience-Derived Evaluation Model." *Journal of Higher Education* 56 (July/August 1985): 363–84.

———. "Integrating Women's History: The Case of United States History Textbooks." *The History Teacher* 19 (February 1986): 211–62.

———. "Its So Opinioney." *Journal of Education* 168, no. 2 (1986): 78–95.

———. "The Journey from Male-Defined to Gender-Balanced Education." *Theory into Practice* 25, no. 4 (Autumn 1986): 227–34.

————. "Phases of Thinking About Women in History: A Report Card on the Textbooks." *Women's Studies Quarterly* 13 (March and April 1985): 35–47.

————. *Women in America: Half of History.* New York: Houghton Mifflin, 1979.

Tinto, Vincent. *Leaving College: Rethinking the Causes and Curses of Student Attrition.* Chicago: University of Chicago Press, 1987.

Trujillo, Carla. "A Comparative Examination of Classroom Interactions Between Professors and Minority and Non-Minority College Students." *American Educational Research Journal* 23, no. 4 (Winter 1986): 629–42.

————, ed. *Chicana Lesbians: The Girls Our Mothers Warned Us About.* Berkeley, Calif.: Third Woman Press, 1991.

Tucker, Sherrie. "When the Blues and the Truth Lay Hiding: Rememory of Jazz in Black Women's Fiction." *Frontiers* 13, no. 2 (1992): 26–44.

Van Maanen, John. *Tales of the Field: On Writing Ethnography.* Chicago: University of Chicago Press, 1988.

Wade-Gayles, Gloria. *No Crystal Stair: Visions of Race and Sex in Black Women's Fiction.* New York: Pilgrim Press, 1984.

————. *Pushed Back to Strength: A Black Woman's Journey Home.* Boston: Beacon Press, 1993.

Weiler, Kathleen. "Freire and a Feminist Pedagogy of Difference." *Harvard Educational Review* 61, no. 4 (April 1991): 449–74.

————. *Women Teaching for Change: Gender, Class, and Power.* South Hadley, Mass.: Bergin and Garvey, 1988.

Westkott, Marcia. "Feminist Criticism of the Social Sciences." *Harvard Educational Review* 49 no. 4 (November 1979): 422–30.

Wills, Gary. "Man of the Year." *New York Review of Books,* November 21, 1991, pp. 12–18.

Wolf, Naomi. *The Beauty Myth: How Images of Beauty Are Used Against Women.* New York: Doubleday, 1992.

Wollstonecraft, Mary. *A Vindication of the Rights of Women.* (1790). Reprint. Troy, N.Y.: Whitston, 1982.

Woolf, Virginia. *A Room of One's Own.* New York: Harcourt, Brace, 1929.

————. *Three Guineas.* New York: Harcourt, Brace, 1938.

Yllo, Kersti, ed. *Feminist Perspectives on Wife Abuse.* Newbury Park, Calif.: Sage, 1988.

INDEX

52–53, 54, 131

Compulsory heterosexuality, 144–50

Connected knowing, 3–4

Consciousness, forced split in, 4

Corrigan, Robert A. (president of San Francisco State University), 53–54

Costa, Alex* (student at Towson State), 137–38

Cotter, Susan* (student at Wheaton), 68, 70, 93, 94, 220

Coulter, Sara (Towson State University), 10, 14, 31, 33, 35, 212, 246

Cox, Ida, 84, 129

Crenshaw, Kimberle, 88

Crowe, Midge (student at Wheaton), 96

Cultural feminism, 222–23

Culture, as term, 15

D'Angelo, Kathy* (student at Towson State), 79

Davis, Angela (San Francisco State University), 51; and authority, 20, 129, 161–62, 213; as community activist, 20; and mastery, 83–86, 87; moves to University of California at Santa Cruz, 247; Wild Women in Music and Literature course, 83–86, 87, 98–100, 129, 159–62, 191, 197–99, 204–5, 208, 211, 216, 242–43, 247n

Denison University, 43

DeSilva, Stanley (student at Wheaton), 43

Dewey, John, 9

Dickinson, Emily, 104–7, 130, 206, 211

"Difference," 14, 15, 23, 166, 170; black and white students and, 114, 223. *See also* "Other," concept of

Dinnerstein, Myra (University of Arizona), 10, 28

Doell, Ruth (San Francisco State University): and authority, 20, 128, 131–34, 138–39, 166; as community

activist, 20, 52–53, 131; The Genetic Revolution course, 128, 131–34, 138–39; and positionality, 166

Donovan, Ted* (student at San Francisco State), 132–34

Doyle, Richard* (student at University of Arizona), 60–61

D'Souza, Dinesh, 4

Dyslexic students, 236

Edgington, K (Towson State University), 34, 35, 221, 233; Honors Freshman Writing course, 179–84; and positionality, 179–84, 189, 212

Elbow, Peter, 102

Ellsworth, Elizabeth, 14, 218, 219

Emerson, Alice (president of Wheaton College), 40

Emory University, 172–78, 191–97, 202, 204, 215, 231

Engelman, Joy (student at Lewis and Clark), 153

Epistemological development: of academic disciplines and institutions, 208–14; and classroom positionality, 214–19; and classrooms, 10; and ethnicity, 5; and feminism, 8; and identity politics, 222–26; political, 47; and social class, 219–21; and women's ways of knowing, 3–4, 7, 11, 42, 95, 224, 225, 227

Ethnicity: and gender, 114–16; and knowledge, 5; and voice, 104–16. *See also* Positionality; Racism

Everywoman's Guide to Colleges and Universities, 32–33

Family violence, 43, 120–22, 144–50

Faulkner, William, 173, 191–97, 204

Feminist pedagogy, 4, 9–10, 11–15; and authority, 19–22, 127–63; Biological Literature course (Towson